Forty years among the bees

C C. 1831-1920 Miller

FORTY YEARS

AMONG THE BEES

— BY —

Dr. C. C. Miller.

---⁕---

CHICAGO, ILL.,
GEORGE W. YORK & COMPANY,
PUBLISHERS,
1903.

Ent. 1970

PREFACE.

Seventeen years ago there was published a little book written by me, the title being "A Year Among the Bees." For several years I have thought of revising it for another edition, but seemed too crowded for time. Upon essaying the task at last, I found that, in the course of the years, matters had changed so much in bee-keeping that most of what was written had to be cast aside, and the task became that of re-writing rather than revising, as but a small portion of the old could be retained. The present work has been much enlarged, allowing a fuller entering into details, and mention is made of some of the different things belonging to the forty years since I began bee-keeping—forty-one years and a half, to be exact—making the present name seem the appropriate one

At the request of the publishers, a brief biographical sketch is given. However much this may be enjoyed by some personal friends, I fear that others may think that the space could have been better filled with something else. But there is this one comfort: There is no law against skipping the first few pages.

With two exceptions, the pictures in this book are from photographs taken by myself or under my immediate supervision, using a No 1 Folding Pocket Kodak. When I say "taken by myself," I do not mean I did all; I merely "touched the button," the Eastman Kodak Co, of Rochester, N Y, "did the rest." I could never dream of doing such exquisite work as they can do in developing and printing. The character of the work secured by the publishers after the completion of the photograph speaks for itself. Even my small part of the work preliminary to "touching the button" has opened up to me a field of pleasure little anticipated. The child delights in his rattle, the millionaire in his steam yacht, I think I would not exchange my little ten-dollar kodak for either rattle or yacht

C C. MILLER.

Marengo, Ill., December, 1902.

Set of Honey-Dishes.

INTRODUCTION.

One morning, five or six of us, who had occupied the same bed-room the previous night during the North American Convention at Cincinnati, in 1882, were dressing preparatory to another day's work. Among the rest were Bingham, of smoker fame, and Vandervort, the foundation-mill man. I think it was Prof. Cook who was chaffing these inventors, saying something to the effect that they were always at work studying how to get up something different from anybody else, and, if they needed an implement, would spend a dollar and a day's time to get up one "of their own make," rather than pay 25 cents for a better one ready-made. Vandervort, who sat contemplatively rubbing his shins, dryly replied · "But they take a world of comfort in it" I think all bee-keepers are possessed of more or less of the same spirit. Their own inventions and plans seem best to them, and in many cases they are right, to the extent that two of them, having almost opposite plans, would both be losers to exchange plans.

In visiting and talking with other bee-keepers I am generally prejudiced enough to think my plans are, on the whole, better than theirs and yet I am always very much interested to know just how they manage, especially as to the little details of common operations, and occasionally I find something so manifestly better than my own way, that I am compelled to throw aside my prejudice and adopt their better way. I suppose there are a good many like myself, so I think there may be those who will be interested in these bee-talks, wherein, besides talking something of the past, I shall try to tell honestly just how I do, talking in a familiar manner, without feeling obliged to say "we" when I mean "I" Indeed I shall claim the privilege of putting in the pronoun of the first person as often as I please, and if the printer runs out of big I's toward the last of the book, he can put in little i's

Moreover, I don't mean to undertake to lay down a methodical system of bee-keeping whereby one with no knowledge of the business can learn in "twelve short lessons" all about it, but will just talk about some of the things that I think would interest you, if we were sitting down together for a familiar chat. I take it you are familiar with the good books and periodicals that we as bee-keepers are blest with, and in some things, if not most, you are a better bee-keeper than I; so you have my full permission, as you go from page to page, to make such remarks as, "Oh, how foolish!" "I know a good deal better way than that," etc., but I hope some may find a hint here and there that may prove useful.

I have no expectation nor desire to write a complete treatise on bee-keeping. Many important matters connected with the art I do not mention at all, because they have not come within my own experience. Others that have come within my experience I do not mention, because I suppose the reader to be already familiar with them. I merely try to talk about such things as I think a brother bee-keeper would be most interested in if he should remain with me during the year.

FORTY YEARS AMONG THE BEES.

BIOGRAPHICAL—BOYHOOD DAYS.

Fifty miles east of Pittsburg lies the little village of Ligonier, Pa., where I was born June 10, 1831. Twenty miles away, across the mountain, lies the ill-fated city of Johnstown, where my family lived later on, and where my only living sister resides at the present day. The scenery about Ligonier is of such a charming character that in recent years it has become a summer resort, a branch railroad terminating at that point. Looking down upon the town from the south is a hill so steep that one wonders how it is possible to cultivate it, while between it and the town flows a little stream called the Loyalhanna, with a milldam upon whose broad bosom I spent many a happy winter hour gliding over the icy surface on the glittering steel; and in the hot and lazy summer days, with trouser-legs rolled up to the highest, I waded all about the dam, the bubbles from its oozy bed running up my legs in a creepy way, while I watched with keen eyes for the breathing-hole of some snapping turtle hidden beneath the mud, then cautiously felt my way to its tail, lifted it and held it at arm's length for fear of its vicious jaws, and with no little effort carried it snapping and struggling to the shore. Ever in sight was the mountain, abounding in chestnuts, rattlesnakes, and huckleberries, and I distinctly recall how strange it seemed, when all was still about me, to hear the roar of the wind in the tree-tops on the mountain eight or ten miles away.

EARLY EDUCATION.

My earliest opportunities for education were not of the best. Public schools were not then what they are to-day, for they were just coming into existence. I recall that we children, upon hearing of a free school in a neighboring village, decided that it must be a very fine thing, for what else could a free school be than one in which the scholars were free to whisper to their heart's content? The teachers, in too many cases, seemed to be chosen because of their lack of fitness for any other calling The one concerning whom I have perhaps the earliest recollection was a man who *distinguished* himself by having a large family of boys named in order after the presidents, as far as the United States had at that time progressed in the matter of presidents, and who *extinguished* himself by falling in a well one day when he was drunk

But with the advent of free schools came rapid improvement, and I made fair progress in the rudiments, even though the advancement of each pupil was entirely independent of that of every other Indeed, there was no such thing as a *class* in arithmetic Each one did his sums on his slate, and submitted them to the "master" for approval, the master doing such sums as were beyond the ability of the pupil, in some cases a more advanced pupil doing this work in place of the teacher. Tom Cole was a beneficiary of mine, and every time I did a sum for him he gave me an apple. I do not recall that I lacked for apples, and apples then and there were worth 12½ cents a bushel

PARENTS

When ten years old I suffered a loss in the death of my father, the greatness of which loss I was at that time too young fully to realize. He was an elder in the Presbyterian church, but for one of those days very tolerant of the views of others He was most lovable in character, and the wish has been with me all through my life that I might be as good a man as my father I think he was chiefly of English extraction, although his ancestors had for many generations lived in this country. His father had tried to make a tailor of him, but he did not take kindly to that business, and became a physician.

My mother was German, her father and mother having both come from the fatherland. Like many others at that day, her education never went beyond the ability to read, and I am not sure that her reading ever went outside of the Bible. Possibly confining her reading to so

Fig. 1.—Home of the Author (from the Southwest).

good a book was one reason why she was a woman of remarkably good judgment, and to her credit be it said that she spared no pains to carry out the dying wish of my father that the children should be allowed to secure an education. She was a faithful Methodist, and although belonging to the two different churches, my parents usually went to church together, first to one church and then to the other.

When my mother married the second time, she mar-

ried a Methodist, and as the children came to years of
discretion they were impartially divided between the two
denominations, three to each (there were six of us—myself and five sisters).

Two years were taken out of my school life to clerk
in a country store three miles away For the first year
I got twenty-four dollars and board, my mother doing
my washing The second year I was advanced to fifty
dollars

BEGINS STUDY OF MEDICINE.

Then I undertook the study of medicine under the
tutelage of the leading—I am not sure but he was the
only—village physician. The Latin terms met in my
reading tripped me badly, and by some means I got it
into my head that if I could spend three months at the
village academy I might be so good a Latin scholar that
my troubles would be overcome. Dr. Cummins was
very insistent that it was vital for my strength of character that having begun to read medicine I should not be
weak enough to be dissuaded from my purpose by a little thing like the lack of Latin, and if I must have the
Latin I could work half time at it, spending the other
half in his office. Possibly he needed an office boy.

ATTENDS ACADEMY

But I was equally insistent that I must have one
uninterrupted term at the academy, and at it I went, taking up other studies as well as Latin. When the term
was completed I felt pretty certain that two more terms
were needed to make a complete scholar of me, and by the
time I had finished the two more terms I had settled into
the determination that I would not stop short of a college
course A college course, however, took money, little of
which I had. At my father's death it was supposed he
had left a fair property, but it was in the hands of others,

and by some means it soon melted away. I kept on at the academy, making part of my college course there.

Fig. 2.—Peabody Honey-Extractor.

ENTERS COLLEGE.

While yet in my teens I taught school in Shellsburg, and afterwards in Johnstown. I entered Jefferson College at Canonsburg, Pa., which college was afterward united with Washington College, and from there went to Union College, at Schenectady, N. Y. This last undertaking was a bit reckless, for when I arrived at Schenectady I had only about thirty dollars, with nothing to rely on except what I might pick up by the way to help me to finish up my last two years in college. I had a horror of being in debt, and so was on the alert for any work, no matter what its nature, so it was honest, by which I could earn something to help carry me through.

WORKS WAY THROUGH COLLEGE

I had learned just enough of ornamental penmanship to be able to write German text, and so got $44 00 for filling the names in 88 diplomas at the two commencements I taught a singing school, I worked in Prof Jackson's garden at seven-and-a-half cents an hour; raised a crop of potatoes; clerked at a town election, peddled maps, rang one of the college bells, and, as it was optional with the students whether they taught or studied during the third term senior, I got $100 00 for teaching during that term in an academy at Delhi, N Y Neither were my studies slighted during my course, which was shown by my taking the highest honor attainable, Phi Beta Kappa, which, however, was equally taken by a number of my class

I secured my diploma, allowing me to write A B. after my name, and left college with fifty dollars more in my pocket than when I arrived there It was not, however, so much what I earned as what I didn't spend that helped me through. I kept a strict cash account, and if I paid three cents postage on a letter or one cent for a steel pen or two blocks of matches, it was carefully entered, and probably a good many cents were saved because I knew if I spent them I must put it down in black ink.

CHEAP BOARD-BILLS

The item that gave me the greatest chance for economy was my board-bill I boarded myself all the time I was in college. My board cost me thirty-five cents a week or less most of the time. The use of wheat helped to keep down the bill A bushel of whole wheat thoroughly boiled will do a lot of filling up The last ten weeks, with less horror of debt before me, I became extravagant, and my board cost me sixty-six and a half cents a week

In the long run, however, I paid dear enough for my board, for its quality, together with a lack of exercise, so affected my health that I never fully recovered from it Strange to say, I was so ignorant that I did not know exercise was essential to health That was before the day of athletics in college.

STUDY AND PRACTICE OF MEDICINE.

After teaching a term in Geneseo, (N. Y.) Academy, I took up the study of medicine in Johnstown, Pa , attended lectures in Michigan University, at Ann Arbor, Mich., and received the degree of M D. I practiced medicine a short time in Earlville, Ill., and went to Marengo, Ill , for the same purpose, in July, 1856.

It did not take more than a year for me to find out that I had not a sufficient stock of health myself to take care of that of others, especially as I was morbidly anxious lest some lack of judgment on my part should prove a serious matter with some one under my care So with much regret I gave up my chosen profession

TEACHING AND TRAVELS

In 1857 I abandoned a life of single blessedness, marrying Mrs Helen M White I spent some years in teaching vocal and instrumental music, and was for several years principal of the Marengo public school. Before devoting my entire time to bee-keeping, I was for one year principal of the Woodstock school, most of the time driving there thirteen miles each morning, and returning to Marengo at night

I traveled two years for the music house of Root & Cady, making a specialty of introducing the teaching of singing in public schools. In 1872 I went to Cincinnati, where I spent six months helping to get up the first of the May musical festivals under the direction of

Theodore Thomas. At the close of the festival I began
work for the Mason & Hamlin Organ Co. at their Chicago house.

FIRST BEES

To go back. July 5, 1861—I was in Chicago at the
time—a swarm of bees passing over Marengo took in
their line of march the house where my wife was She
was a woman of remarkable energy and executive ability,
generally accomplishing whatever she undertook, and
she undertook to stop that swarm. Whether the water
and dirt she threw among them had any effect on the
bees I do not know, but I know she got the bees, hiving
them in a full-sized sugar-barrel

In her eagerness to have the bees properly housed—
or barreled—she could not wait the slow motion of the
bees, but taking them up by double handfuls she threw
them where she wanted them to go. In so doing she received five or six stings on her hands, which swelled up
and were so painful as to make it a sick-abed affair This
was a matter much to be regretted, for ever after a sting
was much the same as a case of erysipelas, preventing her
from having anything whatever to do with handling
bees except in case of extremity.

Previous to that time I had not been interested to any
great extent in bees When a small boy I had cap-
tured a bumble-bees' nest and put it in a little box, but I
do not recall that there was a remarkable drop in the
price of honey on account of there being thrown upon
the market a large amount of honey produced by those
bumble-bees

BEE-PALACE

When I was a little older I remember helping my
stepfather carry home, one night, a colony of bees in a
box-hive (movable-comb hives were not yet invented) the
colony being intended to stock a "bee-palace" This bee-

palace was a rather imposing structure. I think it cost ten dollars. It was large enough to contain about four colonies and was raised about two feet high on four legs. On the top was a hole over which the box-hive was placed, with the expectation that the bees would build down and occupy the entire space. The bottom was made very steep, so that wax-worms falling upon it would, however unwillingly, be obliged to roll out! When a nice piece of honey was wanted for the table, all that was necessary was to take a plate and knife and cut it out, a door for that purpose being in one side of the palace. The plate and knife were never called into requisition, the magnitude of the task of filling that palace being so great that the bees concluded to die rather than to undertake it. Many years after, I saw at the home of an intelligent farmer near Marengo the exact counterpart of that bee-

Fig. 3.— Wide Frame.

palace, which an oily-tongued vender had just induced him to purchase.

Notwithstanding my utter ignorance of bees, I began to feel some immediate interest in the bees in that barrel. I put them in the cellar, and at some time in the winter I went to a bee-keeping neighbor, James F. Lester, and with no little anxiety told him that some disease had appeared among my bees, for I found under them a considerable quantity of matter much resembling coarsely ground coffee. He quieted my fears by telling me it was all right, and nothing more than the cappings that the bees had gnawed away to get at the honey in the sealed combs

In the spring I sawed away that portion of the barrel not occupied by the bees, and when the time for surplus arrived I bored holes in the top of the hive and put a good-sized box over. There were holes in the bottom of the box to correspond with the holes in the hive. I made three box-hives, after the Quinby pattern, with special arrangement for surplus boxes, and they were well made.

"TAKING UP" BEES

When the bees swarmed I hived them in one of the new hives, and later on "took up" the bees in the barrel Altogether I got 93 pounds of honey from the barrel, and am a little surprised to find it set down at 12½ cents a pound Perhaps butter was low just then, for in those days it was a common thing for honey to follow the price of butter.

I left one of the hives with a farmer, and he hived a prime swarm in it, for which I paid him five dollars In the remaining hive I had a weak swarm hived, paying a dollar for the swarm I bought a colony of bees besides these, paying $7 00 for hive and bees

WINTERING UPSIDE DOWN

The bees were wintered in the cellar, and according to Quinby's instructions the hives were turned upside down

That gave ample ventilation, for when the hives were reversed the entire upper surface was open, all being closed below. I doubt that any better means of ventilation could be devised for wintering bees in the cellar. There is abundant opportunity for the free entrance of air into the hive, without anything to force a current through it. Equally good is the ventilation when all is closed at the top and the whole bottom is open, as when the hives with-

Fig. 4.—Heddon Super.

out any bottom-boards are piled up in such manner that the bottom of a hive rests upon the top of a hive below it at one side, and upon another hive at the other side, and the ventilation is perhaps as good when there is a bottom-board so deep that there is a space of two inches or more under the bottom-bars.

SEASON OF 1863.

The four colonies wintered through, and I find charged to the bees' account for 1863 three movable-frame hives at

$2 00 each, three box-hives at $1 00 for the three, and some surplus boxes at 10 to 20 cents each   These surplus boxes held from 6 to 10 pounds each, some of them having glass on two sides, and some having glass on four sides. Small pieces of comb were fastened in the top of each box as starters   I also bought another colony of bees at $7 00, and I bought Quinby's text-book, "Mysteries of Bee-Keeping Explained " I think I had previously read this as a borrowed book   I got 82 pounds of honey, worth 15 cents a pound

I began the year 1864 with seven colonies, which had cost me $23 39, that is, up to that time I had paid out $23.39 more for the bees than I had taken in from them, reckoning interest at ten per cent, the ruling rate at that time   Besides getting new hives that year, I bought a colony of bees for $5 00, and twenty empty combs at 15 cents each. I took 54 pounds of honey, 39 pounds of it being entered at 30 cents, the balance at 25 cents

The year 1865 opened with nine colonies, and the total crop for the season was 10 pounds of honey. Alas! that it was so small, for that year it was worth 35 cents a pound

FIRST ITALIANS

In 1866 I got my first Italian queen, paying R R Murphy $6 00 for her, and the following year I paid $10 00 for another to Mrs Ellen S Tupper, who was at one time editor of a bee-journal   The crop for 1866 was 100¾ pounds of honey, which that year was worth 30 cents

GETTING EVEN

I took 131 pounds of honey in 1867, worth 25 cents a pound, and this for the first time brought the balance on the right side of the ledger, for I began the season of 1868 with seven colonies and had $10 40 ahead besides   It will be seen, however, that bad wintering had been getting in its work, for there were two colonies less than there were three years before.

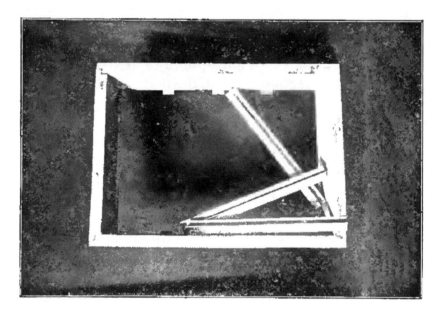

Fig. 5.— T Super.

There was certainly nothing brilliant in being able after seven years of bee-keeping to be able to count only two colonies more than the total number I had started with, together with the four I had bought. But there was a fascination in bee-keeping for me, and it is very likely I should have kept right on, even if it necessitated buying a fresh start each year. At any rate, my friends could no longer accuse me of squandering money on my bees, for there was that $10.40, and the time I had spent with the bees was just as well spent in that way as in some other form of amusement. Indeed, at that time I am not sure that I had much thought that I was ever to get any profit out of the business. Certainly I had no thought that it would ever become a vocation instead of an avocation.

GETS AMERICAN BEE JOURNAL.

In 1869, while away from home,, I came across a copy of the American Bee Journal. I subscribed for it, and also obtained the first volume of the same journal That first volume, containing the series of articles by the Baron of Berlepsch on the Dzierzon theory, has been of more service to me than any other volume of any bee-journal published, and to this day I probably refer to it oftener than to any other volume that is as much as two or three years old

Among the most frequent contributors to the American Bee Journal when I subscribed for it were H. Alley, D. H. Coggshall, C. Dadant, E. Gallup, A Grimm, J. L Hubbard, J M Marvin, M Quinby, A I Root, J H Thomas, and J F Tillinghast, most of which are well known names a third of a century later   G M. Doolittle did not appear on the scene till late in 1870

A. I. Root, under the *nom de plume* of Novice, was then just as full of schemes as he has been since, and was trying a hot-bed arrangement for bees, and in my first communication to the American Bee Journal, in 1870, I wrote, ' I am waiting patiently for Novice to invent a machine for making straight worker-comb ; for as yet I have found no way of securing all worker-comb, except to have it built by a weak colony " At that time he probably little thought that he would come so near fulfilling my expectations, sending out tons upon tons of foundation

ATTEMPT AT COMB FOUNDATION

I made some attempts myself in that line, simply with plain sheets of wax   I poured a little melted wax into a pail of hot water, and when it cooled I took the sheet of wax and gave it to the bees   It was not an immense success   I dipped a piece of writing paper into melted wax, and gave to the bees in an upper corner of a frame where no brood was reared, and for years you could hold that frame up to the light and looking through the comb see the writing that was on the paper. Then when foundation came upon the market, what a boon it was!

VISITS A. I ROOT.

In 1870 I made my first visit to Medina, then several miles from a railroad station Mr Root was then a jeweler, his shop had been burned up, and his house (not a large one at that time) was doing duty as both shop and dwelling Just then he was full of the idea of having maple sap run directly from the trees to the hives I showed him how to use rotten wood for smoking bees, and he thought it a great improvement over the plan he had been using. I do not now remember what his plan had been, but hardly a tobacco-pipe, for I have heard that he has some objections to the use of tobacco Pleased with his newly acquired accomplishment, I had hardly left town when he tried its use, and succeeded in setting fire to a hive by means of the sawdust on the ground. Whether it was burned up or merely put in jeopardy I do not now remember He did not send me the bill for it.

At that time he knew nothing of a bee-smoker, and neither of us then thought that in the next third of a century he would send out into the world three hundred thousand of them!

ADOPTS 18x9 FRAME

In 1870 I made a change in hives. I cannot now tell the size of frames I had been using, but I think the frames were considerably deeper than the regular Langstroth. I say "the *regular* Langstroth," for in reality all movable frames are Langstroths, but the *regular* size is 17⅝x9⅛. J. Vandervort, a man well known among the older bee-keepers as a manufacturer of foundation-mills, had at that time a machine shop in Marengo, and upon his moving away in 1870 I bought out his stock of hives The frames were 18x9, ⅜ of an inch longer than the standard size, and ⅛ of an inch shallower

CHANGE TO REGULAR LANGSTROTH.

So little a difference in measurement could make no appreciable difference in practical results, yet after going on until I had three or four thousand of such frames, the inconvenience of having an odd size was felt to be so great that I felt I must change so as to be in line with the rest of the world, and be able to order hives, frames, etc , such as were on the regular list without being obliged to have everything made to order   The change to the regular size cost a good deal of money, and a good deal more in labor and trouble, extending over several years.

PEABODY EXTRACTOR

In that same year, 1870, I got a honey-extractor. With much interest I made my first attempt at extracting, the supreme moment of interest coming when after having given perhaps 200 revolutions to the extractor I looked beneath to see how much honey had run into the pan beneath   Very vividly I remember my keen chagrin and disappointment when I found that not a drop of honey had fallen   The machine was one of the first put on the market, a Peabody extractor (Fig 2), the entire can revolving, and it had not occurred to me that the same force that threw the honey out of the comb would keep it against the outer wall of the can so long as it kept in motion.   When the can stopped revolving, a fair stream of honey ran down into the pan, and I resumed my normal manner of breathing.

TOO RAPID INCREASE.

I began the season of 1870 with eight colonies, increased to 19, and extracted about 400 pounds of honey. This warmed up my zeal considerably.   In the winter I lost three colonies, so I commenced the season of 1871 with 16 colonies, took 408 pounds of honey, and, the season being favorable, I increased without much difficulty until I reached thirty or forty, and I thought it would be a nice thing to have an even fifty, so I reached *about*

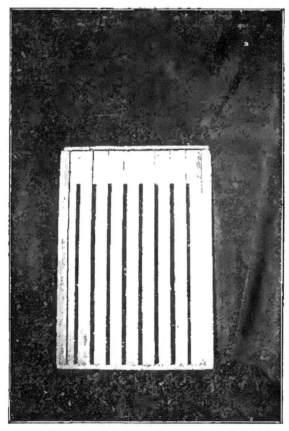

Fig. 6.—Heddon Slat Honey-Board.

that number, for so many of them were weak, that I am not sure exactly how many it would be fair to call them.

I fed them some quite late, too late for them to seal over, and they were put into the cellar with little anxiety as to the result

DISASTROUS WINTERING

In the winter they became quite uneasy, and February 11 I took out five colonies, which flew a little, and then I put them back They continued to become more uneasy and to be affected with diarrhea, and, February 22, I took them all out and found only twenty-three alive They flew a little, but it was not warm enough for a good cleansing flight; and soon after there came a cold storm with snow a foot deep, and by April 1 I had only three colonies living, two of which I united, making a total of *two* left from the forty-five or fifty

It was some comfort to know that nearly everyone lost heavily that winter, but what encouragement was there to continue under such adverse circumstances? I was on the road traveling for Root & Cady all the time with only an occasional visit to my bees, and no certainty of being there upon any particular date, and evidently with no great knowledge of the business if I had been home all the time. To be sure, I may have got enough honey so as to feel that there was no particular money loss, but after eleven years at bee-keeping, and after having bought, first and last, quite a number of colonies, here I was with only two colonies to show for all my efforts!

I do not remember, however, that any question as to continuance occurred to me at that time. Perhaps I didn't know enough to be discouraged Instead of selling off the two colonies and going out of the business, I bought five more colonies early in April They were in box-hives, and one of them died before the season warmed up, so I began the season of 1872 with six colonies These I increased to nineteen, and I think I took no honey With the number of empty combs I had on hand, there was nothing to exult over in this increase, especially as the colonies were not in the best condition as to strength.

Fig. 7.—Two Carrying with Rope.

WINTER IN CINCINNATI.

The thousands who have been charmed by the delightful music rendered under the guidance of the baton of that prince of conductors, Theodore Thomas, at the May Musical Festivals held in successive years in Cinnatti, will have no difficulty in understanding that a congenial, although somewhat arduous, occupation was afforded me when the managers offered me the position of "official agent," charged with doing the thousand and one things needing to be done to carry out their wishes in preparing for the first of these festivals. I began this work in 1872, some six months in advance of the time for the Festival, making my abode in Cincinnati, although I still called Marengo my home. In the winter I went back home, put the bees in the cellar December 7, and then locking up cellar and house for the winter I took my wife and child to Cincinnati, from which place we did not return till late the following May.

The bees were left entirely to their own devices throughout the winter   In the latter part of March the weather at Cincinnati became quite warm, and I wrote to my bee-keeping friend, Mr. Lester, to get him to take the bees out of the cellar   He took them out under protest, for Cincinnati weather and Marengo weather are two different things, and when they were taken out, March 31, they were probably ushered into a rather cold world   They were in bad condition when taken out—bees do not always winter in a cellar in the best possible manner with their owner several hundred miles away—and when I got home in May I found only three of the nineteen left alive

THREE YEARS IN CHICAGO.

Immediately upon the close of the Cincinnati Festival I began work for the Mason & Hamlin Organ Co , at their Chicago office, where I staid three years.   My wife and little boy staid on the farm at Marengo during the summer, and spent the winters with me in Chicago. Notwithstanding the fact that I could have only a few days with the bees each summer, I still clung to them. At least I could lie awake nights dreaming and planning as to what might be done with bees, and I could do that just as well in Chicago as Marengo.

One good thing that resulted from that three years' sojourn in Chicago was an appreciation of country life that I had never had before.   The office, 80 & 82 Adams street, was in the heart of the burnt district left bare by the great fire of 1871, and to one with a love for everything green that grows it was desolate indeed.   A few weeds that grew in a vacant lot hard by were a source of pleasure to me; but my chief delight was to stand and admire a bunch of white clover that grew near Clark street. I think all my years of country life since have been the brighter for the dismal months spent in that burnt district of the great city.

The three colonies that were left in the spring of 1873 were increased to eight in fair condition, and I took perhaps 60 pounds of honey. These eight were put into the cellar Nov 10, and December 10 Mrs. Miller gave the cellar a good airing by opening the inside cellar door so as to communicate with the upstairs rooms, and then she closed up the house to go into the city to spend the winter with me

March 30, 1874, I went out and took them out of winter quarters, and was delighted to find them in superb condition, the whole eight alive, and hardly a teacupful of dead bees in all. These eight I increased to 22, taking 390 pounds of honey Of course they were increased artificially.

I attributed the previous winter's success partly to their having been taken in earlier than ever before, so I decided to take them in still earlier, and went out for that purpose Oct. 29. But the bees decided they would *not* be taken in, and whenever I attempted to take them *in* they boiled *out*. So, just as I had done a good many times before, I had to give up and let them have their own way, leaving Mrs. Miller to get them in when the weather was cool enough for *them*.

November 19 they had a good flight, and November 20 they were taken in by Mr Phillips, a farmer with the average knowledge—or perhaps the average ignorance —of bees, aided by "Jeff," Mrs. Miller's factotum, one of the liveliest specimens of the African race that ever jumped, with considerable more than the average fear of bees. December 12 my wife gave the cellar a good airing, and then it was closed up for the winter.

The winter of 1874-5 was one of remarkable severity, and I felt some anxiety about the bees. The last of
February my wife went out and warmed up the house
and cellar, finding the bees somewhat uneasy, but after
being warmed up and aired they became quiet.   Then
the house was again closed up, and they were left till
April 6, when the men took them out

ITALIANS FROM ADAM GRIMM.

Three of the twenty-two had died, leaving nineteen
to begin the season of 1875   May 10 two colonies were
received from Adam Grimm, for which I paid thirteen
dollars per colony for the sake of getting Italians to
improve my stock, for notwithstanding the several Italian queens I had got, some of my bees were almost black
May 27 I made my first visit, and I did not find the
colonies very strong   Two colonies had died of queenlessness, so that with the two Grimm colonies I had still
only nineteen.

June 25 I visited Marengo again, and was surprised
to find very little gain in the strength of the colonies.
The season had been extremely unpropitious. July 7 I
made another visit, of three days, and found scarcely any
honey in the hives   I made a few new colonies, and by giving empty combs and plenty of room I left them feeling
that there was little fear of any swarming for that
season

TROUBLE WITH SWARMING

But a sudden change must have come over the bees
and the season, and the bees must have built up with
great rapidity, for letters kept coming to me saying that
the bees had swarmed, and Mrs Miller was kept busy
superintending the hiving, "Jeff" doing the work   It
was a mixed-up business for them, for I had left the
queens clipped, and swarms would issue only to return

again, and then in a few days there would be after-swarms, and they didn't know which swarms were likely to have young queens, and which clipped queens. Some swarms probably got away, but in the round up when I went out again, August 10, I found the whole number

Fig. 8.—Carrying with Rope.

of colonies had reached 40, there having been an increase of 12 by natural swarming in addition to the nine colonies I had formed artificially.

BACK TO COUNTRY LIFE.

Clearly, keeping bees at long range was a very unsatisfactory business. City life was also unsatisfactory; a traveling life was worse   So in spite of the reduced chance of making money, I decided for a life in the country, turned my back upon an offer of $2,500 and expenses, and engaged to teach school at $1,200 and bear my own expenses, all because I wanted to be in the country and have a chance to be with the bees all the time. I have never regretted the choice   If I had kept on at other business, I would no doubt have made more money, but I would not have had so good a time, and I doubt if I would be alive now. It's something to be alive, and it's a good deal more to have a happy life.

I did not, however, get away from the city till August 12, 1876, but that was early enough to see that all colonies were well prepared for winter, and to be sure of being with them through the winter

Six of the forty colonies were lost in the preceding winter, and the remaining 34 had given 1,600 pounds of honey, mostly extracted, and had been increased to 99.

IMPROVED WINTERING

The advantage of being at home through the winter was apparent, for in the next four winters the average loss was only 2 per cent, while for the preceding four winters it had been nine times as great. A new factor, however, had come in, to which part of the change was to be attributed   There was chance enough to ventilate the cellar, for two chimneys ran from the ground up through the house, a stove-pipe hole opening from the cellar into each   But the only way to warm the cellar was by keeping fire in the rooms overhead, and by opening the inside cellar-door   One day when I came home from school—I think it was in December, 1876—I found my wife had decided to hurry up the matter of warming the cellar, and had a small stove set up, and throughout the winter there was fire there a good part of the time.

FIRST SECTION HONEY.

In 1877 I gave up extracted honey, the introduction of sections having made such a revolution that it seemed better to go back to comb honey. The sections of that day were crude compared with the finished affairs of the present day. One-piece sections were then unknown, four-piece sections being the only ones, and there was not a remarkably accurate adjustment of the dovetailed parts, so that no little force was required to put the sections together. When the tenon and mortise did not correspond, pounding with a mallet would make the tenon smash its way through.

In order to fasten the foundation in the section, the top piece of the section had a saw-kerf going half way through the wood on the under side   The top was partly split apart, the edge of the foundation inserted, then the wood was straightened back to place. I was not well satisfied with my success in fastening in the foundation, and in 1878 wrote to A I. Root for a better plan, describing minutely the plan I had been using, giving a pencil sketch of the board I used on my lap, with the different parts upon it. In June Gleanings in Bee Culture my letter appeared in full, pencil sketch and all, and he sent me a round sum in payment for the letter, but no word of instruction as to any better way! I hardly knew whether to be glad or mad.

WIDE FRAMES.

The sections were put in wide frames, double-tier, making a frame hold eight sections (Fig. 3) I had an arrangement by which the sections, after having been lightly started together, were all punched into the frame at one stroke, driving them together at the same time, and another arrangement punched them out after they were filled with honey The super in which they were put was the same in size as the 10-frame brood-cham-

ber—in fact there was no difference whatever in the two
except that the bottom-board was nailed onto the brood-
chamber and an entrance cut into it   The super held
seven frames, and that made 56 sections in a super
Lifting these supers when they were filled was no child's
play, especially when loading them on the wagon at an
out-apiary, and unloading them at home, as I had to
do in later years

BROOD-COMBS AS BAITS

In order to start the bees promptly to work in the
sections, a frame of brood was raised from below, and
the sections facing this brood were occupied by the bees
at once if honey was coming in   Care had to be taken
not to leave the brood too long, for if the bees commenced
to seal the sections while it was there they would be
capped very dark, the bees carrying some of the old,
black comb over to the sections to be used in the capping

BEE-KEEPING SOLE BUSINESS

In 1878, at the close of the school year in June, I
decided to give up teaching for a time, and since that
time, more than 24 years ago, I have had no other business but to work with bees, unless it be to write about
them
In 1880 I began out-apiaries in a tentative sort of
way, a few bees in two out-apiaries   In March of that
year my wife died   When the bees were got into the
cellar for winter I closed up the house, took my boy with
me, and went to Johnstown, Pa to spend the winter with
my sister, Mrs Emma R Jones   When I returned near
the close of the following April, deep snow-banks still
surrounded the house, and matters were in anything but
a happy condition in the cellar

DISCOURAGEMENT.

When the bees were ready to begin upon the harvest of 1881, there were 67 colonies left out of the 162 that had been put in the cellar the previous fall. A loss of 59 per cent was additional proof that it is better for the bees and their owner to spend the winter in the same State.

Fig. 9. —Philo Carrying a Hive.

ENCOURAGEMENT.

Beginning 1881 with 67 colonies, I took 7,884 pounds of comb honey, and increased to 177 colonies.

An average of 117 2-3 pounds of comb honey per colony, and an increase of 164 per cent would be nothing so very remarkable in some localities, but I consider it so in a place where there is no basswood, buckwheat, nor anything else to depend upon for a crop except white clover. Certainly it is not the usual thing here, for I have never repeated it since, neither do I expect ever to repeat it unless I should again be so unfortunate as to be reduced to the number of 67 colonies.

AVERAGE YIELD DEPENDS MUCH UPON NUMBERS

In general, I suspect that the number of colonies in a place is not sufficiently taken into account. I remember at one time A I Root commenting upon the case of a beginner with a very few colonies making a fine record, and he thought it was because of the great enthusiasm of the bee-keeper as a beginner. I think instead of unusual enthusiasm it was unusual opportunities for the bees I can easily imagine a place where five colonies might store continuously for five months, and where a hundred colonies on the same ground might not store three weeks. There might be flowers yielding continuously throughout the entire season, but so small in quantity that although they might keep a very few colonies storing right along, they would not yield enough for the daily consumption of more than ten to fifty colonies Remember that the surplus is the smaller part of the honey gathered by the bees Adrian Getaz computes that at least 200 pounds of honey is needed for home consumption by an average colony So far as enthusiasm and interest are concerned, I do not believe my stock is any less of those commodities than it was forty years ago A born bee-keeper never loses his enthusiasm.

TOTAL CROP RATHER THAN PER COLONY.

Some one may possibly ask, "If you can do so much better with 67 colonies, why not restrict yourself to that

Fig. 10.—Colonies Intended for Out-Apiaries.

number?" But I can't do any better; at least not in an average season. For it is not the yield per colony I care for, unless it should be to boast over it; what I care for is the total amount of net money I can get from bees. In the year 1897 my average per colony was 71¾ pounds, only about three-fifths as much as in 1881, but as I had in 1897 239 colonies, my total crop was 17,150 pounds, or more than twice as much as in 1881.

A BAD YEAR.

In the year 1887 my crop of honey was a little more than half a pound per colony, and in the fall I fed 2802 pounds of granulated sugar to keep the bees from starv-

ing in winter   But I could not then tell, neither can I
now tell whether it was because the season was so
bad or because the field was overstocked, for I
had 363 colonies in four apiaries.   Possibly if I had
had only half as many bees, the balance might have been
on the other side of the ledger   But I don't know.

Somewhere there surely is a limit beyond which one
cannot profitably increase the number of colonies in an
apiary, but just where that limit is can perhaps never
be learned   If I were obliged to make a guess, I should
say about 80 colonies in one apiary is the limit in my
locality

If I were to live my life over again, and knew in
advance that I should be a bee-keeper, I never would
locate in a place with only one source of surplus   When
white clover fails here the bottom drops out   Unfortunately the years in which the bottom drops out have been
unpleasantly frequent

In the fall of 1881 I married Miss Sidney Jane Wilson,
who was born on the Wilson farm where one of my out-
apiaries was and is now located   There was some economy in the arrangement, for she could go to the out-
apiary for a day's work, and visit her old home at the
same time

A GOOD YEAR.

Of the 177 colonies with which the year 1881 closed,
two died in wintering, and I sold one in the spring
That left 174 for the season of 1882, and these gave me
16,549 pounds of honey, nearly all in sections   That
was 95 pounds per colony, and the increase was only
16 per cent   Quite a falling off from the amount per
colony of the previous year   But the additional nine
thousand pounds in the total crop reconciled me to the
"per colony" part of the business   It would be interesting to learn how much the difference in the yield per

colony was due to the season, and how much to the increased number, but that is one of the things past finding out.

HEDDON SUPER.

In the year 1883 I tried the Heddon super (Fig. 4) to the number of two hundred. The Heddon super is much in

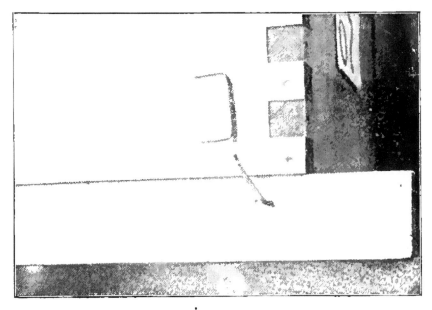

Fig. 11.—Hive-Staples.

form like a T super, but it is divided lengthwise into four compartments. This prevents, of course, the possibility of having separators running the length of the super, so no separators are used. James Heddon and others had reported success in obtaining sections that were straight enough for satisfactory packing in a shipping-case, but with me too many sections were bulged, their neighbors being correspondingly hollowed out. I did not continue the use of this super very long.

T SUPER

In the latter part of the same year I attended the North American convention at Toronto, Canada, and while there D A. Jones showed me the T super (Fig 5). I was much impressed by it The next year I put a number of T supers in use, and the more I tried them the better I liked them I have tried a number of other kinds since, but nothing that has made me desire to make a change.

THICK TOP-BARS.

When attending that same convention, that very practical Canadian bee-keeper, J B Hall, showed me his thick top-bars, and told me that they prevented the building of so much burr-comb between the top-bars and the sections. Although I made no immediate practical use of this knowledge, it had no little to do with my using thick top-bars afterwards I was at that time using the Heddon slat honey-board (Fig. 6) and the use of it with the frames I then had was a boon. It kept the bottoms of the sections clean, but when it was necessary to open the brood-chamber there was found a solid mass of honey between the honey-board and the top-bars It was something of a nuisance, too, to have this extra part in the way, and I am very glad that at the present day it can be dispensed with by having top-bars $1\frac{1}{8}$ inch wide and $\frac{7}{8}$ inch thick, with a space of $\frac{1}{4}$ inch between top-bar and section Not that there is an entire absence of burr-combs, but near enough to it so that one can get along much more comfortably than with the slat honey-board At any rate there is no longer the killing of bees that there was every time the dauby honey-board was replaced

But it would take up space unnecessarily to follow farther the course of the years, especially as these later years are familiar to more of my readers than are the former years, so I will proceed to fulfill my chief purpose in telling about my work throughout the course of the year, reserving, however, the right to refer to the past whenever I like.

SEASONS HAVE CHANGED.

It is only fair to remark, however, that in later years the crops have not been so good as formerly. At least that is true as to the early crop. The fall crop, however, seems to be on the increase. Just why, I don't know, unless it be that there are two important pickle factories at Marengo, and the bees have the range of some two hundred acres of cucumbers. Sweet clover may have a little to do with it.

If the yield of fall honey keeps on the increase, it will hardly do to say there is only one source of honey—

Fig. 12.—Bottom-Board and False Bottom.

white clover. The season of 1902 emphasized the change in seasons. During the proper time for white clover, the bees would have starved if it had not been that they were fed about a thousand pounds of sugar. Clover grew well, but blossoms were scarce. The bloom, however, kept increasing, and during the latter part of August and the first part of September a number of colonies stored fifty pounds and more each. How much of the honey was from clover I cannot tell As late as the last half of October I saw the bees busy on both red and white clover

TAKING BEES OUT OF THE CELLAR.

The difficulty of wintering bees, at the North, is not entirely without its compensations. I am almost willing to meet some losses, for the sake of the sharp interest with which I look forward to the time of taking the bees out of the cellar in the spring I live on a place of 37 acres, about a mile from the railroad station, and on my way down town a number of soft-maple trees are growing How eagerly I watch for the first bursting of the buds, and when the red of the blossom actually begins to push forth, with what a thrill of pleasure I say, "The bees can get out on the first good day!"

In former years I did sometimes bring out the bees earlier, because they seemed so uneasy, but I doubt if I gained anything by it. I have known years when a cold, freezing time came on at the time of maple-bloom and I did not take out the bees for a good many days, but generally I go by the blooming of the soft maples So I watch the thermometer and the clouds, and usually in a day or two there comes a morning with the sun shining, and the mercury at 45 or 50 degrees, with the prospect of going a good deal higher through the day

TAKING OUT WITH A RUSH

This is one of the times when I want outside help, for carrying two or three hundred colonies of bees out

of the cellar is not very light work if it be done with a
rush; and I want them all out as soon as possible so as
to have a good flight before night.   If any should
be brought out too late to fly, it may turn cold before
the next morning, when a lot of bees might fly out to
meet their death. To be sure, I could get along without
outside help by having one of the women-folks help me,
for my hives have cleats on each end, the cleats reaching
clear across the hive, so that a rope can be slipped over
them, and one can take hold of the rope at each side,
making the work not so very hard.   Indeed, the two
women have sometimes rendered efficient service by taking a hive between them, as shown in Fig. 7. An endless
rope is used, making it the work of a very few seconds
to throw the rope over each end of the hive The same
rope may be used to make the work lighter for a single person (Fig. 8).   But the rope is not so quickly
adjusted as when two persons use it.

On the whole, it is better to have a strong man who
can pick up each hive without any ceremony, carry it
directly to its place and set it on its stand.   In this work
the end-cleats of the hive serve an important purpose, for
the carrier can let the full weight of the hive come on his
forearms by having an arm under each cleat, each hand
lightly clasping the hive on the opposite side (Fig 9).

CELLAR AIRED BEFORE CARRYING.

When it is warm enough to carry out bees, it will
be understood that the cellar is likely to become a good deal
warmer than 45 degrees, the temperature near which it is
desirable to keep the cellar throughout the winter So if
carrying out is undertaken without any previous preparation, when the cellar-door is opened the bees will pour out
of the hives and out of the cellar-door, sailing about in
confusion, causing some loss and making the work of
carrying exceedingly unpleasant. This must be avoided;

so the previous evening, as soon as it becomes dusk, cellar door and window are thrown wide open

Having the cellar open the previous night makes it much pleasanter to carry out the bees, which do not generally come out of their hives till some time after being set on their stands. If at any time a colony seems inclined to come out of the hive, a little smoke is given at the entrance. At other times it would be bad to have smoke in the cellar, but as the bees are immediately to have a chance to fly, it does no harm to have the cellar filled with smoke. The hive entrances are left open, and as the hives had been taken into the cellar with covers and bottom-boards just as on the summer stands, the work can be done rapidly.

Before each hive leaves the cellar, I make sure there are live bees in it, by placing my ear at the entrance. If I hear nothing I blow into the entrance That generally brings an immediate response, but sometimes I will blow several times before getting a sleepy reply from a strong colony. That pleases me. If any are dead they are piled to one side in the cellar

PLACING OF COLONIES

Colonies intended for the home apiary are set upon their stands. Those for the out-apiaries are set upon the ground not far from the cellar, being placed in pairs, two hives almost touching, then a space of a foot or more between that pair and the next pair, so as to occupy as little room as possible (Fig. 10) Sometimes some attempt is made to have colonies occupy the same stands they occupied the previous year, but oftener no attention is paid to this. Close attention, however, is paid to selecting the colonies that are to be in the home apiary.

BEST BEES FOR HOME APIARY.

The hives with queens having the best records were all marked the previous fall by having a stick tacked on the front. These are all put in the home apiary. Not that queens will be reared from all of them. The one

Fig. 13.—Entrance-Blocks.

or two very best colonies may furnish all the young queens, the rest will furnish choice drones. By doing this from year to year I ought to have better stock than if I allowed the poorest drones to remain in the home apiary.

TAKING BEES ALL OUT AT ONCE.

Some object to taking all the bees out at the same time, for fear of so much excitement that bees will swarm out and return to the wrong hives. I have never had much trouble in that way. Neither have I had any evil results from putting colonies on stands different from the ones they occupied the previous fall.

I am not sure that I can tell for certain just why there should be this difference in different apiaries, but I think I can see some reason for it. As already mentioned, the cellar is left wide open all night the night before the bees are carried out, and it is possible that just in that little thing lies the secret of the difference. When the weather begins to warm up in the spring, before it is time to carry out the bees. it often happens that there comes a warm day when the outside temperature runs up to 50 degrees or more, and possibly this may continue more than a day   Such times are hard on the ventilation of the cellar.

TEMPERATURE AND VENTILATION.

Please remember that the ventilation of the cellar depends on the difference of the weight of the air in the cellar and the weight of the outside air. Also remember that the difference in weight depends on the difference in temperature. Warm air is lighter than cold air   So when the air outside the cellar is colder and heavier than that inside, it forces itself in and crowds up the warm air, precisely in the same way—although not with the same degree of force—precisely in the same way that water would pour into the cellar if a body of water surrounded the cellar. If the water were lighter than the air, no water would flow into the cellar. So long as the outside air is colder than the inside, ventilation continues.

Suppose, now, that the air in the cellar stands at 45 or 50 degrees, and that the outside air becomes warmed up to the same temperature   There will be an equilibrium in weight, and there will be no ventilation   The air in the cellar is all the time becoming vitiated by the breathing of the bees, and no matter what the ventilation of the *hives,* it can do little good so long as there is no pure air in the *cellar*   The bees become frantic in their desire for fresh air, and if carried out while in this condition they will rush out of the hive, the excitement becoming so great that soon after being put on their stands whole colonies will swarm out. If the cellar has been open all night, they will find little change of air on being carried out, and so will not fly out of the hives for the sake of getting air, but only to take their cleansing flight.

Of course, there is an understanding with the women-folks about the time the bees are taken out, lest they spot the clothes on the line on a wash-day, but the

Fig. 14.— Wagon Load of Bees.

bees have the right of way, and if there is a clash, the wash-day must be postponed.

SIZE OF ENTRANCE.

While the bees were in the cellar, they had an entrance $12\frac{1}{8}$x2 inches, and during the cool days of spring, after they are taken out of the cellar, it is no longer desirable to have so large an entrance. So after the bees have had their first flight, the entrance is closed down to a very small one by means of an entrance-block. Before describing this I must tell you about the hive and bottom-board

CLEATS FOR HIVES

The hive is the ordinary 8-frame dovetailed, only I insist upon having on each end a plain cleat $13\frac{7}{8}$x$1\frac{1}{2}$x$\frac{7}{8}$. There are more reasons than one for having this cleat, rather than the usual hand-holes It is more convenient to take hold of when one wants to lift a hive. Latterly the manufacturers use a very short cleat, which is a great improvement on the hand-hole, but it does not allow one to carry the hive with the weight resting on the whole forearm, as shown in Fig. 9. This way of carrying a hive is one gotten up by Philo Woodruff, the hired man who has helped me for several years, evidently to make the work easier for him. One day he was carrying a hive that had no cleats, only hand-holes, perhaps the only one of that kind he had ever carried He seemed disgusted with it, and as he set the hive down he grumbled, "I wish the man that made them hand-holes had to carry them."

Another advantage of the cleats is the strength it gives to the rabbeted ends of the hive Without the cleat the rabbet leaves the hive-end at the top only 7-16 of an inch thick for more than $\frac{3}{4}$ of an inch of its depth, and the splitting off of this part is unpleasantly frequent With the added cleat the thickness is three times as much, and it never splits off

These cleats, not being regularly made by manufacturers, can only be had by having them made to order, so hives are generally made without them, but quite a number of experienced bee-keepers are quietly using them because of their distinct advantage, notwithstanding the inconvenience of having them made to order.

BOTTOM-BOARD

The bottom-board is a plain box, two inches deep, open at one end. It is made of six pieces of $\frac{7}{8}$ stuff;

two pieces 22½x2, one piece 12⅛x2, and three pieces 13⅞x7½. When so desired, the bottom-board is fastened to the hive by means of four staples 1½ inches wide, with points ¾ inch long (Fig 11).

With such a bottom-board there is a space two inches deep under the bottom-bars, a very nice thing in winter, and at any time when there is no danger of bees building down, but quite too deep for harvest-time. Formerly I made the bottom-board reversible, reversing it in summer so as to use the shallow side, but latterly I prefer to use a false bottom to reduce the space in summer.

It is much easirer to shove in this false bottom or to take it out than it is to lift the hive from its place to reverse the bottom-board The false bottom is made on the same general principle as the bottom-board, only on a smaller scale and very much lighter. The outside dimensions are 18¼x11x1½ It is constructed of two pieces 18¼x1¼x½; one piece 10x1¼x½; two pieces 11x9⅛x¼.

At Fig 12 are seen two bottom-boards, the one at the right being empty as in winter, and the one at the left having in it a false bottom, as in summer. When in use, the closed end of the false bottom is toward the entrance. In an emergency, two dummies or a piece of board may be used in place of the false bottom.

ENTRANCE-BLOCK.

Now for that entrance-block (Fig. 13). It is very simple, made of common lumber, 12 inches long, 3 inches wide, with a notch 1 inch square cut out of one corner. It is put at the entrance against the front of the hive, a little wedge is crowded into the ⅛ inch space at one end, and there you are with an entrance one inch square Hives for the out-apiaries may not have entrances contracted till they are hauled

When the bees are being carried out, if any are noted as suspiciously light, they are marked, and the next day frames of honey are given them If, unfortunately, these are not to be had, sections of honey are put in the hive in wide frames

HAULING BEES.

As soon as the bees have had a good flight, those not in the home apiary are ready to be hauled away. I like to get them away as soon as possible, so as to have advantage of the spring pasturage at the out-apiaries, but sometimes the condition of the roads causes delay I first hauled four colonies at a time on a one-horse wagon, which you may imagine was very slow work That was years ago, and the number has been gradually increased until now 31 colonies are taken at a load (Fig. 14).

WAGON FOR HAULING

A common lumber-wagon is used with heavy springs put under the box; nine colonies are put in the box then a rack (Fig 15) (made in two parts for convenience in handling) is put on the box, and 22 colonies are set on the rack Of the outfit the rack is the only thing that belongs to me, the rest I borrow of a very obliging brother-in-law, Ghordis Stull.

PREPARATION FOR HAULING

All the hives have fixed-distance frames, so no preparation is needed in the way of fastening frames in place before hauling The only thing to do is to fasten the cover and close the entrance The cover is fastened to the hive by two staples (the same as those used to fasten the bottom-board to the hive) one staple at the middle on each side Hives that were brought from the out-apiaries the previous fall have the covers already fastened, for they have never been opened since coming home, unless they were so light as to need feeding. If things were always done just right, there never would be any opened because suspiciously light; but things are not always done just right.

ENTRANCE-CLOSERS.

The entrance is of course closed with wire-cloth, and after trying a good many entrance-closers I have settled down upon the simplest of all. It is a piece of wire-cloth just large enough to close the $12\frac{1}{8}$ entrance and project an inch or so up on the front of the hive. To make the edges at the bottom and at the two ends more firm, and to prevent them from raveling, the wire-cloth is cut about $13\frac{1}{2}$x4, and about $\frac{3}{4}$ of an inch folded over at the bottom and at each end. These edges are folded over the

Fig. 15.—Rack for Hauling Bees.

blade of a saw. When finished, the closer is $12\frac{1}{8}$ inches long or a trifle less, so it will easily fit in the bottom-board   The closer is put in place, a piece of lath 13½ inches long is pushed up against it, and fastened by a nail in the middle of the lath   Then to make it more secure, a nail at each end is placed perpendicularly against the lath and driven a short distance into the outer rim of the bottom-board   The three nails used to fasten the lath are finishing or wire casing nails 2½ inches long or longer   Being so long and not driven in very deep, one can generally pull them out with the fingers.

At Fig. 16, in the middle of the cut, will be seen an entrance-closer, above it being the lath to fasten the closer in place

Before the hives are put on the wagon I make sure there is no possible leak in any of them   This is hardly necessary where everything is in good condition, but some of my covers and bottom-boards are pretty old, and I must plug up any hole that would possibly allow a bee to escape

When the hives are placed on their stands in the out-apiary, the entrance-closers are removed, a little smoke being used if the bees appear belligerent   Then the en-trances are closed with the entrance-blocks

NUMBERING HIVES

Numbers for hives are made in this way   Pieces of tin 4x2½ inches have a small hole punched in each one, near the edge, about midway of one of the longer sides With ½ inch wire nails, nail them on the top of a wooden hive-cover or other plane surface   Then give them a couple of coats of white paint, and, when dry, put the numbers on them, from 1 upward, with black paint. There is room to make figures large enough to be seen distinctly at quite a distance   These tin tags are fas-tened on the fronts of the hives with ¾ or inch wire-nails driven in not very deep, making it easy to change them at any time from one hive to another

I have also used manilla tags with figures printed on them, but the figures are not seen at so great a distance as on the white tin tags. The tin tags cost more in the first place, but are cheaper in the long run, for they last twenty years or more, while the manilla scarcely last a fifth of that time in satisfactory shape.

ORDER OF NUMBERS

When the hives are put on the stands in the spring, the numbers are all mixed up. The first thing to be done is to enter upon the record-book these numbers. The first hive in the first row should be No. 1, the next No 2, and so on; but in the place of No. 1 stands perhaps 231, on the place of No. 2 stands 174, etc. So, on the new record-book I write No 1 (231) on the first page at the top; one-third the way down the page, I write No. 2(174), and so on.

Just as soon as convenient the tags are taken off the hives where they are wrong, and the right ones put on. If on No. 1 the tag says 231, then that tag is taken off and the tag that says 1 is put on.

THE RECORD-BOOK.

I can tell more or less of the history of every colony of bees since I began keeping bees in 1861 At first I kept the record of each colony from year to year in the same book, but for a good many years I have had a new book each year The book I like is 12x5½ inches, containing about 160 pages (Fig. 17). Three colonies are kept on each page, so the book is a good deal larger than I need, for I have never had quite 400 colonies But a good many pages are used for memoranda and other things, and it is better to have too much room in the book than too little. While the size of the book is not so very important, the binding is. If the book were

bound the same as the book in which you are now reading, it would come to pieces if it should be left out long
enough in a soaking rain. Of course a book never should
be left out in a rain, but of course it sometimes is So
I want a book that will suffer no greater harm than to
have the cover come off if it should be rain-soaked It
must be stitched together through the middle, so that the
one set of stitches does the whole business, the first leaf
being continuous with the last leaf, the second continuous with the next to the last, and so on.

HISTORY OF QUEENS.

While the record-book is very important to keep
track of the work from day to day, it is perhaps more
important for the purpose of tracing the history of
queens from year to year. On each page is left a margin
of about ¾ of an inch. In that margin is put the last
two figures of the year in which the queen is born,
'99 if she was born in 1899, 'or if in 1901,
and so on. In that margin is also found anything important to have recorded about the queen
"Very cross" may be in the margin if the workers distinguished themselves in that direction; "seals white" if
the capping of sections was uncommonly white, "dark"
if the workers were unusually dark, etc Especially am I
interested in the memoranda in the margin relating to
swarming and storing You will find *sw* if the colony of
that queen swarmed last year; *no c* if no queen-cells were
found in the hive during the whole of last season *2 k* if
twice I killed queen-cells that were started No doubt the
printer will feel like putting some periods after those con-
tractions Please don't do it, Mr. Printer, for I never
take time to use any such embellishments when making
entries The number of sections stored by the progeny
of the queen the preceding year has a place in this margin, *24 sec* if 24 sections were stored· *160 sec* if so

many sections were stored. If an unusual number of sections was reached, that record follows the queen as

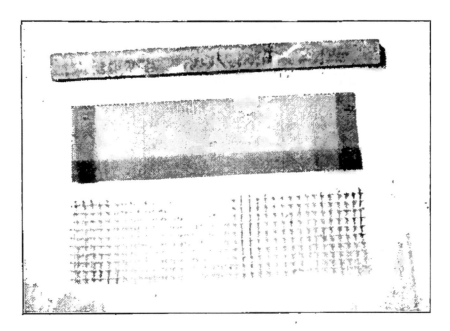

Fig. 16.—Entrance Closers.

long as she lives. For instance, in the year 1902 there may be found in one case in the margin, *44 sec, 60 sec* in *1900, 178 sec* in *99*. That means that the progeny of that queen stored 44 sections in the preceding year, 1901, 60 sections in 1900, and 178 sections in 1899. An unusual record, considering the character of the seasons in 1900 and 1901. If, in the year 1902, a 1900 queen is by any means replaced by a young queen, a line is drawn through the *00* and *02* is written below it.

As soon as I have entered in the record the old numbers that were on the hives, as previously mentioned, I am ready to enter the respective ages of the queens. If, for instance, I find at the beginning, No. 1 (231), I turn to No. 231 in last year's record and find the year set

down for the age of the queen, and put it in the new book
at No. 1.   This I do throughout all the numbers.

ADVANTAGE OF BOOK FOR RECORD.

I do not need to be in the apiary to do this work;
it can be done in the house just as well   Indeed I spend
a good deal of time in the house with my record-book,
studying and planning, perhaps lying on the lounge   I
have two out-apiaries, one three miles north at Jack Wilson's, on the old farm where my wife was born, the
other five miles southeast at cousin Hastings' Frequently I study my book most of the way in going to one
of these apiaries, making my plans, and jotting down
memoranda of what is to be done when I get there
That saves time   Another advantage is that my records
are safe from interference, for with slates, stones, etc.,
in the apiary, there is always danger that records may
be changed, either through accident or mischievous design   One disadvantage of the book is the danger of for-
getting it.   One may forget it at an out-apiary, and then
have to make a special trip to get it   I've done that.

SPRING OVERHAULING

After the bees are hauled to the out-apiaries, I am
ready for spring overhauling as soon as the weather is
right for it   I do not want to open up the hives except
at a time when it is warm enough for bees to fly freely.
Too much danger of chilling the brood.   Sometimes there
may come one good day followed by a week of weather
too bad for bees to fly   So I may commence overhauling
in April, and perhaps not till in May, and if I do commence in April I may not get all done till well on in May.

HIVE SEAT.

Having due regard to my own comfort, I want a
seat when I work at a hive   Mr. Doolittle once tried to

poke a little fun at me in convention, because I acci-
dentally admitted that I sat down to work at bees   If I
were obliged to work all the season without a seat, I
am afraid I would have to give up the business from
exhaustion   Moreover, if I had the strength of a Sam-
son I don't think I should waste it stooping over hives,
so long as I could get a seat.   I generally have three or
four seats about the apiary, and they may not all be of
the same kind.   A common glass-box is more used than
any other.   To make it convenient for carrying, a strap
of leather or cloth may be nailed to two diagonally opposite corners on the bottom   Or the cover may be nailed
on the box with a hand-hole in the middle.   The box
being of three different dimensions, one has a choice as
to height of seat.   It is a little curious to know what a
difference there is in this respect as to the preferences
of different persons   My assistant never uses the highest seat the box affords, while I never use the lowest

Fig. 18 shows a hive-seat with a strap-handle, the
kind I prefer; Fig 19 shows one with hand-hole, which
my assistant prefers.

A DIGRESSION.

Perhaps I ought to digress a little, and tell you about
my help.   Years ago, my wife, her sister Emma, and
sometimes my boy Charlie (I have no other children), all
worked with me at the bees   Those were delightful days.
I think Charlie would have made a very bright bee-
keeper, but somehow he did not take kindly to the business, and has spent his later years in the army and gov-
ernment service   My wife is one of the sort who is
never happy unless she is doing something for someone
else, so for years she has been confined to the house so
as to help make a pleasant home for others, sometimes
of my relatives, sometimes of hers.   At present, in this
year of our Lord 1902, as well as for several years past,
there dwells with us my wife's mother, Mrs Margaret

Wilson, a blessed old Scotch saint, whose presence in the home I feel to be much like the presence of the ark in the house of Obed-Edom, when "it was told king David, saying, The Lord hath blessed the house of Obed-Edom, and all that pertaineth unto him, because of the ark of God" There is with us temporarily a niece who is teaching school, and that completes the household.

ASSISTANT BEE-KEEPER.

So for a number of years Miss Emma M Wilson has given me the only assistance I have had in the apiary The hired man does some such work as carrying out and hauling bees, putting together hives, etc , unloading honey brought from the out-apiary, taking sections out of supers, etc This hired man, whose present name is Philo Woodruff, is in the joint employ of myself and my good brother-in-law, Ghordis Stull. Ghordis has the place pretty well filled with raspberries and strawberries, and he is 'way up in such matters Previous to his occupancy of the place, it was chiefly in grass, for I could give no attention to cultivated crops The only thing I pretend to oversee of the farm work is the cultivation of the rose-beds. I could hardly live without roses and my wife is an expert in chrysanthemums. With the fruit crop I have nothing whatever to do except with the finished product, and only so much of that as we can finish in the house—by no means a small quantity

Miss Wilson was a school-teacher with health run down, and twenty years ago she stopped a year for the out-door life of bee-keeping. She is still stopping. Although never rugged in health, I think she has never missed a day's work in the apiary during all the twenty years, when there was work to be done Small of stature and frail of build, she yet has a remarkable capacity for work, perhaps partly owing to the fact that she is full-blood Scotch, and she will go through more colonies in a day than I can, do my best. I think, however, that the bees prefer just a little to have me work with them. They have more time to get out of my way, and not so many of them get killed.

Fig. 17.—Record Books.

T-SUPER SEAT.

Well, I started in for a digression, but I didn't mean to write a history. We were talking about seats. Another kind of seat is made of an old T-super. A piece of lath is nailed to two opposite diagonal corners, and another piece nailed to the other two corners. That stiffens and strengthens it, so it makes a good seat for one who doesn't like a low seat

HIVE-TOOLS

Of all the hive-tools I have tried, I like best the Muench tool (Fig 20) Its broad semi-circular end with sharp edge can hardly be excelled for the purpose of raising covers and supers, and when the other end is thrust between two frames, a quarter turn separates the frames with the least possible effort Beside the hive-tool for opening the hive and starting the frames, if the hives are to be cleaned out another tool is needed

After trying a number of different things for hive-cleaners, I have been best satisfied with a hatchet, the handle sawed short, so that it will not be in the way when working in the bottom of the hive, the edge dull and a perfectly straight line, and the outside part of the blade also ground to a straight line and at right angles with the edge This right-angled corner is to clean out the corners of the hive. In cleaning, the hatchet is moved rapidly back and forth, or rather from side to side, the blade being held at right angles to the surface being cleaned The weight of the hatchet is quite a help, something like a fly-wheel in machinery.

It would be a nice thing to clean the propolis out of all hives every spring, because I am in a region for profitable propolis production if it ever comes to be a staple article of commerce, but it takes some time to clean the hives, and it is not done every spring.

CLEANING HIVES

If the hives are to be cleaned, an empty clean hive is ready in advance The empty hive is placed at right angles to the hive to be overhauled, the back end of the empty hive near the front end of the other hive, thus leaving plenty of room for my seat beside the full hive, and leaving the empty hive within easy reach

OPENING HIVE.

A single puff at the entrance if the smoker is going well, or two or three puffs if it is yet scarcely under headway, notifies the guards that they needn't bother to come out if they feel a little jar. The cover is cracked open the least bit at one corner by the tool, then the other corner is cracked open and the cover lifted. It could be lifted without using the tool twice, simply prying up one corner enough, but that would jar the bees more, and excite them. The desire is to get along with the smallest amount of jar and smoke possible, for the queen is to be found, and too much smoke or jarring will set the bees to running so the queen cannot be found. As soon as the cover is raised, a little smoke is blown across the tops of the frames, not down into the hive. While it

Fig. 18.—Hive-Seat with Strap-Handle.

is bad to use too much smoke, it is also bad to use too little, for if the bees are once thoroughly aroused it takes more smoke to subdue them than it does to keep them under in the first place.

TAKING OUT FRAMES.

When the cover is removed the dummy is taken out. If the dummy was on the near side, the frames are all crowded to that side, allowing me to lift out the farther frame Whether that farther frame is now to be put into the empty hive depends upon circumstances. It is to be put in if the next frame contains brood, otherwise not. For I want the brood-nest to begin with the frame next to the farther outside frame, at least that is generally the way.   Then I can tell at any time afterward how many frames of brood are in a hive, merely by finding where the brood begins on the side next me. One after another the frames are changed into the empty hive, making sure that at least those containing brood maintain their original relative positions

When the old hive is empty, then it is set off the stand and the other takes its place. The order of proceeding may be changed by first setting the full hive off the stand and putting the empty one in its place Or the change may be made when half the frames have changed their places. The last makes the lifting a little lighter, but takes more time

The empty hive is now to be cleaned out, the hatchet being used for all but the rabbet, which is a separate contract. Propolis is used in large quantities in my locality, and the trough formed by the tin rabbet will, in the course of years, become completely filled

In the matter of propolis, there is a difference in bees as well as localities   The worst daubers I ever had were the so-called Punics or Tunisians from the north of Africa One colony put so much propolis at an upper entrance that I rolled up a ball of it somewhere between the size of a hickory nut and a black walnut.

To clean out the rabbet, the small end of the hive-tool is well adapted. Holding it perpendicularly, with the edge of the tool diagonally in the trough, I play it backward and forward until the trough is emptied of propolis.

The empty hive is now used to take the place of the next hive to be overhauled, which in its turn is cleaned and then used again, and so on.

While the frames are being changed from one hive to the other, observations and necessary changes are made. If there is no cleaning of hives, then the work is shortened. The dummy is taken out, and one frame is also taken out so as to leave freer working room. This one frame may be put in an empty hive standing convenient; or it may be leaned against the hive being operated on, or against an adjoining hive. If the dummy was on the near side, then the frames are all pushed toward me, two or three being started at a time, and when all are started the tool is pushed down between the farther frame and the side of the hive, and all the frames at one push shoved toward me enough to give plenty of room at the farther side. If the frames are Hoffman (a few hives contain Hoffman frames) then it is necessary to start each frame separately before it can be lifted out

WATCHING FOR QUEEN.

As the frames are being handled, the thing that receives closer attention than anything else is to see the queen so as to know whether she is clipped or not. For if a colony should have an unclipped queen there is a fair chance that it might swarm and decamp, and it is possible that almost any colony may have superseded its queen the previous fall, leaving it with an unclipped queen.

IMPLEMENT FOR CLIPPING.

If the queen is unclipped, of course I clip her. Nearly always I use a pair of scissors for clipping, although I

have tried a knife   The strongest argument in favor of
the knife is that a knife is always on hand. But it is as
easy to have a pair of scissors on hand. They may be
tied to the record-book, and the record-book is sure to be
always on hand   Most of the time I have had a pair
of embroidery scissors tied to my record-book with a
string long enough to allow the scissors to be freely used,
but I have been surprised to find that much larger scissors will do very good work   Latterly I have used a
common pair of gentleman's pocket scissors, and I am
not sure but I like them as well as the embroidery scissors. It is just as easy to have a pair of these as a
knife constantly in the pocket. To make good work clipping, a knife should be very sharp, and I find it is harder to
have a *sharp* knife constantly on hand than a sharp pair of
scissors   Neither is it so necessary that the scissors be
sharp

FINDING QUEEN

Before a queen is clipped she must be found   I have
seen some attempt at rules for finding a queen, but after
all is said, you must do more or less hunting for a queen
if you would find her. I generally begin looking on the
first frame of brood I come to—hardly worth while to
look on any frame before the brood is reached—and as
I raise the frame out of the hive I keep watch of the
side next me. Then when the frame is lifted out of the
hive, before looking at the opposite side, I glance at the
nearest side of the next frame in the hive; for it requires
scarcely any time to do this, and if she happens to be in
sight it will be a saving of time to lift out immediately
the frame she is on   Not seeing her on the frame in the
hive, I look over both sides of the frame in my hand,
and continue thus through all the frames   Although it
was not worth while to look for her on any comb before
the brood-nest was reached, it is worth while to look for
her on the comb or combs remaining after passing over

those that contain brood, for in trying to get away from the light she will go onto the outside combs.

Fig. 19.—Hive-Seat with Hand-Holes.

This trying to get away from the light on the part of the queen, by going from one comb to the other, makes me go over the combs as rapidly as possible without looking too closely, for if I do not see her with a slight looking, the chances are that she is on another comb, and I count it better to run the chance of going over the combs again, rather than to go too slowly. For if one goes over the combs *slowly enough*, it is a pretty safe thing to say that the queen will be driven clear to the other side of the hive.

My assistant, however, who is an expert at finding queens, holds a different theory, and as a consequence her practice is different   She thinks it better to go more slowly and make sure of finding the queen first time going over.   She takes more time to go over the combs the first time, but she doesn't often have to go over the combs a second time, so perhaps one way is as good as the other.

If the queen is not found the second time going over, she *may* be found the third time, but it is quite possible that she is hid in such a way that it may be impossible to find her with long searching   So it is economy to close the hive, and try it again another day, or at least to wait half an hour.

AIDS TO FINDING QUEEN

If, for some special reason, it is very important to find the queen without any postponement, sometimes the combs are put in pairs.   Two of the combs are put in an empty hive, the two being close together, then another pair is put an inch or more distant from the first pair, and the remaining combs in the hive on the stand are arranged in pairs the same way   Wherever the queen is, it will not be long before she will be in the middle of whatever pair of combs she is on   Going on with work at another hive, I return after a little, and look again for the queen   Lifting out the comb nearest me, I look first on the side of its mate in the hive, and if I do not see the queen there, I quickly look on the opposite side of the comb in my hand   I am pretty sure to find her in the middle of one of the pairs.

If the pairs are sufficiently separated from each other (I don't mean the two combs of each pair separated, for the two combs in each pair should be as close together as possible, but that one pair should be far enough from another pair so that the bees should not communicate), the bees will after standing long enough, show signs of uneasiness by running over the combs, all but the one pair that has the queen on, and the quietness of the bees on that one pair is sufficient warrant for seeking the queen there.

If the bees get to running, it is hardly worth while

Fig. 20.—Muench Hive-Tool.

to continue the search for the queen until they have quieted down. Sometimes she will be on the side or the bottom of the hive, and will be found only by lifting out all the combs.

BEE-STRAINER.

A strainer may be used for straining the bees through
and leaving the queen A queen-excluder is fastened
to the bottom of an empty hive-body, and that makes
the strainer The strainer is set over a hive-body in
which there is a frame of brood but no bees—at least it
must be certain that the queen cannot possibly be in the
hive-body under the strainer Then all the bees are
shaken and brushed from the combs into the strainer
The workers will go down through the excluder, being
hurried by a little smoke if necessary, while the queen will
be left in the strainer

On the whole the queen is generally found so easily
by the ordinary looking over the combs that it is seldom
that any other plan is resorted to

It happens once in a great while that the queen is on
the cover when it is lifted off the hive, so it is well to
glance over the under surface of the cover as it is removed from the hive Once in a great while I have
known the queen after no little searching to be on the
shoulder or some other part of the operator. How she
managed to get there I don't know

CATCHING THE QUEEN

When the queen is found, she must be caught before
she is clipped. I want to catch her by the thorax or just
back of the thorax, and if she is in motion, by the time
I reach for the thorax it will have passed along out of
reach. So I make a reach more as if attempting to catch her
by the head, and the movements she makes is likely to
bring my thumb and finger down on each side of her
thorax, and in that position she is held firmly on the
comb (Fig 21) There is no danger of hurting the
queen by giving a pretty hard squeeze on the thorax, and
indeed there is not so very much danger if the hold is

farther back and the abdomen gets a little squeeze.

Then the thumb and finger are slid up off the thorax, at the same time pressed together, and this gives me a grip on the wings, when she is lifted from the comb, fairly caught (Fig. 22).

All this is done with the right hand, generally, although occasionally she is caught with the left hand. At any rate, she is now shifted to the left hand, and held between the thumb and finger, back up, head and thorax between thumb and finger, head pointing to the left, ready to clip (Fig. 23).

CLIPPING THE QUEEN.

Then one blade of the scissors is slipped under the two wings of one side, and they are cut off as short as they can conveniently be clipped (Fig. 24).

Fig. 21.—Catching the Queen.

The queen will be just as helpless about flying if only the larger wing on one side is clipped, and clipping the

one wing will not mar her looks so much, but when a
queen is scurrying across a comb, or when you get just
a glimpse of her in the hive, it is much easier to tell at
a glance that she is clipped if both wings on one side
are cut off.

ADVANTAGE OF CLIPPING

Although nowadays the practice of clipping has become quite general, there are a few who doubt its ad-
visability. I would not like to dispense with clipping if I
kept only one apiary and were on hand all the time,
and with out-apiaries and no one to watch them it seems
a necessity If a colony swarms with a clipped queen,
it cannot go off. True, the queen may possibly be lost,
but it is better to lose the queen than to lose both bees
and queen

If there were no other reason for it, I should want
my queens clipped for the sake of keeping a proper record
of them. A colony, for example, distinguishes itself by
storing more than any other colony I want to
breed next spring from the queen of that colony
But she may be superseded in the fall after that big
harvest, and if she is not clipped there is no way for me
to tell in the following season whether she has been
superseded or not   Indeed I can hardly see how it is
possible to keep proper track of a queen without having
her clipped

Sometimes when a queen is being found, she will
quickly run under and out of the way, giving one a mere
glimpse of her, so that it is not easy to say whether it was
a queen or a worker that was seen, in which case the
missing wings aid in recognizing her To this, however, it may be replied that there is less need to find
queens where they are not kept clipped.

BEE-SMOKERS.

You who have used smokers ever since you began working with bees hardly know how to appreciate them At least it is doubtful if you appreciate them as much as you would if you had done as I did when I first began bee-keeping, going around with a pan of coals and a burning brand on it, or else a lighted piece of rotten wood (indeed this last was quite an improvement over the first), the only bellows I had being a sound pair of lungs. Any one of the various makes of smokers I have tried will do quite satisfactory work. I have used up more Clark smokers than any others Although low in price, the Clark is really more expensive than any other It works beautifully while new, but the "new" wears off entirely too soon. The bellows becomes incapacitated by reason of the smoke sucked into it, and then there is no good way to clean it out.

CONTINUOUS AND CUT-OFF BLAST

The Bingham, Cornell, Crane, and others, are all good. The cut-off blast lengthens the life of a smoker, but shortens its blast The continuous blast, as in the Clark, allows one to send the smoke with more force, but, as already mentioned, shortens the life of the smoker, because the bellows become foul with smoke The Crane has the advantage of the full strength of blast without the weakening of the cut-off, and works in perfection for a long time. Still, in the course of time, the metal valve becomes dirty, and it must be cleaned Fortunately the part containing the valve can be taken off, allowing all to be made just as clean as when new. It takes quite a bit of time to do this, but it is time well spent, and one cleaning a year, even with heavy use, is sufficient. Those who do not care for so strong a blast will prefer a Bingham, Corneil, or other smoker with a cut-off, never needing to be cleaned, while those who like the strong blast will be willing to spend the time occasionally cleaning the Crane

CLEATS ON SMOKERS

Using a smoker all day long is a hard thing on the muscles that work the bellows, and the stiffer the spring of the bellows the more tiresome the work. But unless the spring be quite stiff, the smoker will drop out of the hand when the grasp is relaxed so as to allow the bellows to open   I think it was W L Coggshall who suggested little cleats on the smoker, and these cleats have given great satisfaction   They are merely strips of wood one-fourth inch by one-eighth, extending across the upper end of each bellows-board and half way down the sides (Fig 80). The sharp edges of the cleats cling to the fingers, allowing the spring to be—I don't know just how much weaker, but I should guess only half as strong as without the cleats. Some smokers are made with a channel cut in the bellows-board, but that doesn't begin to compare with the cleats

SMOKER-FUEL

It is a matter of much importance to have plenty of the right fuel and lighting material   Time is precious during the busy season, and it is trying on the temper to have to spend much time getting a smoker started, or relighting it when it has gone out. There are a great many different things that can be used for fuel, and it is largely a matter of convenience as to what is best for each one   Pine needles, rotten wood, sound wood, excelsior rammed down hard, planer shavings, greasy cotton-waste thrown away along the railroad, peat, rags, corn-cobs, old bags—in fact almost anything that will burn may be used in a smoker. Whatever is used, however, there should be a good stock of it on hand thoroughly dry, with no chance for the rain to reach it.

Fig. 22.—Caught!

GREEN FUEL.

And yet there are times when something green is better. When a continuous and strong smoke is wanted, after a hot fire has been started in the smoker, it is a good thing to fill the smoker with green sticks from a growing tree. The hot fire and the continuous blowing makes it burn freely, and the smoke from green wood is sharper than that from dry.

But it is only on special occasions that it is desirable to have green wood, and it should at all other times be not only dry but very dry. Nothing is better as a standard fuel than sound hard wood sawed into proper lengths and split up into pieces about a quarter of an inch thick. The only objection is that such wood is rather expensive, for it takes a great deal of time to prepare it. Much the same thing without the cost of preparation may be had at any woodpile where hard wood has been chopped—I mean the chips to be found there—and that has been the favorite smoker-fuel "in this locality" for some time. When the weather is dry, the chips may be picked up in the chip-yard and filled directly into the smoker, but a stock is always kept on hand well covered up, ready to use immediately after the heaviest shower of rain.

SMOKER-KINDLING

When live coals are at hand in the cookstove, nothing is handier than to put a few of them in the smoker to start the fire. These are not always at hand. I have used for kindling carpenter's shavings, kerosene, rotten wood of some hard wood, especially apple, that kind of rotten wood that is somewhat spongy and will be sure to burn if the least spark touches it—all these have given more or less satisfaction, but nothing quite so much as saltpeter-rags. Like the right kind of rotten wood, the least spark will light a saltpeter-rag so that it will be sure to go, but it is not so slow in its action as the rotten wood, and makes a much greater heat, so that chips of sound hard wood will be at once started into a secure fire.

SALTPETER-RAGS.

To prepare the saltpeter-rags a crock is kept constantly standing, containing a solution of saltpeter. The strength of the solution is not a matter of great nicety.

A quarter or half a pound of saltpeter may be used to a gallon of water, and if it evaporates so that the solution becomes stronger, water may be added. A cotton rag dipped in this solution will be ready for use as soon as dried. As a matter of convenience, quite a lot of rags are prepared at a time. They are wrung out of the solu-

Fig. 23.—Ready for Clipping.

tion and spread out to dry in the sun, and when thoroughly dry are put in the tool-basket, which always contains a supply. When taken out of the crock, the rags may be wrung quite dry, thus containing not so much saltpeter, or they may be wrung out just enough so the

liquid will not run off on the ground and waste, in which
condition they will be strongly dosed with saltpeter.

A plentiful supply of dry smoker-fuel, with a corresponding stock of saltpeter-rags, is a great saving of
the "disposition."

POUNDING BEES OFF COMBS

Mention was made of getting bees off combs. Sometimes shaking is used altogether, sometimes brushing,
and sometimes both The weight of the comb has something to do with the manner of shaking The most of
the shaking—in fact all of the shaking, unless the combs
be very heavy—is done as shown in Fig 26 Perhaps
it might better be called pounding bees off the comb
The comb is held by the corner with one hand, while
the other hand pounds sharply on the hand that holds the
comb By this manner of pounding I can get almost
every bee off a comb with a few strokes, unless the comb
be too heavy.

DOOLITTLE'S PLAN OF SHAKING.

With a very heavy comb, G M Doolittle's plan is
better, and is the one used Let the ends of the top-bar
be supported by the first two fingers of each hand, the
thumbs some distance above Keeping the thumb and
fingers well apart, let the frame drop, and as it drops
strike it hard with the balls of the thumbs, then catch
it with the fingers, raise it and repeat the operation The
bees are jarred both up and down, and don't know which
way to brace themselves to hold on, so a very few shakes
will get most of them off

BEE-BRUSHES,

Sometimes it is not desirable to get all the bees off,
in which case, or with very light combs, no brushing is

needed. But if all the bees are to be cleaned off, and the combs are not very light, then brushing must be resorted to. I know of no brush better than one made of some growing plant, such as asparagus, sweet clover, goldenrod, aster, etc. No little bit of a thing, but a good, big bunch, well tied together with a string (Fig 27).

But like many a thing that costs nothing, these weed brushes are too expensive, for they dry up so that a fresh one must be made every day, and that takes a good deal of time. So I generally use a Coggshall brush (Fig 28) The essential thing about a Coggshall brush is that it must be made of long broom-corn with a very thin brush, and not trimmed at all at the ends. One of these is always in the tool-basket.

Of course no shaking or pounding of combs is admissible if queen-cells are on the combs that are considered of any value.

TOOL-BASKET.

The tool-basket spoken of is simply a common splint basket (Fig. 29). At different times I have had different arrangements for carrying the things most generally needed, at least two different tool-boxes having been made for that special purpose with separate compartments for the various articles. But the basket is lighter, and although things get a little mixed up in it, it seems to have the preference at present At one time I tried to keep an outfit at each apiary—smoker, hive-tools, etc.— so that there should be no need to carry anything from one apiary to another, but one gets used to tools and prefers to use the same ones day after day, so the basket is used.

CONTENTS OF TOOL-BASKET.

Of course, the number of objects carried in a basket must be somewhat limited. The bulkiest part is the apron, sleeves and gloves of my assistant. The record-book must always be present. Then there will be smokers, hive-tools, hammer, cages, matches (although matches are always kept covered with the fuel in each apiary), saltpeter-rags, nails, and any other light objects that may happen to be needed at any particular time. Of course there will be heavier articles, not convenient to carry from one apiary to another, and each apiary must have its own, as a hive with a closed entrance and a robber-cloth, ready to contain at any time frames of brood or honey safe from robbers Generally, however, there will be no need to be so careful against robbers, and the one or two frames lifted out of a hive will be leaned up against it, taking pains to stand any frame where the hot rays of the sun may not strike too directly upon it, and to stand it up straight enough so it will not sag with its own weight.

RESTING FRAME DIAGONALLY IN HIVE.

With one frame out of the hive there will be room enough for the rest to be moved about in the hive, and returned to it as soon as examined. Sometimes when it is desired to set a frame back in the hive very quickly, or when a queen has been caught and is held in the fingers, so that the frame must be handled by one hand, it is convenient to set the frame in the hive resting diagonally, as shown in Fig 36. The frame is lowered till one end of the top-bar rests upon one rabbet, and then the bottom-bar is allowed to rest upon the other rabbet.

Perhaps oftener, however, I use both hands to handle a frame, even while holding a queen in one hand While searching for the queen the frame is held in both hands, and as soon as she is seen the end of the frame held by the right hand is rested upon the hive, the right hand catches the queen, and she is then allowed to run upon the leg of my trousers, upon the thigh (it is an exceedingly rare thing that a laying queen will offer to fly), and then I catch her in the hollow of my right hand, holding her in the hollow formed by the three fingers, while with the thumb and forefinger I am free to handle the frame at leisure.

BEES BALLING QUEEN.

When a colony is being overhauled, it sometimes happens that the queen is found balled. This balling is likely more because the colony, being frightened, is seeking to protect the queen than because of any hostility to her. Fig. 30 shows a queen thus balled, or rather the balling bees are shown, the queen being hidden by them. The ball is small, whereas a ball of bees bent on the destruction of a strange queen is likely to be as large as a hickory-nut, or larger.

Fig. 24 —Clipping the Queen.

Whether the object of the bees be to protect the queen or not, anything that tends to excite them suffi-

ciently may lead them to do violence to the queen So
when I find the queen thus balled, I always close the
hive immediately, not generally touching it again till
the next day, when everything will be found all right.

MAKING RECORD.

After the overhauling of a colony is completed, a
record thereof must be made If May 10, 1902, should
be the date of the visit, and if I should clip the queen at
that visit, I would make the entry, May 10 cl q (01),"
which means that I clipped the queen May 10, and that
she was a queen reared in 1901. If, later in the season,
I should clip a queen reared that same season, the entry
would be, "cl q (02)," meaning that the queen was reared
in 1902 In either case the year of the birth of the old queen
in the left-hand margin has a line drawn through it, and
the birth-year of the new queen is written under it If
I find a clipped queen in the hive, then the entry is, "q
cl," which means the queen was already clipped It
might not seem important to enter that the queen was already clipped, but if I do not find her the first or second
time looking over the combs I leave it till another day,
leaving a blank after the date, and that keeps me in mind
of the fact that I have not yet seen the queen

After clipping the wing of the queen I put her on
the top of a frame directly over the brood-nest If you
hold her on your finger over the brood-nest she displays
a great degree of perverseness and persists in crawling
up your hand, right away from her proper home So I
let her crawl upon a leaf, little stick or other object, lay
this on the frames, and she will directly go down into the
cluster

On this first visit I also generally enter in the record-book the amount of brood present If the record is
"2 br," or "3 br," it means that two combs or three combs
are fairly well filled with brood—at least half filled with

brood. If the record is "br in 2," that means that brood is found in two combs, but that at least one of them is less than half full. So you will see that "br in 3" might be a good deal less than "2 br," for "2 br" might mean two very full combs, and at the least will be as much as one very full comb, while "br in 3" may mean that there is only a little spot of brood in each of three combs.

Any other item that needs especial mention will be recorded, but generally there is no record made beyond those mentioned.

MENDING COMBS.

In handling the combs, if any are found with drone-comb or with holes in them, and if we are not too crowded for time, the defects are remedied. Very likely I may turn over these combs to my assistant, who mends them before they are returned to the hive. The usual plan is to mend them in this way:

She takes a common tea-knife with a thin, narrow, sharp blade, cuts out the piece of drone-comb if the hole is not already made, lays the frame over a piece of worker-comb, (this piece of worker-comb may be the part or whole of some old or objectionable comb), with the point of the knife marks out the exact size and shape of the hole, removes the frame, cuts out the piece and crowds it into the hole.

Or, the following plan may be used, especially if the frame is wired: After the hole is made, (the mice have probably made the holes in the wired frames), the cells on one side are cut away to the base for a distance of $\frac{1}{8}$ to $\frac{1}{4}$ inch from the hole, and a piece of foundation cut to the right size is placed over the hole and the edge pressed down upon the base that surrounds the hole. The foundation must not be too cold. Before fall these patches cannot be detected, unless by the lighter color where the foundation has been used.

HIVES AND FRAMES.

Now that the apiary is all in running order, you may want to take a look at it. You "don't think it looks remarkably neat?" Neither do I. If I had only a dozen colonies and were keeping them for the pleasure of it, I should have their hives painted, perhaps ornamented with scroll work, but please remember that I am keeping them for profit, and I cannot afford anything for looks. I suppose they would last longer if painted, but hardly enough longer to pay for the paint. Besides, in the many changes constantly taking place, how do I know that I may not want to throw these aside and adopt a new hive?

CHANGES IN HIVES

I have already changed five times, having begun in 1861 with a full-sized sugar-barrel, changing the next year to Quinby box-hives, then to a movable-frame hive made by J. F. Lester, and afterward when J. Vandervort, the foundation-mill man, came and lived perhaps a year in Marengo, I bought out his stock of hives. I supposed they were the exact Langstroth pattern, but they had frames 18x9 inches, not different enough to make any appreciable difference in results, but different enough so that they were not standard, and after I had a few thousands of them on hand and wanted to change to the regular Langstroth size, the trouble I had would be hard to describe. I still have some of them, but not in regular use. These hives were 10-frame, and in course of time I cut them down and made them 8-frame. Then I changed to the 8-frame dovetailed hive, and I don't know what the next change will be

Another reason for not painting hives is that I am afraid bees do not do quite so well in painted as in unpainted hives

Except the full-sized cleat already mentioned on each

end, my hives are the regular dovetailed. But the frames are Miller frames.

Fig. 25.—Home from the Out-Apiary.

LOOSE-HANGING FRAMES.

For a good many years handling frames was much slower work than it is to-day, because for a good many years I had loose-hanging frames. In moving the frames from one side of the hive toward the other, each frame had to be moved separately. It would not do to shove two or more at a time, because in so doing bees would be mashed between the frames. Then when the frames were returned to place each one had to be carefully adjusted, judging by the eye when it was at the right distance from its neighbor. This was slow work, and when done with the utmost care it was only approximately exact. There was no dummy to lift out to make extra room; and the frames had to be crowded together so as to make room to get a first frame out. That disarranged the spacing of

several of the frames, even if there were no other occasion
for disarranging them.

Then there came a time of struggling for some self-
spacing arrangement, closed-end, partly-closed-end, and
what not. I tried a good many different kinds. Closed-
ends were probably warmer for wintering, and were certainly self-spacing, but it took time to avoid killing bees,
and the trouble with propolis was no small matter. Half-
closed-ends were the same in kind, only different in
degree.

Of these last the Hoffman is probably the most popular, and I put in use enough to fill a few hives, and most
of them are still in use. When new they work very
nicely, but as propolis accumulates the difficulty of handling increases, and the frames become more and more
crowded, until it is almost impossible to get out the
dummy, the easier thing being to pry out with a good
deal of force the first frame, either with or without the
dummy. Indeed, the difficulty of getting out the frames
is so great, that the sight of a set of Hoffman frames
when the cover is removed always produces something
like a shudder.

Although I could not have anything in the line of
closed-ends, I wanted the advantage of the self-spacing,
and not finding anything on the market to suit me I
was, in a manner, compelled to adopt something of my
own "get-up," and so for several years I have used with
much satisfaction the Miller frame (Fig 95)

The frame is of course of the regular Langstroth
size, 17⅝x9⅛. Top-bar, bottom-bar, and end-bars are
uniform in width, 1⅛ inches throughout their whole di-

mensions. The top-bar is $\frac{7}{8}$ inch thick, with the usual saw-kerf to receive the foundation, and close beside this is another kerf to receive the wedge that fastens in the foundation. The length of the top-bar is $18\frac{5}{8}$ inches, and $\frac{7}{8}$x9-16 is rabbeted out of each end to receive the end-bar. The end-bar is 8 9-16x$1\frac{1}{8}$x$\frac{3}{8}$. The bottom-bar consists of two pieces, each $17\frac{5}{8}$x$\frac{1}{2}$x$\frac{1}{4}$. This allows $\frac{1}{8}$ inch between the two parts to receive the foundation,

Fig. 26.—Pounding Bees Off Comb.

making the bottom-bar $1\frac{1}{8}$ inches wide when nailed.

In Fig. 95 the frame is upside down, one-half of the bottom-bar nailed on, the other half above, while below is seen the long strip that serves as a wedge to fasten in the foundation.

SPACING-NAILS.

The side-spacing, which holds the frame at the proper distance from its next neighbor, is accomplished by means

of common wire-nails   These nails are 1¼ inches long
and rather heavy, about 3-32 inch in thickness, with a head
less than one-fourth inch across.   By means of a wooden
gauge which allows them to be driven only to a fixed
depth, they are driven in to such a depth that the head
remains projecting out a fourth of an inch.

Each frame has four spacing-nails   A nail is driven
into each end of the top-bar on opposite sides, the nail
being about an inch and a half from the extreme end of
the top-bar, and a fourth of an inch from its upper surface.   About two and a fourth inches from the bottom
of the frame a nail is driven into each end-bar, these nails
being also on opposite sides.   Hold the frame up before
you in its natural position, each hand holding one end of
the top-bar, and the two nails at the right end will be on
the side from you, while the two nails at the left end will
be on the side nearest to you

The object of having the nails so heavy is so that
they may not be driven farther into the wood when the
frames are crowded hard together   Once in a great while
the wood is split by having so heavy a nail driven, and if
such a nail could be obtained it would be better to have a
lighter nail with a head a fourth of an inch thick, so that
it could be driven automatically to place without the need
of a gauge, and without the possibility of being driven
farther in by any amount of crowding.

END-SPACING

The end-spacing is done by means of the usual
frame staple, about three-eighths of an inch wide   The
staple is driven into the end-bar, immediately under the
lug of the top-bar   This lug being only half an inch long,
there is room for a bee to pass between the end of the
lug and the upper edge of the hive-end, so no propolis is
deposited there   I like this feature as much as some
dislike it.   They complain that with so short a top-bar

the frames drop down in the hive—a nuisance not to be tolerated. I do not have that trouble, although the hold of the top-bar on the tin support is so slight that if the work were not exact I can easily imagine the frames dropping down. Possibly those who complain do not have very exact work. I am not sure but I would put up with a little dropping down of frames, rather than to have the ends of the top-bars glued.

It will be seen that while the frames are automatically spaced very firmly, the points of contact are so small that the frames are always easily movable. Those points of contact are the thin metal edges upon which the top-bars rest, the two end-staples, and the four nail-heads. The same spacing is in use in other frames, only staples are used for side-spacing instead of nails. The staples do not seem quite so substantial, and there is

Fig. 27.— Weed Brushes.

more danger, when the frames are crowded hard to-gether, that the staples may be driven in deeper, or that the head of the staple may dig into the adjoining wood

The top-bar and end-bar being 1⅛ wide, and the spacing of the nails ¼ inch, the frames are spaced just 1⅜ from center to center   It is just possible that a little wider spacing than 1⅜ might be better, but 1⅜ is the general fashion, and so far as possible I like to adopt standard goods   I may be asked, then, why I should use a frame not regularly made by manufacturers. Possibly prejudice has a little to do in the case, but I think the Miller frame enough better than anything I can find listed, that I prefer to be out of fashion so long as I can find nothing listed that is quite close to what I want

USING STANDARD GOODS

In general I think it is best to adopt standard goods. They can be more cheaply made, and it is more convenient to get them.   It cost me no small sum to change my frames so little as to make them only ⅛ of an inch less in length and an eighth of an inch more in depth, but I made the change, and made it solely because my frames were not of standard size   Years ago I changed from four-piece to one-piece sections solely because I wanted to be in fashion, although I think I prefer the one-piece now

WORKING FOR IMPROVEMENT

At the same time it is one's privilege—perhaps one's duty—to make some effort toward improvement, if one can only keep from thinking that a thing is necessarily an improvement because it is different from what has been. The things and plans gotten up by me that were different from others would make a pretty long list. Unfortunately, a full trial has in most cases convinced me that my supposed improvements were no improvements, at all, and so they were cast aside   A few, however, have stood the test, the Miller feeder and the Miller

introducing cage having become standard articles on the
price-lists, while bottom-starters, the robber-cloth, bot-

Fig. 28.—Coggshall Brush.

tom-board, and some other things have had from my
brother bee-keepers a reception of which I have
no reason to complain.   While the tendency towards
something different needs to be kept in bound, it would
be a sad thing if no changes had been made, and we were
set back just where we were a quarter or a half century ago.

GETTING COMBS BUILT DOWN TO BOTTOM-BARS.

While upon the subject of frames, I may as well tell
how I manage to have them entirely filled with straight
combs which are built out to the end-bars and clear down
to the bottom-bars, a thing I experimented upon for a
long time before reaching success.   The foundation is cut
so as to make a close fit in length, and the width is about

half an inch more than the inside depth of the frame. The frame is all complete except that one of the two pieces of the bottom-bar is not yet nailed on. The frame is laid on a board of the usual kind, which fits inside the frame and has stops on the edges so that when foundation is laid on the board it will lie centrally in the frame. The half of the bottom-bar that is nailed on lies on the under side. The foundation is put in place, and one edge is crowded into the saw-kerf in the top-bar. Then the lacking half of the bottom-bar is put in place, and a light nail at the middle is driven down through both parts. Then the frame is raised and the ends of the two halves of the bottom-bar are squeezed together so as to pinch the foundation, and nailed there. Then the usual wedge is wedged into the fine saw-kerf in the top-bar.

FOUNDATION SPLINTS

Now we are ready for the important part. Little sticks or splints about 1-16 of an inch square, and about ¼ inch shorter than the inside depth of the frame, are thrown into a square shallow tin pan that contains hot beeswax. They will froth up because of the moisture frying out of them. When the frothing ceases, and the splints are saturated with wax, then they are ready for use. The frame of foundation is laid on the board as before: with a pair of plyers a splint is lifted out of the wax (kept just hot enough over a gasoline stove), and placed upon the foundation so that the splint shall be perpendicular when the frame is hung in the hive. As fast as a splint is laid in place, an assistant immediately presses it down into the foundation with the wetted edge of a board. About 1½ inches from each end-bar is placed a splint, and between these two splints three others at equal distances (Fig 31). When these are built out they make beautiful combs, and the splints do not seem to be at all in the way (Fig 32).

A little experience will enable one to judge, when putting in the splints, how hot to keep the wax. If too hot there will be too light a coating of wax.

It must not be understood that the mere use of these splints will under any and all circumstances result in faultless combs built securely down to the bottom-bar. It seems to be the natural thing for bees to leave a free passage under the comb, no matter whether the thing that comes next below the comb be the floor-board of the hive or the bottom-bar of the frame. So if a frame be given when little storing is going on, the bees will deliberately dig away the foundation at the bottom, and even if it has been built down but the cells not very fully drawn out, they will do more or less at gnawing a passage. To make a success, the frames should be given at a time when work shall go on uninterruptedly until full-depth cells reach the bottom-bar.

To a very limited extent I have used strips of wax instead of wood, but it is doubtful as to the improvement without using too much wax.

In Fig. 32 will be seen two such frames of splinted foundation that have been built out and filled with honey. The upper one is built out solid to the frame all around, while the lower one has a hole at one of the lower corners, through which a queen can play hide-and-seek.

In Fig. 33 are two that have been built out and filled with brood. They are built out solid to the wood, excepting one hole in each at one of the lower corners, but these two holes are covered up by the fingers so that you cannot see them. Look carefully at the frame at the left hand, and you will see at least three places where the capping is slightly elevated, because of the splints beneath.

BROOD TO THE TOP-BAR.

Incidentally your attention may be called to this comb as a fine specimen of one well filled with brood. It is literally *filled*, all the cells, sealed and unsealed, containing brood. It shows that there is no necessity for shallow frames to have brood clear to the top-bar. At the time when it is desired to get bees to start work in sections, the brood will be up so high in the combs that bees will start in the sections just as promptly with standard frames as with those that are shallower. *After* the bees have been at work storing for some time, the brood in the standard frame will not be as near the top-bar as in a shallow frame, but that will be no hindrance to the *continuance* of storing in supers

Please do not understand that all my combs look like the four in Figs 32 and 33   Many of them do, but more do not, because so many of them were built in seasons of comparative dearth.

There is another way to get combs built down to the bottom-bar   Suppose you have a comb with a passage-way under it more or less of its length.   Cut it free from the bottom-bar, and then cut straight across an inch or more above the bottom-bar, then turn this piece upside down ·and let it rest on the bottom-bar   The bees will immediately fasten this piece to the bottom-bar (of course it must be at a time when bees are working freely), and very soon they will fill in the gap above the piece.

HIVE-DUMMY.

A good dummy is a matter of no light importance   It is handy to fill up vacant space, its chief use being to make an easy thing of removing the first comb from a hive With self-spacing frames there can be no crowding to-gether of the frames so as to give one of them extra room, as is the case with loose-hanging frames, and if a hive be filled full of self-spacing frames it will be about impossible to remove the first frame after a fair amount of propolis is present   A dummy at one side is the thing to help out.

An eight-frame dovetailed hive is 12⅛ inches wide inside. Eight frames spaced 1⅜ inches from center to center will occupy 11 inches, leaving at one side a space of 1⅛ inches, abundance of room to lift out the first frame easily. A dummy put into that space will keep the bees from filling it up with comb, and it ought never to be difficult to lift out the dummy. If a dummy a trifle more than a fourth of an inch thick be put in, leaving a fourth

Fig. 29.—Tool-Basket.

of an inch between dummy and frame, there will be left between the dummy and the side of the hive a space of a little more than half an inch, a space that the bees will never fill with comb in such a place. As propolis accumulates, however, this space will become less.

The dummy should be light and at the same time quite substantial, and the one I use fulfills these requirements (Fig. 42). The principal board of the dummy is 16⅛x8⅜x5-16, of pine. The other parts are of some

tougher wood   The top-bar is 18⅞x5-16x5-16   Each
end-cleat is 8⅜x½x5-16.

It will be seen that the dummy is neither so long nor
deep as a frame.   That makes it easier to handle, and being at the side of the hive it never makes any trouble.
While the cut-off top-bars in the frames work nicely, they
do not work so well in dummies, as I found upon trying
a number of them.

HIVE-COVERS.

At the risk of losing caste as a bee-keeper, I am
obliged to confess that I never got up "a hive of my own,"
never even tried to plan one, but I have tried no little
to get up a hive-cover to suit me   A hive is so seldom
moved that I care less for its weight, but when I, or, more
particularly, my female assistants, have to lift covers all
day long, when hot and tired, a pound difference in
weight is quite an item   The first covers I had for
movable-frame hives were 8 inches deep and weighed
about 18 pounds   Needless to detail the different covers
I have devised and tried, with upper surface of tin, oil-
cloth, and wood, painted and unpainted   Although I
don't paint hive-bodies, I want covers painted   Most of
my covers just at present are the common plain board
cover, and I don't like them   Some of them are of two
boards united at the middle by a V-shaped tin slid into
saw-kerfs, and I like these still less   A new board cover
is a nice thing   After a little it warps, and then it isn't a
nice thing   Put a cleat on each end so it cannot warp—
cast-iron cleats, if you like—and it will twist so that there
will be a grinning opening at one corner to allow bees to
walk out and cold to walk in, to say nothing of robber-
bees

TIN COVERS WITH DEAD-AIR SPACE

I have fifty covers that I like very much   They are
double-board covers, the boards being ⅛ thick, the grain

of the upper and lower boards running in opposite directions, with a ⅜ dead-air space between them; at least it would be dead-air if it were not for cracks, and I do not consider the cracks a necessary part if the covers were properly made. The whole is covered with tin and painted white. The lower surface is perfectly flat, with no cleat projecting downward, for such cleats do not help rapid and easy handling. Such a cover is light, safe from warping and twisting, is cooler in summer than the plain

Fig. 30.—Balled Queen.

board cover, and warmer in winter. The greatest objection is the cost; I think they cost 25 cents or more each.

Two of these tin covers will be seen at Fig. 37, the one at the right showing the under surface of the cover

ZINC COVERS

Fifty other covers are made on the same plan and covered with zinc These are not painted So long as they remain whole there is no need of paint, and whenever there seems to be a possibility of their approaching anything like a leaking condition they can be covered with paint. The same might be said of the tin, only I expect the zinc to stand the weather unpainted much longer than the tin would

At Fig 38 may be seen two of these zinc hive-covers The one at the right shows the upper or zinc surface The left one shows the under or wood surface, and if you look at the right end of this last cover you will see that the upper layer of thin board projects three-fourths of an inch so as to serve as a handle. One of these covers weighs five pounds

A cover sent me by the A I. Root Co covered with paper and painted, has been in use two years, and so far it seems to stand as well as zinc or tin   Possibly this paper may do as well as the metal and save expense   I would rather pay a good price for a good cover, rainproof, bee-proof, non-warping, non-twisting, with a deadair space, than to take a poorer cover as a gift

The hundred covers I have mentioned were made specially to order, but I am glad to see that the A. I. Root Co have now on their list a cover made on the same principle.

HIVE-STANDS

My hive-stands are simple and inexpensive (Fig 39) They are made of common fence-boards 6 inches wide Two pieces 32 inches long are nailed upon two other pieces or cleats 24 inches long. That's all. Of course the longer pieces are uppermost, leaving the cleats below. Two similar cleats, but loose, lie on the ground under the first-mentioned cleats. This makes it equivalent to cleats of two-inch stuff, with the decided advantage that only the loose cleat will rot away by lying on the ground, without spoiling the whole stand. These stands are leveled with a spirit-level before the hives are placed on them, (sometimes not till afterward), being made perfectly level from side to side, with the rear one two inches higher than the front. Each of these stands is intended for two hives, with a space of 2 to 4 inches between the two hives. It is much easier to level a stand like this than to level one for a single hive. There are other advantages.

HIVES IN PAIRS.

This putting in pairs is quite a saving of room; for if room were allowed for working on each side of each hive, only two-thirds the number could be got into the row. But so far as the bees are concerned, it is equivalent to putting in double the number; that is, there is no more danger of a bee going into the wrong hive by mistake, than if only a single hive stood where each pair stands. If hives stood very close together at regular intervals, a bee might by mistake go into the wrong hive, but if a colony of bees is in the habit, as mine sometimes are in the spring, of going into the south end of their entrance, they will never make the mistake of entering at the north end, as you will quickly see if you plug up, alternately, the north and south ends of the entrance. When the north end is closed it does not affect the bees at all, but close the south end, and dire consternation follows. To the bees the pair of hives is much the same as a single hive, and they will not make the mistake of entering the wrong end.

A space of 2 feet or so is left between one pair of hives and the next pair, so as to leave plenty of room for a seat.

GROUPS OF FOUR HIVES.

In two of the apiaries there is a still further economy of room by placing a second row close to the first, the hives standing back to back. That, you will see, makes the hives in groups of four. I do not know of any arrangement that will allow a larger number of hives to stand on a given surface. The difference in the amount of travel in the course of a year in such an arrangement as compared with one without any grouping, is a matter not to be despised.

SHADE.

Trees shade most of the hives at least a part of the day, and at one end of the home apiary the trees were so thick that I cut out part of them. I had previously thought that shade was important, and that with sufficient shade there was never any danger of bees suffering from heat, but after having combs melt down in a hive so densely shaded by trees that the sun did not shine on it all day long, I changed my mind. I value the shade these trees give, not so much for the good it does the bees, but for the comfort of the operator working at them. I don't believe bees suffer as much from the hot sun shining directly on the hives, as they do from having the air shut off from them by surrounding objects. I have had combs melt down in hives, the honey running in a stream on the ground, one of the hives at least being in a shade of trees so dense the sun never shone on it, and I suspect it was for lack of air. A dense growth of corn was directly back of the hives, and a dense growth of young trees and underbrush in front. I didn't know enough to notice this, although when working at the bees my shirt would be as wet as if dipped in the river. I had the young trees thinned out and trimmed up, the corn-ground in grass, so,

Fig. 31.—Foundation with Splint Supports.

the air could get through, and I now work with more comfort, and no comb has melted down for 20 years.

Sometimes I have found it desirable to shade one or more hives singly. An armful of the longest fresh-cut grass obtainable is laid on the hive-cover, and weighted down with two or three sticks of stove-wood. But I do not think anything of the kind is needed on double covers.

MOVABLE SHADE.

For hives that are not in the shade, especially during certain parts of the day, a movable shade (Fig. 58) is a great comfort to the operator when the sun shines with blistering heat. Four standards are made of 7-16 inch rod-iron. Take a piece of the iron 6 feet 2 inches long; bend the upper end into a ring or eye, and sharpen the

lower end.   Twelve inches from the point or lower end
bend the rod at right angles.   Two inches higher up bend
again at right angles, leaving the rod straight except that
knee of two inches, upon which you can set your foot and
drive it in the ground as when spading.

The cloth used for the shade is about as large as an
ordinary bed-sheet, and is usually the linen lap-robe,
which is always at hand, and on which a string is kept
tied on each corner so as to be always ready to set up in
a twinkling   This string has both ends tied around the
cloth at the corner, leaving the string in the form of a
loop   The loop is thrust through the eye of the standard,
looped back over the eye, and there you are

When the sun is not far from the horizon, only two
standards are used, from which the lap-robe hangs as a
wall between the operator and the sun.

FEEDING MEAL.

I used to read about feeding meal in the spring.   I
tried it, put out rye-meal, and not a bee would touch it;
baited them with honey, and if they took the honey they
left the meal   Finally, one day, I saw a bee alight on a
dish of flour set in a sunny place   It went at it in a
rollicking manner as if delighted.   I was more delighted.
At last I had in some way got the thing right, and my
bees would take meal   The bee loaded up, and lugged off
its load, and I waited for it and others to come for more.
They didn't come, and that was the first and last load
taken that year   I cannot tell now exactly when the
change came about, neither do I know that I have done
anything different, but I have no trouble now in getting
the bees to take bushels of meal   I suppose the simple
explanation is that there was plenty of natural pollen for
the few bees I had in the first years, but not enough for
the larger number of colonies I had later.

About as soon as the bees are set out in the spring, I begin feeding them meal, although some years I do not offer any substitute for pollen. For this purpose I like shallow boxes, and generally use old hive-covers 4 inches deep. These are placed in a sunny place about a foot apart, one end raised three or four inches higher than the other. This may be done by putting a stone under one end, although I generally place them along the edge of a little ditch where no stone is needed, and they can be whirled around as if on a central pivot. One feed-box is used for every 10 to 20 colonies, although I am guided rather by what the bees seem to need, adding more boxes as fast as the ones already given are crowded with bees.

SUBSTITUTES FOR POLLEN.

I can hardly tell what I have not used for meal. I have used meal or flour of pretty much all the grains, bran, shorts and all the different feeds used for cows in this noted dairy region, including even the yellow meal brought from glucose factories for cow-feed, although, if this last were known, it might be reported that I filled paraffin combs with glucose and sealed them over with a hot butcher-knife. I think this glucose meal is perhaps the poorest feed I have used. As to the rest I hardly know which is best, and I have of late used principally corn and oats ground together, partly because I was using that for horse and cow feed, and partly because I think it may be as good as any.

When the feed-boxes are put in place, in the morning, (and I commence this feeding just as soon as the bees are out of the cellar), I put in each box at the raised end about four to six quarts (the quantity is not very material) of the feed. The more compact, and the less scattered the feed the better. The bees will gradually dig it down till it is all settled in the lower end of the box,

just the same as so much water would settle there.   This
may take an hour, or it may take six, according to circumstances.   As often as they dig it down, I reverse the
position of the box, just whirling it around if it stands
on the edge of the ditch   This brings the meal again at
the raised end of the box   When the bees have it dug
down level there is little to be seen on the top except the
hulls of the oats, and what fun it is to see the bees bur-
row in this, sometimes clear out of sight.

It is always a source of amusement to see the bees
working on this meal, and the young folks watch them
by the half-hour.   By night the oat-meal and finer parts
of the corn are nearly all worked out, and after the bees
have stopped working, the boxes are emptied, piled up,
one on top of another, and at the top, one placed upside
down so that no dew or rain may affect them   If I think
it is not worked out pretty clean, I may let them work it
over next day, putting three or four times as much in a
box.   When the bees are done with it, there will be
empty oat-hulls on top, and the coarse part of the corn on
the bottom.   It does not matter if it is not worked out
clean, for it is fed to the horses or cows afterwards

After the first day's feeding, the boxes must be filled
in good season in the morning, or the bees annoy very
much by being in the way, and throughout the day, while
the bees are at work, if I go among the feed-boxes to
turn them, or for any other purpose, I must look sharp
where I set my feet, or bees will be killed, as they are
quite thick over the ground, brushing the meal off their
bodies and packing their loads.   Before many days the
meal-boxes are deserted for the now plenty natural pollen,
although if you watch the bees, as they go laden into the
hives, even when working thickest in the boxes, you will
see a good many carrying in heavy loads of natural pollen

It seems to be a beneficent natural law, that bees do
not like to crowd one another in their search for pollen or

nectar, or else the meal-boxes would be untouched and all the bees would work upon the insufficient supply of pollen. In consequence of this law it is necessary to furnish a sufficient number of boxes, for although the bees will work quite thick if only 5 boxes are left for 150 colonies, they will work scarcely thicker if only one box is left.

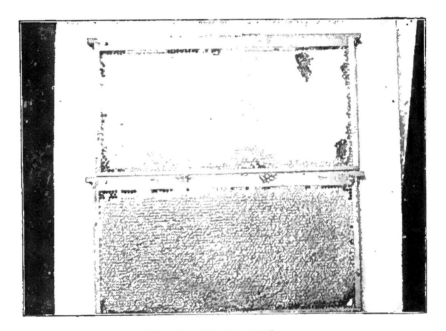

Fig. 32.—Combs of Honey.

OUT-DOOR FEEDING.

I have fed barrels of sugar syrup in the open air, and it is possible that circumstances may arise to induce me to do it again, but I doubt.

There are serious objections to this out-door feeding. You are not sure what portion of it your own bees will get, if other bees are in flying distance. Considerable experience has proved to me that by this method of feeding, the strong colonies get the lion's share, and the weak colonies very little. Moreover, I have seen indications that part of the colonies get none, both of the weak and strong. You are also dependent on the weather, as wet and chilly days may come, when bees cannot fly

As already mentioned, when the bees are brought out of the cellar, colonies are marked that are suspiciously light, and their immediate wants supplied as soon as possible But with 8-frame hives there will be a good many colonies that will run short of stores before there is any chance for them to supply themselves from outside.

STIMULATIVE FEEDING

Some would say that I ought to practice stimulative feeding for the sake of hastening the work of building up the colony. But it takes a good deal of wisdom to know at all times just how to manage stimulative feeding so as not to do harm instead of good; and I am not certain that I have the wisdom .

Whatever else may be true about spring feeding, I am pretty fully settled in the belief that it is of first importance that the bees should have an abundant supply of stores, whether such supply be furnished from day to day by the bee-keeper, or stored up by the bees themselves six months or a year previously Moreover, I believe they build up more rapidly if they have not only enough to use from day to day, but a reserve or visible supply for future use If a colony comes out of the cellar strong, and with combs full of stores, I have some doubts if I can hasten its building up by any tinkering I can do. So my feeding in spring is to make sure they have abundant stores, rather than for the stimulation of frequent giving.

RAPID CONSUMPTION OF STORES

After so many years of experience in that line, I am nevertheless still surprised sometimes to find how rapidly the stores have diminished under the constantly increasing demands made by brood-rearing So there is little danger of getting too much honey in the hive It is not enough to have sufficient to last till the white clover harvest begins. To be sure, that might be all right so far as the building up of the colony is concerned. But no honey will be put in the supers so long as there are empty cells in the brood-chamber, and it is better to have enough honey left in the brood-chamber so that the first white honey shall go straight into the supers.

SURPLUS COMBS OF HONEY.

Nothing is better than to have plenty of full combs of sealed honey saved over from the previous year, with which to supply any colony that may need them. If I were as good a bee-keeper as I ought to be, there would always be enough of these so that nothing else would be needed to take their place. But I am not as good a bee-keeper as I ought to be, and while some years I may have all the extra combs of honey that can be used, at other times they may run short, even to not having enough to supply the pinching wants of colonies just taken from the cellar There may, however, be some combs at least partly filled that have been taken from colonies that died in winter, or from the uniting of colonies in spring, and these may supplement the number of combs saved up from the previous year.

FEEDING SECTIONS OF HONEY.

When the combs of honey are all gone, the next best thing is to give sections in wide frames. This seems like an extravagant thing to do; but if the sections contain dark or objectionable honey, and if they can be cleaned out and used for baits, there is no very great extravagance about it I have given sections by sliding them under the bottom-bars, a thing very easily done with bottom-boards two inches deep, but such sections are ruined for use as baits, and all you can do with the empty comb in them is to melt it into wax

FEEDING TO FILL COMBS.

If neither combs of sealed honey nor suitable sections are to be had, then feeding with Miller feeders is in order But colonies that need feeding in spring are not always very strong, and a weak colony makes rather poor work on a feeder at that time   Instead of distributing feeders to all the colonies that need feeding, they are limited to a small number of the very strongest, whether these need feeding or not.   Then filled combs are taken from these strong colonies and given to the needy colonies whether at home or in the out-apiaries, for the feeders are generally used only at home.

It may be that these strong colonies are already well supplied with honey   Whatever honey they have is taken from them, unless it be in combs containing brood, and empty combs given in place   The feeder is put directly on the brood-chamber   After the bees get a fair start on the feeder an upper story with empty combs may be given, but just at first they will make a better start without this second story.   When the feeder is put on, 5 or 10 pounds of sugar is poured in, and an equal quantity of water poured on the sugar   It is much better to have the water hot   It would be well to fill the feeder full, but in that case a good portion of it would be left to get cold, and faster work will be done if no more is given each day than will be taken that day   Very often when I go around to the feeders next morning I find most of them with sugar still in the feeder, but the liquid all taken.   That doesn't matter, more water can be added Indeed 12 or 15 pounds of sugar may be put in the feeder, and then each day only so much water as the bees will use out that day. For they are not likely to do much at night unless the weather be quite warm.

WHOLESALE FEEDING.

There come times, however, when the feeding must be rushed, and there can be no puttering with getting one colony to store for another. One of those times came in the year 1902. The second week in June, at the time when in a good season there ought to be lively work piling on supers, I found nearly every colony on the point of starvation. If there was any difference, the strongest colonies were the worst. The combs were filled with brood, requiring large daily consumption, stores in the hive were exhausted, and not enough for daily supplies

Fig. 33.—Combs of Brood.

coming in. It would hardly be proper economy to have combs filled with honey saved up for such emergencies, seeing that they are not expected to come often, so the whole force of feeders, some fifty, were put into action

Part were put in the home apiary and part taken to the out-apiaries   When going to an out-apiary a bag of sugar was taken along.   Water was put in the wash-boiler on the cook-stove and a good fire built under it A good-sized tin pail was filled half full or more with the heated water, then sugar was poured in till the pail was nearly full, and it was stirred with a stick till fairly well dissolved, which did not take very long   The syrup was then poured into the feeder on one of the hives, a pail half full of water was taken in and poured into the boiler, and then another colony was fed, and this was continued till all the feeders were supplied   The next day or so the feeders were shifted to another set of hives, till all were fed

FEEDING IN JUNE.

You will notice this is considerably different from the early spring feeding.   The colonies were stronger in June, the weather warmer, and the bees made rapid work carrying down the feed   It was better to dissolve the sugar before putting it in the feeders (perhaps it is better at any time), for then there was no danger of having dry sugar left in the feeder   Perhaps there was no real gain in using hot water when the colonies were strong and the weather warm.   I tried cold water in some cases, and it worked all right, only it took more stirring

ORIGINAL MILLER FEEDER

Most of my feeders are of the original pattern (Fig. 40)   At Fig 41 is seen one of them dissected   The lower part is an ordinary section-super.   On this rests the feeder proper, with the little board at one end removed, also the little board at one side, so as to show the inside wall under which the syrup may flow, and the outside wall, which lacks enough of coming to the top so that the bees can come up over it and go down into the feed.

Fig. 34.—Part of Home Apiary (from Northwest).

IMPROVED MILLER FEEDER.

The improved Miller feeder of the catalogs, instead of being all in one has two parts, and the bees go up through the middle. I thought it was an important improvement to allow the bees to go up the middle instead of up the two sides, because the heat ought to be greater at the middle. After a thorough trial of the two, side by side, I am obliged to admit that the improvement is one in theory only, and that the bees go up the sides whenever they will go up the middle, and it seems a little better to have the feed all in one dish.

If it were not for the expense of keeping two sets of feeders, I should like to keep a set of division-board feeders, for there may come times when it is cool and bees will not take feed readily from a Miller feeder, yet would take it from a division-board feeder, because closer to the brood-nest But most times I should prefer the Miller, so that has the preference.

CROCK-AND-PLATE FEEDER.

I have used the crock-and-plate feeder (Fig. 43), and it answers a very good purpose It has the advantage that any one can make a feeder at a minute's notice with materials always ready to hand Take a gallon crock, fill it half full of granulated sugar, then fill nearly full with water, all the better if stirred till dissolved, cover over the crock a thickness of flannel or other woolen cloth, or else four or five thicknesses of cheese-cloth; over this lay a dinner-plate upside down: then with one hand under the crock and the other over the plate quickly turn the whole thing upside down. Of course a smaller quantity of feed may be used if desired

The feeder is then set over the frames of a colony, an empty hive-body placed over, and all covered up so no bee can get to it except through the regular hive-entrance.

WATERING-CROCK.

This crock-and-plate feeder is a good one for those who like out-door feeding, if only a small quantity is to be fed It also makes a good watering-place for bees, if one does not mind the trouble Generally, however, I prefer a six-gallon crock standing upright with a few sticks of firewood in it for a watering-crock (Fig 44). A little salt thrown into the water helps to keep it sweet, and prevents it from being a breeding-place for mosquitoes Perhaps the bees like it better with the salt.

LACK OF SYSTEM.

I would like to say that I am very methodical about overhauling and seeing to the building up of colonies, from the time they are placed on the summer stands, till the honey harvest begins, but it would hardly be in accordance with facts. Conditions of bees or weather may make a difference in course of action. Possibly some other duties aside from the direct care of the bees may make a difference. So when I attempt to tell things just as they are, my want of system confronts me and makes the task somewhat difficult

At this point I fancy I can hear some of my good friends saying, "Why don't you keep a smaller number of colonies, so that you can have system enough to be able to tell a straight story, and derive more pleasure and profit?" I know it would be more pleasure; as to the profit, I doubt. If I had so few that I could at all times do every thing by a perfect system, I am afraid I should have part of the time a good deal of idle time on my hands. Neither is it fair for me to charge my lack of system entirely to the number of colonies Some of it comes from ignorance in not knowing how to do any better, some of it from changing plans constantly, and perhaps some of it from lack of energy in doing every thing just at the right time.

DIVISION-BOARDS.

In former years I made some attempt to keep the bees warmer by the use of a division-board, closing down to the number of combs actually needed at the time by the bees I was disappointed to find no clear proof that any great good came from it. Since then the experiments of Gaston Bonnier have shown that combs serve as good a purpose as a division-board, so the trouble of moving a division-board from time to time to accommodate the size of the colony is avoided

VERY WEAK COLONIES IN SPRING.

I have had, one time and another, a good many very weak colonies in the spring, and I am puzzled to know

what to do with them.   It seems of no use to unite them,
for I have united five into one, and the united colony
seemed to do no better than one left separate   About
all I try to do, is to keep the queen alive till I find some
queenless colony with which to unite them

One year I took the queens of five or six very weak
colonies, put them in small cages, and laid the cages on
top of the frames, under the quilt, over a strong colony
When I next overhauled this colony, its queen was gone,
probably killed by the bees on account of the presence of
other queens, but the queens in the cages were in good
condition, and became afterward the mothers of fine
colonies   I had put two of the queens in one cage, as I
was short of cages, and did not attach much value to the
queens, and these two did as well as the others   Of
course this was an exception to the general rule

In my locality I do not think the colonies can ever
become strong and populous too early in the season.
Theoretically, at least, then, I see that every colony as
soon as it comes out of the cellar, has plenty of stores to
last it for some time   I know this is a very indefinite
amount   Perhaps I might make it more definite by saying, for an ordinary colony, the equivalent of two full
combs of stores   If they have not so much I supply
them   I formerly thought it desirable to have any feed
given them as far as possible from the brood-nest, so
that they might have the feeling they were accumulating
from abroad   Further observation makes me place less
confidence in this

STRONG VERSUS WEAK COLONIES

I think that with increasing years I have an increasing aversion to weak colonies.   At the time of the honey
harvest, 40,000 bees in two colonies will not begin to
store as much as the same bees would do if they were all
in one colony.   Of course you have thought of that, but

possibly you have not noticed so clearly that something like the same rule holds good about building up in spring. Take a colony that comes out of the cellar with only enough bees to cover two combs. It will remain at a stand-still for a long time. Indeed, it may not stand still, but may become weaker, so that it will not have as much brood June 1 as May 1, with a possibility of peg-

Fig. 35.—Part of Home Apiary (from Southwest).

ging out altogether before the harvest opens. On the other hand a colony with bees enough to cover well three frames is likely to hold its own, beginning to increase slowly as soon as weather permits; and if it has bees enough to cover four frames it will walk right along increasing its brood-nest.

GIVING BROOD TO STRONGER.

Shall I take frames of brood from strong colonies to give to the weaklings? Not I. For the damage to the

strong colonies will more than overbalance the benefit to
the weaklings   If any taking from one colony to give
another is done in the spring, it will be to take from the
weak to give to those not so weak   If one colony has
four frames of brood and another two, taking from the
stronger a frame for the weaker would leave both so
weak they would not build up very rapidly, whereas taking one from the two-frame colony and giving it to the
four-frame colony would make the latter build up so much
faster that it could pay back with interest the borrowed
frame.

GIVING BROOD TO WEAKER

Not till a colony has six or eight frames of brood is
it desirable to draw from it brood for weaker colonies,
and there's no hurry about it then.   When a colony has
its hive so crowded with brood that the queen seems to
need more room, then a frame of brood can be taken
from it to help others   The first to be helped are not
the weakest, but the strongest of those with less than
four frames of brood   When the three-framers are all
brought up to four frames, it is time enough to help the
weaker ones   Toward the last the little fellows can be
helped up quite rapidly   Perhaps a colony with two or
three brood (if you will allow me to use brood for short
when I mean frames of brood) has had brood taken from
it, leaving it with only one brood   It has stood so for
several weeks, and now it can have three or four brood
given to it, setting it well on its feet

When brood is thus taken, generally the adhering
bees are taken with the brood, of course making sure
that no queen is taken.   Where a single brood is given
with adhering bees to a colony, I have never known any
harm to come to the queen of the reinforced colony   In
rare cases I have had the queen killed when several
frames of brood have been given at a time to a very weak

colony. A precautionary rule is that when more than one brood is given at a time, each one is taken from a different colony.

GIVING SECOND STORY.

When a colony is beginning to be crowded and there are no colonies needing help, and sometimes even when others do need help, a second story is given. This second story is given below. Putting an empty story below does not cool off the bees like putting one above. The bees can move down as fast as they need the room. Indeed this second story is often given long before it is needed, and sometimes two empty stories are given, for it is a nice thing to have the combs in the care of the bees. They will be kept free from moths, and if any are mouldy they will be nicely cleaned out ready for use when wanted.

Fig. 36.—Comb Resting Diagonally in Hive.

Sometimes when a colony is very strong and a story of empty combs is given below, a frame of brood is taken

from the upper story and put below, an empty comb being put in its place above   But unless the colony is very
strong, this hinders rather than helps the building up.

I may say here that after a good deal of experience
with colonies having two stories, I find that there is no
trouble from having the queen stay exclusively in one or
other of the stories   She passes up and down freely,
keeping filled with brood in both stories as many combs
as the bees will care for.

SUBSEQUENT OVERHAULING.

Any overhauling subsequent to the first, is an easy
matter.   As a broodless frame was left at the farther side
at the first overhauling, and the brood-nest commenced
with the next frame, I can count that the bees will continue this arrangement, only in some cases there will be
brood found in the outside frame   So in any examination after the first, I commence at the near side and when
I come to the first frame of brood, I need go no further,
for I know that the brood-nest will occupy all the rest of
the combs except the outside one   If they have not plenty
of feed, of course it can be given, although it may not
often be necessary to give stores the second time, for in
this locality they can get good supplies from fruit-bloom,
I suppose they can forage upon 10,000 fruit-trees without
going a mile

If, however, the first frame of brood I come to, contains only sealed brood, I must look further to see whether
they have eggs or very young brood, for it is possible
they may have become queenless.   If eggs are plentiful,
but no unsealed brood, I know that they have a young
queen which has commenced laying, and I must find her
and clip her wing

If there is nothing but sealed brood, and no eggs, I
am not sure whether they have a queen or not, and it is

not safe to give them one till I do know, so I give them, from another colony, a comb containing eggs and young brood. I make a record of giving them this young brood thus: "May 20, no eg gybr," and in perhaps a week I look to see in what condition they are. If I find queen-cells started I am pretty sure they have no queen

QUEENLESS COLONIES

What shall be done in that case depends. If the colony is weak, it is at once broken up, brood and bees being given wherever they may be needed, and I heave a sigh of relief to think I am rid of the weakling. If it is strong—an accident may have happened to the queen of a strong colony at the last overhauling—it may be broken up and the brood and bees distributed where they will do the most good, but more likely a weaker colony with a good queen will be united with it   Just possibly, the queen-cells started may be allowed to go on to completion.

BROOD AS A STIMULANT.

If it happened that they had a virgin queen when the young brood was given them, the presence of this brood is supposed to stimulate the queen to lay the sooner, and I may find eggs on this later inspection. It may be, however, that I shall find neither eggs nor queen-cell, in which case I consider it probable that they have a queen which has not yet commenced to lay, and they are left for examination later.

LAYING WORKERS

Although laying workers are not so likely to be found early in the year, it is still possible. In some cases the scattered condition of the brood awakens immediate suspicion   This scattered condition is shown in Fig. 59, but the picture does not clearly show how the sealed brood projects above the surface like so many little marbles, being thus projected because drone-brood is in worker-cells.

Often the presence of laying workers can be detected before there is any sealed brood, by the fact that drone-cells are chosen in preference to worker-cells, that is, drone-cells will be filled with eggs or brood—perhaps two or more eggs in a cell—while plenty of unused worker-cells seem handy Eggs in queen-cells are also likely to be found, and if you find a queen-cell with more than one egg in it you may be pretty sure laying workers have set up business. Sometimes a dozen of eggs may be found in one queen-cell An egg in a queen-cell with no other brood or eggs present is a pretty sure sign of laying workers

TREATMENT OF LAYING-WORKER COLONIES

When a colony of laying workers is found early in the season, about the only thing to do is to break is up, and it matters little what is done with the bees They are old, and of little value Indeed, there are never any very young bees with laying workers, when the bees are Italians or blacks, and it may be the best thing in all cases to break them up, distributing the bees and combs to other colonies.

Yet if a strong colony is found at any time with laying workers, and if, for any reason, it may seem desirable to continue the colony, a queen-cell, or a virgin queen just hatched may be given, for it is not easy to get them to accept a laying queen.

DRONE-LAYING QUEENS.

Drone-brood in worker-cells may be present with no laying workers—the work of a drone-laying or failing queen. The brood in that case, however, will not be so scattering as in Fig. 59. Such a colony is more amenable to treatment, and can be well utilized by uniting with a weak colony having a laying queen.

Fig. 37.—Painted Tin Hive-Covers.

RECORD ENTRIES.

While care is taken to omit no entry in the book that will be of future importance, there is really not such a great deal of writing done, as will be readily understood when it is remembered that only one page is allotted to three colonies, allowing only 22 square inches for each. It is seldom that a colony requires more than its allotted space in the season, hardly half the space being used on the average. There is a great deal of monotony about the entries, and there are a few words which are so frequently used that abbreviations aid much in saving room and time for making the entries. Some abbreviations that are constantly used are as follows: b for bees, br for brood, c or qc for queen-cell, g for gave, k for killed or destroyed (kc means I destroyed the queen-cells), q for queen, s for saw, but sc means sealed queen-cell, t for took, v for virgin queen, ☐ for super.

PLACE FOR PENCIL

To make sure of having a pencil always handy to make entries, it is tied to the book, as also is a pair of scissors for clipping queens unless the latter is replaced by a pair of pocket scissors. A strong string is put in the middle of the book, passed around the back and tied, and to this is tied a long string that holds the pencil, and another for the scissors. To prevent the scissors hanging open with its two sharp points, a common rubber band is so fastened on the handles as to hold them together While the band holds the scissors together when not in use, its elasticity allows their free use when needed.

KILLING GRASS.

This is a good time to salt the ground at and about the entrances of the hives, to kill the grass, although too often I leave it till it has to be cut with a sickle Grass growing in front of the hive annoys the bees, and that growing at the side annoys the operator, especially if the operator is of the female persuasion, and the grass is wet with dew or rain

HARBINGERS OF HARVEST.

There are certain things always noticed by a bee-keeper, with much interest, as heralding the beginning of spring or of the honey-harvest Among these are the singing of frogs, the advent of bluebirds, and the opening of various blossoms. With me the highest interest centers in white clover As I go back and forth to the out-apiaries, I am always watching the patches of white clover along the roadside. If your attention has never been called to it, you will be surprised to find how long it is from the time the first blossom may be seen, till clover opens out so bees will work upon it. I usually see a stray blossom days before it seems to have any company. In my location I do not count upon anything usually besides white clover for surplus, so no wonder I am interested in it.

Fig. 38.—Zinc Hive-Covers.

VARIOUS HONEY-PLANTS.

Yet there are a good many other plants whose help, all taken together, is not to be despised. If I kept only a few colonies, it is quite possible that I might secure some surplus from more than one of them.

Dandelions help no little in brood-rearing.

Raspberries are eagerly visited by the bees, but there are not enough of them to give a noticeable amount of raspberry honey. It is a very pleasant sight to see the bees thickly covering a field of raspberries in full bloom (Fig 45).

Red clover may yet be of importance Whether it be the change in the bees or the change in the season I do not know, but formerly I never saw a bee on red clover except at rare intervals, and now it is quite common I think it may be that the bees are different

Alsike clover is little cultivated here

SWEET CLOVER

It is hard to tell just how much, but I think the bees gather quite a little from sweet clover (Fig. 46). The earlier part of the sweet clover bloom is probably of no great value, because it comes at the same time as white clover, but it continues after white clover is gone, thus making it of greater value. It has a habit of throwing out fresh shoots of blossoms on the lower part of the stalk after the whole stalk has gone to seed and appears dead, and thus it continues the blooming season till freezing weather comes on A branch of this kind will be seen at the right in Fig. 46 I value sweet clover for hay

Alfalfa (Fig 47) is little known here It is a rare thing to see a bee at work upon it, and I think it is generally understood that it does not yield nectar east of the Mississippi But the experiment station says that if the land in Illinois be inoculated with some of the soil from the proper alfalfa regions of the West, it will grow as well here. If they can make changes in its growth, is it not just possible that it may yet become a honey-plant here?

GIANT WHITE CLOVER.

A new honey-plant has been mentioned a good deal in foreign bee-journals, a giant white clover, called Colossal Ladino (Fig 48) I succeeded in getting some seed from Switzerland, sowed a few of them in the window in the winter, and had the plants blooming in the summer of 1902. For the purpose of comparison you will see in Fig. 48, at the right, a branch of red clover, and at the left a plant of common white or Dutch clover, both grown on the same ground.   As you will see by looking at the picture, the new plant has leaves as large as those of red clover, and in appearance I think they are identical   The blossom, however, which you will see toward the left, looks precisely like a large white clover blossom   The habit of growth, too, is that of the common white clover, running along the ground and taking root as it goes.   A look at the picture will show this, the roots being seen coming from the stalk at the left.

Just how much value there is in this new clover I do not know   As will be seen, it grows much larger than the common white, but only as its leaves and leaf stems are larger, for it does not grow up and throw out branches like red clover

LINDEN, CATNIP, GOLDENROD, ASTERS, HEARTSEASE.

Linden or basswood (Fig 49) is a scarce article, the flavor of linden honey being seldom perceptible in any honey stored by my bees   I take great pleasure, however, in the sight of a row of lindens running from the public road up to the house (Fig. 50).

Catnip (Fig 51) is scattered about, in some places quite plentiful where it has the protection of hedges, for which it seems to have a great liking   It has a long season.

Goldenrod (Fig 52) grows in abundance in several varieties, and while other insects may be seen upon it in great numbers, a bee is seldom seen upon it   Much the same may be said of the asters (Figs. 53 and 54).   In some other places both these plants are said to be well visited by the bees.

The summer of 1902 was very wet, and for the first time in my observation heartsease (Fig. 55) was busily worked upon by the bees. Possibly the same thing might occur any very wet season.

CUCUMBERS.

I think the white clover crop, for some reason, is more unreliable than it was years ago. Some years there is a profusion of clover bloom, but there seems to be no nectar in it. As some little compensation, I think there is more fall pasturage than formerly. One reason for this is that two pickle factories are located at Marengo, and my bees have the run of one or two hundred acres of cucumbers. And yet I must confess that I am not at all sure what cucumber honey is. Sometimes the honey stored at the time of cucumber bloom is objectionable in flavor, and sometimes the flavor is fine. Two or three years the bees at the Hastings apiary stored in the fall some fine honey, remarkable for whiteness, and I've no idea what it was gathered from. On the whole I am in a poor honey region, and would have sought a better one long ago but for ties other than the bees.

ARTIFICIAL PASTURAGE

I have made some effort to increase the pasturage for my bees. Of spider-plant I raised only a few plants. It seemed too difficult to raise to make me care to experiment with it on a larger scale Possibly if I knew better how to manage it, the difficulty might disappear. Or, on other soil it might be less difficult to manage The same might be said of the other things I have tried My soil is clay loam, and hilly, although I live in a prairie State. I am at least a mile distant from prairie soil. I have tried Alsike many times, and never had a good stand but once ; perhaps an acre then. I had an acre of as fine figwort as one would care to see. It died root and branch the second winter; even the young plants that had come from seed the previous summer. It was on the lowest ground I had, very rich, and much like prairie.

When the boom for Chapman's honey-plant (echinops spherocephalus) was on, I was among the first to get it, and I succeeded in having a large patch. Bees were on it in large numbers, but close observation showed that a great proportion of them were loafing as if something about the plant had made them drunk. I concluded I did not get nectar enough from it to pay for the use of the land, to say nothing of cultivation.

One year I raised half an acre of sunflowers, and I have tried other things, but have given them up.

Fig. 39.—Hive-Stand.

APPLE-BLOOM.

Quite likely if a second crop of apple-bloom came a month or two later than the usual time, I might get some

surplus from that ; but coming so early I think there are
hardly bees enough to store it   Still, the bees are at this
time using large quantities of honey for brood, and so
the apple-bloom is of very great value.   Another advantage is that the great quantity of bloom has somewhat
the effect of prolonging its time, for the latest blossoms,
that with a few trees would amount to little or nothing,
are enough to keep the bees busy   So it happens that
often I can scarcely recognize any interim between fruit-
bloom and clover.   A few items from a memorandum for
1882 may be interesting·

MEMORANDA OF 1882

Apr 4 —Last bees taken out of cellar
May 8 —Plum-bloom out   Bees still work on meal
and sugar syrup.
May 10 — Wild plum, dandelion, cherry pear, Si-
berian, Duchess of Oldenberg.
May 31 —Saw first clover blossom
June 5 —Apple about done
June 12 —Commenced giving supers
June 13 —Clover full bloom—plentiful
June 20 —Locust out
Aug 1 —Clover failing.
Aug. 5 —Robber bees trouble

You will notice that the earliest apple-bloom
(Duchess of Oldenberg) commenced May 10, while the
Janets and other late bloomers were still in blossom on
June 5, several days after the first clover was seen, making about four weeks of apple-bloom.   Possibly this was
unusual—certainly the clover lasted unusually long, being about 7½ weeks from the time the bees commenced
working on it, for they do not seem to commence work
till after the blossoms have been out some time

TIME FOR GIVING SUPERS.

You see that I did not commence putting on supers till 12 days after I saw the first clover-blossom, and if I

Fig. 40.—Original Miller Feeder.

had had only a dozen colonies, I might have waited later, but with a large number I must commence in time so that all shall be on as soon as needed. Usually I put on supers as nearly as convenient to ten days after seeing the very first white clover blossom. A little time before bees commence work in supers, little bits of pure, white wax will be seen stuck on the old comb about the upper part, yet I hardly wait for this, but go rather by the clover.

Another year (1884), I saw the first clover-blossom on May 21, apple being still in full bloom; and I commenced putting on supers June 2. One year, I remember, clover failed on July 4, the earliest I ever remember.

MEMORANDA OF 1901.

Turning to another year, the year 1901, I give a few entries:

March 17.—Bluebirds, prairie chickens, robins, larks
March 25 —Frogs.
April 5 —Soft maple.
April 28.—Dandelion.
May 1 —Hard maple, plum.
May 2 —Cherry
May 5 —Apple.
May 6 —Strawberry.
May 23 —White clover
June 20 —Sweet clover.
June 29.—Linden.

WHITE CLOVER UNCERTAIN

That year, 1901, had perhaps the finest show of white clover bloom ever known, but it was a dead failure, perhaps on account of the terrible drouth, although sometimes white clover blossoms bountifully and fails to yield honey when nothing that can be seen in the way of weather is at all at fault About the middle of August the bees began storing, perhaps from cucumbers and sweet clover, and gave a surplus of 16 pounds a colony It would have been better to have had it all stored in brood-frames, I think.

The following year, 1902, was still more exceptional. As already told, the bees would have starved in June but for feeding, yet later on they did some good work, some colonies, yielding as much as 72 sections. The bulk of this was stored toward the last of August or later

Fig. 70 is from a photo taken Oct. 1 In the picture the bee appears to be perfectly still, but these are not moving pictures, and I assure you that that bee was in very lively motion when taken.

OVERSTOCKING.

To a bee-keeper who has more bees than he thinks advisable to keep in the home apiary, pasturage and overstocking are subjects of intense interest. The two subjects are intimately connected. They are subjects so elusive, so difficult to learn anything about very positively, that if I could well help myself, I think I should dismiss them altogether from contemplation But like Banquo's ghost, they will not down. I must decide, whether I will or not, how many colonies will overstock the home field, unless I make the idiotic determinatoin to keep all at home with the almost certain result of obtaining no surplus. I do not expect ever to have any positive knowledge upon the subject, because if I could find out with certainty just what number of colonies a given area would support in one year, I have no kind of assurance that the same kind of a year will ever occur again. So I act upon the *guess* that in my locality it is never wise to have more than 100 colonies in one apiary, and possibly 75 would be better.

SURPLUS ARRANGEMENTS.

The first surplus honey I obtained worth mentioning was secured in boxes holding somewhere from 6 to 10 pounds. The boxes had glass on one or more sides, and were placed on the top of box-hives. Then for a year or more my surplus was extracted honey obtained with the old Peabody extractor (Fig. 2), in which the whole affair, can and all, revolves.

SECTIONS.

Then I started on sections of the four-piece kind, and later used the one-piece. I have used the $4\frac{1}{4}x4\frac{1}{4}x1\frac{7}{8}$

size much more than any other   I have used a few hundreds of the tall sections, but my market does not seem
to like them any better, if as well, as the square sections
I have tried 4¼ square sections of several widths, 1 15-16
inches wide, 7 to the foot, also 8, 9, and 10 to the foot.   I
have made some trial of plain sections, but for my market
I am not sure that there is advantage enough in them to
make me change from the two-bee-way sections

T SUPERS.

The T supers I use are 12⅛ wide inside, just right
for 8-frame hives.   Just why I adopted this size I do not
know, for at that time I was using 10-frame hives, and it
was a little awkward to use a super so much narrower
than the hive   But at least part of the time I used only
eight frames in the 10-frame hives.

The separators used are plain wood, and are generally bought new every year, for it is about as cheap to
buy new as to clean the old, and more satisfactory.   The
usual follower fills out the super, wedged in with a plain
stick   I do not believe this kind of a wedge is so good
as super-springs, and I hope to change to springs in the
near future.   The T tins are not fastened to the super,
but loose (Fig. 5)

SECTIONS READY IN ADVANCE.

The work of getting sections and supers ready for
use has been all done long before the time for putting on,
and something will be said about how that work is done.

At the time the supers are needed for putting on the
hives, they are all nicely piled up in the store-room of the
shop, ready to carry out, not less than four supers ready
for each colony.   Even with that number prepared, I was
once caught short in the harvest time—not a pleasant
thing   Very likely they will not all be used, but some al-

lowance must be made for unfinished sections, and some supers will be put on rather late when it is not certain anything at all will be done in them. So remembering the old adage, "It is better to be ready and not go than to go and not be ready," it is well to be prepared with a good number, even if they are carried over to a later year, and I have had sections used satisfactorily after they had been filled five years.

Fig. 41.—Miller Feeder Dissected.

SHOP FOR BEE-WORK.

The shop (Fig. 71) in which the filled supers are stored is a plain wooden building 18x24, two-story, with a bee-cellar under it. The bee-cellar, however, has not been used for a few years, not because it might not be better to use it, but because it is more convenient to have the bees all in the one cellar under the dwelling-house. The upper story is used for storing empty supers, hives and other articles not very heavy, or such as are not often needed   The outside door opens into the middle of the east side of the house into a store-room, immediately in front of you as you enter are the stairs leading to the upper story, and at your right a door opens into the work-room.   In this work-room is a coal-stove, and the room, being ceiled up, is comfortable in the severest weather.

ROOM FOR QUEEN.

Up to the time of putting on supers the queen has had unlimited room with the design of encouraging the rearing of as much brood as possible.   When the harvest begins, she may have as much as 6, 9, 11, even up to 14 frames well occupied with brood and eggs.   A good deal depends on the season, as well as the queen   At one time I thought I ought to be able to make a success of continuing the two stories of brood-frames throughout the harvest.   It seems that when a colony is so strong as to have 12 or 14 frames of brood, there ought to be no difficulty in having good super-work done by putting the supers above the two stories; and one season of failure the only super I had filled was on a two-story colony.   But I was never able to have that thing repeated, and whatever the reason may be, I have not been able to make a success of putting comb-honey supers on two-story colonies   Even if the two-story plan would work all right it involves much extra lifting.

REDUCING TO ONE STORY.

So before putting on supers the colonies are reduced to one story each.   If a colony has 9, 10, or more frames of brood, all but 8 are taken away.   The surplus frames of brood are given to those which have less than 8 frames of brood each the effort being to have in each hive 8 frames well filled with brood when a super is given   The season may be such that it will not be possible to have as many as 8 brood in each hive. A colony strong enough to have 6 frames well filled with brood is likely to be in condition for good super-work, but the work will be better if it has 7 or 8. On the other hand the season and the early condition of the bees may be such that when each colony is brought up or down to its 8 frames of brood, a considerable surplus of brood may be left.

DISPOSAL OF EXTRA BROOD.

Circumstances will decide what shall be done with this extra brood. It may be needed for building up nuclei, or for new colonies. It may be piled up temporarily in piles of three, four, or five stories each, to be used later

Fig. 42.—Hive-Dummy.

in any manner desired. It does not take three times as many bees to care for the brood in three stories as it does

to care for the brood in one story.   If two or three stories
of brood with adhering bees are piled up, in two or three
weeks there will be enough bees there so that when reduced to one story it will be all right for super-work
Or, it may be left just as it is, and allowed to store in
combs for the next spring's use

BURR-COMBS.

At the time of putting on supers, it is desirable that
there shall be as little inducement as possible toward the
building of burr-combs between top-bars and supers.   A
very strong inducement of that kind consists in the presence of any beginnings of such combs already there
Formerly I had a space of ⅜ of an inch over top-bars,
and if a super of sections were placed directly on the hive,
burr-combs in abundance would be built.

HEDDON HONEY-BOARD.

In such conditions the Heddon slat-honey-board
(Fig 6) was a boon. Between the top-bars and the honey-
board was a mass of burr-combs filled with honey, making a disagreeably dauby, sticky, dripping mess when the
honey-board was removed; but the space between the
honey-board and the bottoms of the sections was left beautifully free from burr-combs, so the section bottoms were
left clean   This while everything was new; for if the
honey-boards were put on a second year without cleaning
there would be the beginnings of burr-combs between
honey-board and sections, or more than the beginnings if
the honey-boards had gone more than one year without
cleaning   So at some time before putting on the honey-
boards they were carefully cleaned   But cleaning the
honey-boards was not enough.   The tops of the frames
had to be cleaned as well, and this cleaning was done with

a common garden-hoe, an assistant smoking the bees out of the way while the top-bars were hoed.

CORRECT BEE-SPACE.

It was a great step in advance when we learned that instead of a space of ⅜ of an inch there should be only ¼ inch, or perhaps a shade less. In other words we learned that a bee-space, or that space in which bees were least inclined to put either comb or propolis, was a scant quarter of an inch. With a correct bee-space between top-bars and sections, we can dispense entirely with anything in the shape of a honey-board. There will be a little trouble with the building of bits of comb under the sections, but not enough to make it worth while to use a honey-board. But that trouble will be greatly aggravated if there be any beginnings of burr-combs on the tops of the frames when supers are given. So the tops must be cleaned off wherever there is anything to clean off before the supers are put on the hives.

THICK TOP-BARS.

Another thing that may help to keep down burr-combs is the thickness and width of top-bars. My top-bars are ⅞ thick and 1⅛ wide, leaving a space of ¼ inch between them. There are more burr-combs than I like built between them, and I have wondered whether any other space would be better. If the sides as well as the tops of the top-bars were cleaned off at the time of giving supers, it would help to keep the bottoms of sections clean, but I doubt its paying.

THICK TOP-BARS FOR WHITE SECTIONS.

Even if the ⅞ thickness of top-bar were of no other advantage, I should want it for the sake of keeping the cappings of the sections white. At one time I had wide-frames of sections facing brood-frames (the brood-frames were used to bait the bees up into the supers), and if the brood-frames were left there till the sections were sealed, the sealing would be almost if not quite as dark as the sealing of brood-combs The bees seem to carry bits of the old, black brood-combs to use in capping the sections So the thick top-bar increasing the distance of the sections from the brood-combs helps to keep the former whiter

NO EXCLUDER UNDER SECTIONS.

"Before putting on the super, would you advise me to put a queen-excluder (Fig. 56) over the brood-chamber?" It would increase the space between the brood-combs and the sections, and in that way would be a further help toward prevention of dark cappings on the sections, and it would make a sure thing as to preventing burr-combs on the bottoms of the sections But I don't believe there would be enough advantage in both ways to pay for the excluders

I think I hear you say, "But wouldn't it pay to use excluders for the sake of keeping the queen out of the supers?" I may reply that the queen so seldom goes up into a super that not one section in a hundred, sometimes not more than one in a thousand, will be found troubled with brood. So on the whole I hardly think that all the advantages to be gained from using excluders would pay for the time and trouble of using them I need not consider so very much the cost of them, for I have a lot on hand lying idle At one time I thought I had a plan for prevention of swarming by the use of excluders, and was so sanguine about it that I got 150 of them. I think a great deal of queen-excluders, and wouldn't like to do without them, but I did not need 150 of them, for my excluder-swarm-prevention plan did not turn out to be a howling success.

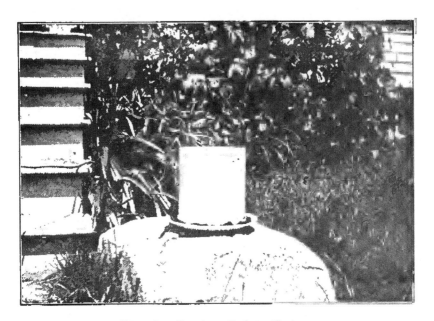

Fig. 43.—Crock-and-plate Feeder.

EXPERIMENTING ON TOO LARGE SCALE.

Allow me to digress long enough to confess that one of my weaknesses is being a little too sanguine about new plans while they are yet in the raw, and so experimenting on too large a scale. More than one crop of honey has been lessened by means of some foolish project that I thought might increase the crop. But I haven't done as badly as I might have done, for my good wife has acted somewhat as a balance-wheel, advising me to "go slow" and not experiment on too large a scale, and she has always been abetted by her sister, who is perhaps over-conservative. I could have tested my plan with 15 excluders just as well as with ten times that number, but I knew the plan would work, and I couldn't wait! I think I

didn't consult my wife about ordering the 150 excluders.
As I grow older I may learn caution, and experiment on
a smaller scale, but being only just turned of seventy too
much should not be expected of me

PLEASURE OF EXPERIMENTING

As an offset to the mischief done by experimenting
on too large a scale, I may say that one of my keenest enjoyments is the working out of problems connected with
bee-keeping   There is never a time, summer or winter,
when I am not cooking one, or more schemes, plans or
projects connected with the business   Good it is that my
pastor (his name at present is the Rev A. J. van Page)
is a very interesting preacher, else it would be a harder
task than it is for me to keep my thoughts from wander-
ing off upon some new scheme for getting better queens
or whiter sections while he is trying to tell me how I
ought to live.   No doubt more money could be made at
bee-keeping if everything in the business were fully settled and we knew beforehand just exactly the right step
to take in any given case, but there wouldn't be nearly the
fun in it

BROOD IN SECTIONS

It may be asked why it is that I have so little trouble
with queens laying in sections, while some others are
much troubled in that way.   Possibly the thickness of top-
bars may have something to do with it, but it may be that
the amount of foundation in sections has a bearing on the
case   Some use small starters in sections, while my sections are filled as full as possible with foundation   When
drone-comb is absent from the brood-nest, there seems
such a desperate desire for drone-brood that I have known
the queen to leave the brood-nest and fill with eggs a
patch of drone-comb two or three frames distant from the

brood-nest.   On the same principle she would go up into the sections if drone-comb were there, and nearly always when I find brood in the sections it is drone-brood.   With small starters in sections there is plenty of chance for building drone-comb, but when the sections are full of worker foundation there is no chance for it, hence no special temptation for the queen to go above unless very much crowded for room.

Fig. 44.— Watering-Crock.

PREPARING SUPERS OF SECTIONS.

This work is done in the winter, or at least so early in spring that it will not interfere with other work, but as an understanding of it may help just a little toward understanding some of the summer work, I will talk about it here.

CLEANING SUPERS AND T TINS.

The propolis is scraped from the supers by means of the hatchet already mentioned.   Cleaning T tins is another matter. The plan used is the invention of my assistant, and I think I can not do better than to let her tell about it by copying the following article which she wrote for Gleanings in Bee-Culture

"When we commenced work in the shop, the first super I filled with the nice clean sections, I looked at the T tins all covered with propolis and thought to myself, 'If we are to have sections unstained by propolis it will never do to put them on these dirty T tins But, oh dear! it will be an endless task to scrape them all I can never do it.' Just then a happy thought struck me Why not boil the propolis off? Sure enough, why not?

"I repaired to the kitchen, placed the wash-boiler on the stove (one we use for such work), filled it with water and T tins, then went back to the shop to work, and left them to boil at their own sweet will, delighted to think I had such an inspiration. In about an hour I went back to the kitchen to see how my T tins were progressing I fully expected to see them all nice and clean, and was most bitterly disappointed to find that they looked even worse than they did when I put them in, as the propolis was more evenly distributed all over them.

"I next tried scrubbing them with a broom in the boiling water, but it would not work. I meditated awhile, then concluded I would try concentrated lye, providing Dr Miller did not object. I did not know what effect the lye would have on the tins He said I might try it I put the boiler back on the stove to try once more. I did not feel quite so sanguine as I poured in part of a can of concentrated lye

"I did not leave it this time, but anxiously watched to see what effect it would have. It brought it off pretty well, but was not quite strong enough. I put in the rest of the can of lye, and, Eureka! the propolis disappeared as if by magic I stirred the tins with the poker to insure the lye reaching all parts of them; then with the tongs I lifted them into a tub and rinsed them off with cold water, and set them up in the sun to drain, as bright and clean as when they came from the tinner's

"I filled up the boiler with T tins again, and so on, until the strength of the lye was all used up, when I turned it out, filled up the boiler afresh, and began all over again, continuing until they were all done. I used a can of lye to a boiler of water.

"Every time I fill up a super with the nice clean T tins I feel more than paid for the work it took to make them so. I am pretty sure that washing-fluid would clean them almost if not quite as well as the concentrated lye, providing it were used strong enough, although I have never tried it. However, I think I should prefer the lye, as it does the work most thoroughly and does not hurt the T tins in the least, that I can see.

"If you have a lot of dirty T tins I advise you to clean them in this way, and see if you are not as delighted as I was to see them come out so bright and clean   Be sure to use plenty of water in rinsing them off "

WETTING SECTIONS.

The well-known Hubbard section-press is used for putting the sections together   If the sections are fresh from the manufacturer and as good as they ought to be, they can be put together at once without any preparation If they have been held over from the previous year they may be so dry that too many of them will break in folding The joints of these are wet in a somewhat wholesale manner. If they are crated in such a way as to be favorable for it, the whole crate of 500 are wet before being taken from the original package, one side of the crate being removed so as to expose the edges of the sections. If the crate is not of the right kind for this, then the sections are taken from the crate and put in the proper position

in an empty crate lying on one side with the top and one
end removed   Of course the sections do not lie flat, but
on their edges, the grooves of each tier corresponding
with the grooves of the other tiers, so that a small stream
of water poured into the grooves at the top will readily
find its way clear through to the bottom   If necessary
the sections must be wedged together, so there will be no
room for water to get between them only at the grooves.

A pint funnel is specially prepared for the work.   A
wooden plug is pushed in from above, projecting below
two inches or less   The lower end of the plug is whittled to a point, and either by means of a bad fit or by
means of a little channel cut in one side of the plug, there
is just leak enough so that when the funnel is filled there
will be a continuous fine stream of water running from
the point of the plug   Holding the funnel in one hand
I pour into it *boiling* water from a tea-kettle held in the
other hand at the same time holding the funnel so that
the stream from the point of the plug shall be directed
into the grooves, moving the funnel along just fast
enough so that the water shall be sure to go clear through
to the bottom   Cold water will not work well

FOLDING SECTIONS

Sometimes I put sections together myself, but generally some boy or girl does the work unless my wife be
pressed into service   The operator seated at the machine (Fig 57) has a pile of sections laid at a convenient
height at her left hand, the sections piled so that the ends
correspond   As fast as the sections are taken from the
press they are neatly piled in order on a board at the right
of the operator   (I know that some throw the sections
indiscriminately into a basket as they leave the press, and
it seems this ought to take less time, but I think in the
long run my way saves time)   It is desirable that the

board upon which the sections are piled should be light, as no great strength is required, and sometimes several thousand folded sections will be piled up ahead, and it is pleasanter to handle the light board. A dummy or almost any board will answer, but oftener wood-zinc queen-excluders are used. One of these is of such size that there may be placed upon it side by side three rows of sections with ten sections in each row. Upon these are placed three other rows, break-joint fashion, with nine sections in each row, and this piling up may continue till the upper rows contain four or less each. Generally the piling goes no higher than to have six sections in the upper rows, making 120 sections a board-full. As fast as one board is filled another takes its place, and the filled board is piled up, unless Miss Wilson is putting in foun-

No. 45.—Field of Raspberries in Bloom.

dation at the time and is ready for a fresh board-full of sections.

SIZE OF STARTERS IN SECTIONS

Foundation for sections comes from the factory in sheets large enough to fill several sections. At different times the sheets have been of different sizes, but for some time past they have measured $3\frac{7}{8} \times 15\frac{1}{2}$ This size is just right to make four top-starters $3\frac{1}{4}$ inches deep, and four bottom starters $\frac{5}{8}$-inch deep. Occasionally a bottom-starter of this depth makes trouble by lopping over, but not often, and a shallower starter is more likely to be gnawed down by the bees. Moreover, I think the deeper the bottom-starter the more promptly the two starters are fastened together

With two starters of this size in a $4\frac{1}{4}$ section, there should be a space of $\frac{1}{8}$ inch between the two if it were not that the space is made larger by the melting away of the edges of the starters when they are put in the section (Fig 60)

CUTTING FOUNDATION

I have one time and another used different plans for cutting   A simple way and one that is quite satisfactory, is the following: Take a board 18x12 inches or larger, on one end nail a block as a stop for the ends of the sheets of foundation to rest against, and on one side nail four blocks about $2\frac{1}{4}$ inches long as stops for the one edge of the foundation to rest against   It is well also to nail one of these $2\frac{1}{4}$-inch blocks on the other side near the stop at the end, so as to make a space of $7\frac{7}{8}$ inches in which the ends of the foundation shall be confined, otherwise the foundation has a disagreeable habit of sluing off to one side when the first cut is made at the other end. Of course these stops are to be nailed on the upper surface of the board and not on the edges   The two blocks that are nailed nearest the end-stop are to be tight against it, the others at such intervals as to allow for cutting the

3^1_4 starters. The size of these blocks is not important, ⅝ square being a good size. With a rule of any con-

Fig. 46 — Sweet Clover

venient length ½x¼, this rule being used to guide the knife in cutting, the machine would now be ready for the foundation if one had an eye accurate enough to put the rule in the right place. In order to do this quickly and accurately, nails against which to place the rule at the right places are partly driven in on both sides; 2½-inch wire finishing-nails are good for this purpose. The board is to lie before you, having the side with the four stop-blocks nearest you. Drive a nail into each side of the board so that there shall be a space of just 3^1_4 inches between the end-stop and the nail. I don't mean you shall mark a point 3^1_4 inches from the end-stop and drive your nail there, for that would make 3¼ inches from the end-stop to the *middle* of the nail, whereas it should be 3¼ from the stop to the nearest *side* of the nail. The distances of the other nails from the end-stops will be as follows: 6½, 9¾, 13, 13⅝, 14¼, 14⅞. Now your cutting-board is all ready for work.

Two knives are needed, one to be heating while the the other is cutting. For heating I use a common kerosene lamp put in a box deep enough so that when a board is laid over the top of it and a knife is laid on that board the end of the knife-blade shall be directly over the lamp, nearly or quite touching the top of the chimney. I don't know what kind of a knife is best. A Barlow knife makes good work, but I think I like better a common tea-knife with a thin steel blade broken off, so it is 2½ or 3 inches long, and somewhat square at the point.

Preparatory to cutting, the foundation must be carefully and evenly placed on the board. Take five sheets and even them up true and nice, and lay the pile with one end tight against the end-stop and one side against the side-stops. Now lay a similar pile close beside it. Beginning at the right-hand end, place your rule against the left-hand side of the nails, and with a quick stroke make a cut with the knife held flat against the rule. If you don't look out you'll hold the rule so that you'll cut a piece off the tip of the thumb or finger of the left hand, but you'll not be likely to do it many times. If you are not careful to hold the knife flat against the rule you will be likely to cut into it. To avoid this I have tried covering the rule with tin, but do not like it so well. The rapidity of the stroke is important. If your knife is hot enough you can cut clear down through at one stroke, but that's bad. The edges of the foundation will be melted together, and you will have trouble getting them apart. Turn down your lamp, and get it so three or four strokes will be needed.

When the boardful is cut I take a super with a bottom in it, gather up and put into it the 40 bottom-starters, also the 40 top-starters, making them in a neat pile.

Instead of using a single rule, I have for some time preferred to have a rule for every cut, making a saving of time. Take seven rules and lay them on the board on the proper places for cutting On the ends of the rules, at each side, lay a thin strip of wood 15 inches long or longer—a one-piece section without the grooves does nicely—with one end of each strip tight up against the end-stop Now nail together in this position, clinching the nails You will use this with the other side up, the rules above, the side-strips below (Fig 61). Of course the guide-nails are not needed with this arrangement. In the picture three of the rules appear all right, but the other four, which are very close together, look as if they were all one

The cutting-board rests on a little work-table (Fig 62), which is quite convenient for this and other purposes

A plan for cutting that is highly commended, which I have not yet had the opportunity to try, may be still better. It is to use a mitre-box with cuts at the proper places, and cut the foundation with a corrugated bread-knife

The sections being folded and the foundation cut, we are now ready for putting starters in the sections. This is the work of Miss Wilson, and she is an expert at it After trying a number of foundation-fasteners, I have found nothing with which I can do better work than with the Daisy fastener.

DIVISION OF LABOR.

I may remark in passing that when I speak of doing things it does not always mean that I do such things personally, for it may be that some one else does the work entirely But when any new implement is to be used or new plan tried, I first carefully study it up and try to learn just how it ought to be used, and then I instruct the one who is to make a specialty of that part of the work, and in a short time the specialist far exceeds the instructor Miss Wilson can put in, I think, five starters to my one, my son Charlie, when a little chap, could distance me in putting together sections; and I think Philo can beat me at taking sections out of supers.

PUTTING STARTERS IN SECTIONS

The Daisy foundation-fastener is so well known that I need say nothing about the use of the machine itself As the operator sits at the machine with a small pile of starters in the lap, a boardful of sections is at the left hand at a convenient height, the side of the board toward the operator (Fig 87).   The bottom-starter is put in first, then the top-starter   When the section has its two starters, it is put directly into the super.   With a starter as deep as $3\frac{1}{4}$ inches it would hardly do to throw the section in a basket.   Formerly the sections when filled were placed in order on a board the same as the board from which they were taken, and it was a separate job afterward to fill them in the super

PUTTING SECTIONS IN SUPERS

By means of an implement of my own devising, which for want of a better name may be called a "super-filler" (Fig 63), the separate job of filling sections in supers is now entirely dispensed with, and the sections go directly from the Daisy fastener into the super, taking no more time to be put into the super than it would take to put them on a board.   Indeed, I think it takes a little less time, for there is not the same need of care in placing the sections so other sections will not be knocked off the board, but the sections are shoved into place in the super in a sort of automatic way. Then, too, it is a comfort to

Fig. 47.—Alfalfa.

get them directly into the super, for while on a board, even for a short time, there is always danger of some mishap by which a boardful may tumble over and come to grief.

SUPER-FILLER.

I'll tell you how to make a super-filler. Take a board as large as the outside dimensions of your super or larger (The one in the picture is a board hive-cover) Nail a cleat on one end of the board, and another cleat on one side, as in the picture These cleats may be ½ by ¼ inch, but the dimensions are not important Now put a super on the board, shoving one corner snug up in the corner made by the cleats. With a lead-pencil, mark on the board, on the inside of the super, where the sides of the super come Put eight sections in the super, four on each side, with the three T tins in their proper places With a pencil rule across the board each side of each T tin, so as to show where the T tins come. Now take off the super and its contents, and get six strips, each 11½ inches long and ¼ inch square Nail these on as shown in the picture, so as to keep at equal distances from the pencil-mark of the super at each side, and about a fourth of an inch distant from the marks made for the T tins The super-filler is now complete.

It stands at a convenient height at the right-hand side of the one who operates the Daisy fastener, with the side-cleat at the farther side (Fig 87). A super is placed on it with one corner of the super tight against the angle made by the cleats, but no T tin is yet put in the super As the sections come from the fastener they are placed in the super at the end toward the back of the operator When the first row of six is completed, the T tin is slipped under these sections into its proper place In like manner a second row of sections and a T tin; then a third row and a T tin, and lastly the fourth row Then without rising, the operator lifts this filled super to one side and gets an empty one.

PUTTING IN SEPARATORS.

Generally these filled supers are not separatored till the day's work of fastening foundation is done. Then a small table is used at which the operator sits. This table is made of three hive bottom-boards, or boards 21x14. Stand two of the boards on end; nail the other board on top; nail light boards on one side for a back, or brace with two pieces of lath diagonally; and there's your table (Fig. 62). Being convenient for other purposes, several of these little tables are on hand. The table is placed

Fig. 48. Colossal Ladino Clover.

near a pile of supers to be separatored, and the separators are filled in.

TOP SEPARATORS.

As the sections now stand, there is some space between them endwise, allowing them to be out of square, and making a convenient place for the bees to deposit a disagreeable quantity of propolis. To remedy this, there is crowded in at the top between each two rows of sections a little stick 11½ by ¼ by scant ⅛. Then the follower is wedged in, and when all are done the supers are carried into the south room or store-room, and piled up to await the harvest time.

BAIT-SECTIONS.

Bait-sections are put in enough supers so that the first super put on each hive shall be baited Generally only one bait-section is in a super, the bait being in the center, and these baited supers are piled in the store-room where it will be convenient to reach them first. The total count in the store-room will be such that each colony can have an average of about four and a half supers if it wants them. There is no great probability of that, but it will do no harm to have some of them left over till a year or more later

SATISFACTION IN HAVING SUPERS READY.

There is a feeling of real satisfaction in seeing the larger part of the store-room filled with piles of supers ready to go on the hives How many times I have counted them and admired the nice even piles reaching to the ceiling! Perhaps I should not appreciate them so much if I had not, years ago, felt the annoyance of running out of sections or foundation right in the middle of the honey season, waiting days for it, and the honey wasting.

Having spent thus much time telling what was done the previous winter, let us get back to warmer weather.

GIVING ADDITIONAL SUPERS.

Understanding now that each colony has had a super given to it about ten days after the very first white clover blossom has been seen, the further history of this super and its possible successors is a matter that varies so much in different seasons that it is difficult to tell it straight. By the way, you may think that I'm always thrilled with the sight of the first clover blossom. I'm not. Scarcely ever a thrill. The colonies are never all of them as strong as I would like for the beginning of the harvest, and that first clover blossom is merely a warning that the time for building up for the harvest is becoming very short.

UNCERTAINTY OF SEASONS

As to giving additional super-room, it is a thing that may or may not be. That first clover bloom may have so few successors that there will be no harvest; or bloom may be abundant with no nectar. So sometimes it happens that after it becomes a clear case that the harvest is a failure, the supers are taken off as innocent of honey as when they were put on. Oftener it happens that the bait-section in each super is filled and sealed and not a cell drawn out in the other sections. From that up, the seasons will vary so that the average number of sections to each colony will be 10, 24, 48, and up to not such a great way from 100, although these latter seasons do not come with any alarming degree of frequency.

If one could know in advance just what the season was going to be, one could tell a good deal better what to do in the way of giving additional super-room. One may give so much room that there will be an undue propor-

tion of unfinished sections at the final taking off, or one
may leave the bees so crowded for room as to lose part
of the crop   I am not likely to make the latter mistake,
which I consider a good deal worse than to have too many
unfinished sections

GUESSING ABOUT MORE SUPER-ROOM.

On the whole, there is a mixture of judgment and
guess-work as to putting on any super after the first.
Perhaps the nearest to a general rule in the matter is to
give a second super when the first is half filled   If, however, honey seems to be coming in slowly, or if the colony
is not strong, and the bees seem to have plenty of room
in the super, no second super is given, although the one
already there may be nearly filled with honey   On the
other hand, if honey seems to be coming with a rush, and
the bees seem crowded for room, a second super may be
given, although there is very little honey in the first
These same conditions continued, a third super may be
given when the second is only fairly started and the first
not half full, and before the first super is ready to take
off there may be four or five supers on the hive.

RISKING IN GOOD SEASON

In the year 1897—a remarkably prosperous year—
there were at one time on the hives in the Wilson apiary
an average of four supers to each colony, some colonies
with less than four and some with more, and not a finished super in the lot   As I would lie at night thinking it
over, I would say to myself, "What if there should come
one of those sudden stops to the flow that sometimes occur, and you should be caught with those tons of honey
with scarcely any sections finished in the lot?   Wouldn't
you wish you had gone a little slower, and had the bees
finish up what they had, rather than to coax them to

spread over more territory?" And then the cold chills would run up and down my back. But the sudden stop didn't come, and the crop was finished in good style. The supers were all well filled with bees, and although I took some chances as to unfinished work, I feel pretty

Fig. 49.—Linden or Basswood Blossoms.

sure that if I had allowed less room it would have been at a loss. But that was a very exceptional case.

Usually, in a fair season, when the harvest is in full blast and fairly along, there will be three or four supers upon each hive. That does not mean, by any means, that

there will be that number of finished supers to each
colony, for very likely the last super given will have very
little honey in it when the harvest is over.   But it will
not do to let the bees be crowded for room, and if all the
sections on the hive are about full, if the harvest has not
entirely closed an empty super must be given, in case they
might need it.

SUPERS FOR OUT-APIARIES.

If there is guessing about the number of supers to
put on in the home apiary, there is still more guessing as
to the number to be taken when starting to an out-apiary.
If I take a smaller number than needed, I may have to
take a special trip for more   If I take more than are
needed, I will hardly want to take them back home with
me, and they are put in piles and covered up in the hope
that they may be used the next time   But there is some
danger of their being affected by rain when piled up at
the out-apiary, so there is trouble either way   On the
whole it is better to take too many than too few, and so
there are generally some extra ones at the out-apiaries

To take supers to the out-apiaries, they are piled up
on the wagon in five piles, a lath is nailed from top to
bottom on each pile, and they are braced on top with lath
(Fig. 64).   Fifty empty supers can be taken at a load,
but it is not often that as many as forty filled supers are
taken at a load

ADDING SUPERS UNDER OR OVER.

As the harvest advances I am more chary about giving room, and it is only given when the sections already
on are pretty well filled   Suppose toward the last of the
season I come to a colony that has its sections nearly all
filled.   There is a possibility that the bees may be able to
finish up what they have and a few more in an additional
super, but the great probability is that they will do no

more than to finish what they have.   Although that probability may amount to almost a certainty, I do not act upon it, but go for the possibility and give the extra super. But I put it on top of the others, so that the bees will not commence work in it unless actually crowded into it.

During the early part of the harvest, so long as there is a reasonable expectation that each additional super will be needed, the empty super is put under the others, next

Fig.—50. Row of Lindens in Bloom.

to the brood-chamber.   Work will commence in it more promptly than when an empty super is placed on top, and that greater promptness in occupying the new super may be the straw to turn the scale on the side of keeping down the desire for swarming.   But when a super is put on toward the close of the season, not because it seems really needed, but as a sort of safety-valve in case it might be needed, I do not wish to do anything to coax the bees into it, so it is put on top, and the bees can do as they

please about entering it. It is true that if an empty
super is put under the others at a time when the harvest
is nearing its close, the bees may not do a thing in it, but
merely go up and down through it and keep to work in
the super above   But it is not so well to have them working so far from the brood-nest with empty space beneath
    No bait-section is needed in any super after the first

SWARMING NOT DESIRABLE.

If I were to meet a man perfect in the entire science
and art of bee-keeping, and were allowed from him an
answer to just one question, I would ask for the best and
easiest way to prevent swarming, for one who is anxious
to secure the largest crop of comb honey. There are localities where a large crop of honey is secured in the fall, and
in such place, or in any place where the honey-flow is long
enough, a larger crop may be secured by increase, but I
am not so sure about that. If a man in such a place
starts in the spring with 75 colonies, he may get a larger
crop by increasing early enough to 150, supposing 150
colonies to be the largest number his field will bear, but
would he not have a still larger crop if he had the 150 all
through the season and made no increase? However that
may be, in my locality, which bee-keepers generally would
consider a poor one, where white clover is the chief if not
the only source from which a crop may be expected, and
where the harvest is all too short, if, indeed, it comes at
all—in such a place I am satisfied that more honey can be
harvested by commencing in the spring with the largest
number the field will bear, and holding at that number,
always providing that the means taken to keep down increase shall in no wise interfere with the best work on the
part of the bees
    If I were working for extracted honey, I suppose the
matter might be managed, to a great extent, if not to the

fullest extent, by simply giving abundance of room in
every direction but with comb honey, I do not believe
that an abundance of room in the brood-nest is compatible
with the largest yield of surplus

Or, if I were working for extracted honey, I might at
the beginning of the harvest put all the brood over an excluder in an upper story, leaving the queen on empty
frames below, but that would hardly work for comb-
honey production.

MANAGEMENT OF SWARMING COLONIES.

From my first using movable frames, I think I have
kept my queens' wings clipped, so my experience in having natural swarms with flying queens has been very
limited   But my experience in having swarms issue
where and when I did not want them, has been very large
Only extreme modesty and humility prevents my being
very proud of so large an experience   If I should ever
reach that point where I shall be equally successful in
preventing swarms, I make no promise to be either modest
or humble

So long as success in prevention of swarms has not
been reached, it remains an important matter to know the
best thing to do when swarms do issue.   Under ordinary
circumstances some one must be on hand to watch for
swarms.   For several years I have had no watching for
swarms, and have had no swarms except those which
swarmed in spite of my efforts to prevent them   Yet if I
had only the one apiary, it is just possible that I might
allow swarming, at least so far as to allow the bees to
swarm and then return to their old hives.   At any rate
there are a great many so situated as to allow their bees to
go thus far in swarming, and I feel pretty sure that for
them there may be some interest in knowing what I did

when swarms did issue, so I will give an account of my
management when I formerly allowed the bees to swarm

WATCHING FOR SWARMS.

With as many as 100 colonies in an apiary, the one
who is on watch can hardly be allowed to do anything
else.   The regular noise is so great among so many that
the added noise of a swarm is hardly noticed, so sight,
not hearing, must be depended on   I have gone on with
my regular work and taken a look once in five or ten minutes along the rows to see if any swarms were out, but
it is not a very satisfactory way of doing   A bright boy
or girl can watch very well, if faithful   It is not necessary, of course, to watch all day, and the weather has
much to do with the hours at which swarms may be expected   On a hot morning a swarm may issue as early as
6 o'clock, but this is exceptional, and if the weather has
been cloudy through the day, clearing off bright and
warm in the after part, a swarm may issue after 4 o'clock
Ordinarily, however, it is not necessary to be on the lookout before 8 a. m, or much after 2 p m   I had a swarm
issue once in a shower, but that is so unlikely to occur
that I would not think it worth while to keep any watch
at such a time
The watcher will soon learn the points of advantage
from which he can easily command a view of the whole
apiary, not needing to stir from his seat unless a swarm
issues.   Sometimes, however, there is so much playing
going on among the bees, that there is no alternative but
to travel about and take a close look at each colony that
shows unusual excitement   It is an advantage at this
time to have the hives in long rows.   I have 30 or 40
hives in a row   At the middle is a shady place to sit
A clock or watch lies in open sight so that a look at every
hive may be taken once in five minutes.   If there is no

time-piece to go by, the watcher may become interested
in something else, and think the five minutes not up when
double that time has passed; but having the time measured out, he is free to read or do anything else between
times.　At each five minutes, the watcher, who is sitting

Fig. 51.—Catnip.

at the middle of the middle row, rises, glances along the
back row to the north end; then, along the middle row to
the north end; then, stepping forward, glances along the
front row to the north end; then along the same row to
the south end; then to the south end of the middle row;

and lastly to the south end of the back row. All this has taken less time than it takes to write it, and the watcher is ready to sit down till another five minutes is up.

If, however, unusual commotion is seen—and, sighting along the rows in this way, it can easily be seen—the watcher goes to the hive for a closer look Up to the middle of the day or later, there is not often much excitement, unless there be a swarm, but after this time so many colonies take their play-spells that the watcher needs to spend most of his time on his feet

ONE-CENT CAGES.

The watcher is provided with a number of queen-cages. These are easily made and the material costs less than a cent apiece. I take a pine block, 5x1x½-inch, and wrap around it a piece of wire-cloth 4 inches square The wire-cloth is allowed to project at one end of the block a half inch The four sides of this projecting end are bent down upon the end of the stick and hammered down tight into place. A piece of fine wire about 10 inches long is wrapped around the wire-cloth, about an inch from the open end, which will be about the middle of the stick, and the ends of the wire twisted together. I then pull out the block, trim off the corners of the end a little so that it will easily enter the cage, slide the stick in and out of the cage a number of times so that it will work easily, and the thing is complete (Fig. 65). When not in use, the block is pushed clear in, so as to preserve the shape of the cage Such cages can be carried in the pocket without danger of being injured.

FINDING QUEEN OF SWARM.

When the watcher finds a swarm issuing, he is pretty dull if he does not become interested in looking for the queen I do not know of any sure way to find the queen, but she is not often missed. I think I can find her most easily by watching on the ground in front of the entrance. Very frequently she comes out at the back end of the hive or at the side, when the hive is raised on blocks. Rarely

Fig. 52.—Vase of Goldenrod.

she may be found at some distance from the hive, on the ground, with a group of bees about her. If not found, she is most likely in the hive, and the swarm may re-issue in a day or two. She may be lost, but at this particular time her loss is not so very great. There is no danger of the swarm being lost; it will return to the hive in a few minutes, although I have known them to cluster for half an hour or more before returning. It may happen, sometimes, that a swarm may go into a hive whose colony has swarmed a little while before, and where it is always peacefully received. I do not like this doubling up, but I do not know that I lose anything by it, for the bees can store up just as much in one hive as another

When the watcher finds the queen, she is caged. Either the cage is held down for her to run into, or she is caught and then caged. After the queen is in the cage, the block is pushed in an inch or so, and the cage put where the bees can take care of it. Usually it is thrust into the entrance, close up against the bottom-bars, so that if a cool night should come there will be no danger that the bees will desert it.

The watcher keeps a little memorandum book, and puts down in it the number of the colony that swarmed; for it might make bad work if it should be forgotten and neglected until the emergence of a young queen to lead out an absconding swarm.

DOOLITTLE'S PLAN.

Some years ago Mr G. M Doolittle gave a plan for management of swarming colonies when no increase was desired. I do not think that he uses it now. I do not know that I shall ever use it again, and yet it was valuable to me, and for some circumstances nothing may be better. The plan, in brief, was this· The queen being caged and left in the hive, all queen-cells are cut out in five days from the time the swarm issued, and five days later all queen-cells are again cut out and the queen set at liberty.

I used this one season with great satisfaction, and I do not remember that any colony thus treated swarmed again

VARYING DOOLITTLE'S PLAN.

The next season I varied the plan Instead of leaving the queen with the colony to remain idle for ten days, I took her away and gave her to a nucleus, a new colony, or wherever a queen was needed At the end of the ten days I returned her to the colony, placing her directly upon a comb taken from the middle of the brood-nest. Often, however, I gave them a different queen, for after an absence of ten days, I doubt if they could tell their own queen from any other. Besides, they were in a condition to take any queen without grumbling

After the first year, however, I had some colonies swarm again after the queen was given them Whether it was the season, the change in the plan, or some other cause, I am unable to say.

PUT-UP PLAN.

I then adopted a plan which relieved me of the necessity of hunting for and cutting out queen-cells. No matter how careful I might be, there was always a possibility that I might overlook a queen-cell, although this very rarely happened, if ever But it took a good deal of valuable time I give herewith the plan, which I think an improvement:

When a swarm issues and returns, it is ready for treatment immediately; although usually it is put down in my memorandum of work to be done, and the time set for it may be the next day or any time within five days, just as suits my convenience. The queen is caged at the time of swarming, and left in the care of the bees, as already mentioned.

Within the five days, I take off the super, and put most of the brood-combs into an empty hive. Indeed, I may take all the brood-combs, for I want in this hive all the combs the colony should have. In the hive left on the stand, I leave or put from one to three frames, generally two. These combs must be sure to have no queen-cells, and may be most safely taken from a young or weak colony having no inclination to swarm The two combs are put in one side of the hive, two or three dummies placed beside them, and the rest of the hive left vacant.

The question may be asked, "Will not the bees build comb in this vacant part of the hive?" No; at least they do not for me. Queenless colonies are little given to comb-building, and not at all inclined to make a fresh start in a new place.

If I did not do so at the time of taking out the frames, I now shake the bees off from about half the frames, not being particular to shake them off clean. These bees are of course shaken off into the hive on the stand The supers are now put on this hive with its two or three frames of brood, the cover is put over the supers, and the "put-up" hive filled with brood is placed over all.

GETTING THE BEES TO DESTROY QUEEN-CELLS.

A plenty of bees will be left to care for the brood, the queen will commence laying, all thought of swarming is given up, and every queen-cell torn down by the bees In perhaps two days I take a peep to see if the queen is laying, for it sometimes happens that at the time when I "put up the queen" (as I call the operation I have just described), there is already a young queen just hatched, and then the old queen is pretty sure to be destroyed In this latter case I may remove the young queen and give them a laying one, or I may let the young queen remain

PUTTING DOWN THE QUEEN.

In ten days from the time the swarm issued—sometimes ten days from the time I "put up the queen"—I put

down the queen. If, by chance, a young queen is in the
upper hive, I do not like to put her down until she com-
mences laying and her wing is clipped, for fear of her taking out a swarm. It seems a foolish operation for them

Fig. 53.—Two Asters.

to swarm when there is nothing in the hive from which
a queen can be reared, but I have had it happen. The
operation of putting down is very simple. I lift the hive
off the top, place it on the ground, remove the supers,
take the hive off the stand, place it on one side, put the

hive containing the queen on the stand, and replace the supers.

You will see that this leaves the queen full chance to lay from the minute she is uncaged, and at the time of putting down there will be as much brood as if the queen had remained in her usual place. Most of the bees, of course, adhered to the lower hive when the queen was put up, but by the time she is put down quite a force has hatched out, and these have marked the upper hive as their location. Upon this being taken away, the bees, as they return from the field, will settle upon the cover, where their hive was, and form a cluster there; finally an explorer will crawl down to the entrance of the hive below, and a line of march in that direction will be established immediately In a day or two they will go straight to the proper entrance.

GOOD CHANCE FOR NUCLEI.

We left, standing on the ground, the hive with its two combs, which had been taken from the stand These two combs, when the queen was put up, probably had a good quantity of eggs, and brood in all stages. They now contain none but sealed brood, some queen-cells and a pretty heavy supply of pollen Or, it may be that eggs from a choice queen were given, and the queen-cells are to be saved A goodly number of bees adhere to the two combs and I know of no nicer way to start a new colony, than simply to place the hive in a new location. Or, the bees may be shaken off at the old stand and the combs used again to do duty as they have done during the last ten days, or given to a nucleus which needs them.

I may remark in passing, that these queenless colonies will produce queen-cells not excelled by those of a swarming colony, and not surpassed in excellence by those produced by any of the best plans used by queen-breeders.

In short, I do not believe it is possible to have better   It must be remembered, however, that all of them are not of

Fig. 54 —Three Asters.

equal excellence.   For the bees will continue to start cells for several days, and the last ones started will be from larvæ too old to make good queens.   You may be able to distinguish these cells by their poorer look, or if you give the bees several cells, among them at least one or two of the finest looking, they will make no mistake in making the proper selection.

WORKING OF QUEENLESS BEES.

It may be objected that this keeping bees queenless for ten days makes them work with less vigor.   I am not sure but it ought, but I must confess I have had no strong proof of it come directly under my own observation. So far as I could tell, these bees seemed to work just as hard when their queen was taken away as before. In the spring of 1885 one colony was, by some means, left entirely away from the proper rows—some three rods from any other colony. I took it away, put it in proper line, and left to catch the returning stragglers a hive containing one comb, this comb having no brood and very little if any honey. This colony having been a very weak one, very few bees returned to the old spot, but these few surprised me by filling a good stock of honey in empty comb, before they were put with the rest of the colony.

Swarms treated on this "putting up" plan often swarmed again, but if they did they were put up again. An objection to the plan was that these "put-ups" were in the way and had to be lifted down when anything was done with supers. Still, for any one who allows the bees to swarm, and who does not object to the lifting, the plan is a good one.

GIVING NUCLEUS TO SWARM.

A plan that has seemed to be as satisfactory as any other, although it is not always convenient to use it, is upon the issuing of a swarm to pick up the queen so as to have her out of the way, remove the old hive from the stand and place on the stand a nucleus in a regular hive. The supers are put upon this hive, and the swarm is left to return at its leisure. This takes little time and trouble, and there is no danger of further swarming. I have seen it stated that when the swarm returns the queen of the nucleus may be killed, but that does not occur "in this locality."

PREVENTION OF SWARMING.

I don't quite like that heading. It may be understood to mean that I am entirely successful in profitably preventing swarming, and I am not certain that I have yet attained to that. I say *profitably* preventing it, for there might be such a thing as preventing it in a way that would hardly pay. If a colony disposed to swarm should be blown up with dynamite, it would probably not swarm again, but its usefulness as a honey-gathering institution would be somewhat impaired Swarming might also be prevented by means of such character as to involve an amount of trouble that would make it unprofitable; or it might be prevented in such a way as to have a very unprofitable effect upon the honey-crop. The thing I am after is *profitable* prevention.

NO DELIGHT IN SWARMS.

I have read of the great delight felt by the bee-keeper at the sight of an issuing swarm, the bees whirling and swirling in delirious joy, but such things do not appeal to me. I do not like swarming. I never did. I don't think I ever shall. In my forty years of bee-keeping experience, I think I never looked upon the issuing of a swarm with feelings other than those akin to pain, unless it might be the first swarm I ever had.

BAD MANNERS OF SWARMS.

I am not an expert at hiving swarms. They don't act nicely for me. After I have climbed a tree with laborious pains and shaken down a swarm with a hive under it at just the right place, the swarm instead of entering in a well-mannered sort of style will just as like as not keep flying back every time it is shaken down, unless it should take it into its head to give me more exercise by taking another tree. I got a Manum swarm-catcher, but I do not remember that I ever used it with success. One day when I was trying to use it, J T. Calvert, the energetic business man of the A. I. Root Co., was here.

He helped me   He made a catcher of his hands and put
the bees in the catcher by main strength. But they
wouldn't stay "catched," and they didn't   So I don't like
swarming, even if I didn't think it interfered with the
honey crop.

WHY DO BEES SWARM?

Upon no other subject connected with bee-keeping
have I studied so much, tried so many plans, or made so
many failures, as with regard to prevention of swarming
If I knew all about just what makes a colony swarm, I
would be in better shape to use preventive measures; but
I don't know all about it   Of course I know that want
of room and want of ventilation may hasten swarming,
and possibly some other things of that kind, but after all
there is a good deal of mystery about the whole affair.

VENTILATION AND ROOM.

I think it is of some use to take pains to see that the
bees are never really cramped for room. I believe that
raising the hive on blocks $\frac{3}{4}$ of an inch or
more is a good thing   It is also a good thing to rear
queens from stock that has shown little inclination to
swarming. Indeed, with room enough and ventilation
enough it is possible that bees would never swarm. Some
one will say to me that bees may swarm with a hogshead of room. Yes, but the combs may be in such condition that the queen will be cramped for room, even in a
hogshead.

NON-SWARMING PILES.

For a good many years I have been in the habit of
having in each apiary one or more colonies whose hives
were kept as a sort of store-house where extra frames of
brood or honey could be put, to be drawn from as occasion required, but often there has been no drawing, and

these "piles" have grown to be four or five stories high with an immense force of bees. I never knew one of them to swarm. But the ventilation was as immense as the force of bees, for each story had formerly an entrance as large as the lower entrance, and perhaps the super-

Fig. 55.—Heartsease.

abundance of ventilation was the secret of their not swarming.

YOUNG QUEENS AND SWARMING.

It was said that colonies with queens of the current year's rearing would not swarm, and one year I supplied all the colonies of one apiary with young queens about the beginning of the honey harvest. It didn't work.

Once when a colony swarmed and returned to its hive, I removed its queen and gave it a queen that I think had not been laying more than two or three days Within three days that queen came out with a swarm. It seems the condition of the colony has more to do with the case than the condition of the queen C J H. Gravenhorst, late editor of *Deutche Illustrierte Bienenzeitung,* gives what I think is the truth about young queens and swarming: A given colony will not swarm with a queen of this year if the queen was reared *in this colony;* if reared elsewhere it may swarm. Why that difference he did not know. But some have claimed exceptions to this rule

TAKING TWO FRAMES OF BROOD WEEKLY.

One season I kept eight brood-combs in the hive, and every week or ten days took out two of the central combs, replacing them with foundation or empty combs This was to give the queen so much room that there should be no desire to swarm It was successful in most cases, but there were too many exceptions to make the plan reliable.

TAKING AWAY ALL BROOD.

Afterward I carried the same thing to its extreme limit in a good many cases, taking away all the brood One frame of brood, however, was left for two or three days, perhaps a week, for fear the bees would be discouraged and desert an entirely empty hive. This one frame of brood was then taken away because it was the common thing for the bees to start queen-cells on it. Yet it is just possible that no swarming would have taken place, in spite of the queen-cells

FORCED SWARMING.

This plan has come into great prominence lately under the name of *forced, shaken,* or *brushed* swarms. Gravenhorst, the great German authority, practiced and advocated it more than a quarter of a century ago. L. Stachelhausen was earnest in his advocacy of the plan in this country, and E. R. Root, editor of Gleanings in Bee-Culture, took it up with great enthusiasm. Probably a good many had done more or less at it independently, for it would naturally suggest itself that taking away all the brood would leave a colony in much the same condition as if they had swarmed; and in actual practice most of those who have tried the plan have found bees no more inclined to swarm after it than after natural swarming.

Fig. 56.—Queen-Excluder.

FORCED VERSUS NATURAL SWARMING.

Many have found the plan a material advance over natural swarming. One very great advantage is sufficient to commend it; the bee-keeper is master of the situation, and is not dependent upon the whims of the bees as to when they shall swarm—an inestimable boon to those who have out-apiaries, and indeed to any one who does not wish the trouble of watching for swarms.

STRONGER FORCE IN FORCED SWARMING.

It also gives the bee-keeper control over the number of bees that shall remain with the swarm. In natural swarming there may be too few bees go with the swarm for best results in storing, while there may still be not enough for any hope of good work in the parent colony, with a possibility of this latter force being still further divided by after-swarms In the case of a forced swarm, all the bees may be allowed to remain on the old stand except merely enough to care for the brood which is taken away, put on a new stand, and with the addition of a queen or a queen-cell allowed to start out on its career as an independent colony.

SHAKING OFF ALL BEES.

Or, the forced swarm may be made still stronger, by giving it *all* the bees, and distributing the brood to nuclei, weak colonies, or wherever it will do most good   In no case, however, would it be a prudent thing in this locality to follow the recommendation of some, by putting the brood on a new stand without any bees, trusting to the warmth of the weather to hatch out young bees fast enough to care for the brood   If such a colony—if you can call it a colony—should not fall a prey to the robbers, there would in most cases be a serious loss of brood from starvation and chilling

NO FORCED SWARMING TILL QUEEN-CELLS STARTED.

In no case did I practice this forced swarming till I found by the presence of queen-cells that the bees were thinking of swarming. There would be less labor in the long run (supposing that all were to be swarmed sooner or later), to do up the whole business at a suitable time, without waiting for the bees to take the initiative. Indeed, conditions may be such in some localities that there might be a loss to wait for queen-cells.

But the harvests here are such that it is usually better to have swarming delayed Moreover, a good many of my colonies, if let alone, will go through the entire season without attempting to swarm, and such colonies are the very ones that give the best yields, and forced swarming would be practiced upon them only at a loss.

DISADVANTAGE OF FORCED SWARMING.

With all the advantage forced swarming has over natural swarming, it still leaves something to be desired. As already said, those colonies which hold their force intact throughout the entire season are the ones that give the best results. It is true that in forced swarming the entire force of bees may be left on the old stand, but there are thousands of prospective bees in the brood taken away. If you take away that brood to-day, you are taking away the bees of to-morrow, and of twenty more days to come.

"But the bees that emerge to-morrow do not emerge as field-bees, and will not be field-bees till they are sixteen days old. If the harvest closes in sixteen days the additional force will only be a lot of useless consumers" While the first part of your statement may be true enough, I cannot say as much for the second.

BEES DO 1HE WORK MOST NEEDED.

While the bees that emerge to-morrow may do no field-work for sixteen days, they begin housework at a very tender age—housework that would have to be continued by older bees if this brood were taken away. As fast as one of these young bees is ready to begin housework, it takes the place of an older bee, which can now go afield. I know that, as a general rule, the different departments of work are done by bees of certain ages, but I also know that bees accommodate themselves to circumstances I have seen bees at five days old carrying in pollen because there were no older bees in the hive to perform that duty, and we all know that in early spring nursing and housework are done by bees several months old

So it is reasonable to believe that at least to a certain extent the necessities of the case rather than the matter of absolute age decides what duties a bee shall perform; and the logical conclusion from that is that the larger force of bees we have in a hive the more storing we shall have, even if a good many of the bees be quite young

Without, perhaps, giving any satisfactory reason for it, I am also quite of the opinion that better work is generally done when bees are allowed to go right along rearing brood at their own sweet will; for toward the close of the harvest they, of their own accord, curtail work in that direction.

NON-SWARMING PREFERRED TO FORCED.

While I yield to no one in my appreciation of the advantages of forced swarming over natural swarming, I believe that the advantages of no swarming whatever over forced swarming are as great as the advantages of forced over natural swarming.

So you will hardly blame me if instead of resting content with forced swarming I continue to pursue that will-o'-the wisp—in the opinion of many—non-swarming.

Fig. 57.—Folding Sections.

KEEPING COLONIES QUEENLESS.

The next season after practicing the removal of two frames of brood, I settled upon a plan which I felt pretty sure would prevent the possibility of swarming. It was a no less radical measure than to keep the colony queenless. I reasoned that as I had never had a queen hatched inside of eleven days from the time the queen was taken away, or from the time the bees started queen-cells, the colony was safe from swarming if once in ten days I took away their brood and gave them fresh; also, that it was only bees over two weeks old that worked in the field; add to this the three weeks that it took from the egg to the full-fledged worker, and it was five weeks or more from the

time the egg was laid till the bee became a gatherer
Clearly, then, only such bees as came from eggs laid five
weeks or more before the close of the honey harvest were
available as gatherers. Why not have the colony queenless during this five weeks? So I took away the queen
leaving in the hive three combs, one of which contained
eggs and brood in all stages, the other two containing
nothing from which queen-cells could be started

Once in ten days the comb of young brood with its
queen-cells was taken away and a fresh one given them,
and at the close of the five weeks, which was about the
close of the harvest, the queen was returned

NOT A SUCCESS.

As a preventive of swarming, it was a complete success. Not one colony thus treated swarmed; how could
they? As a means of securing a large crop, I think it was
an egregious failure, although I can hardly tell with great
definiteness, the season itself being a failure. Possibly
the absence of the queen itself had something to do with
lessening their stores, but I doubt it. But when all combs
of brood but one were taken away, a large force of prospective bees were taken away that would have hatched out
in from one to twenty-one days

If I had allowed four or five frames of brood, changing every ten days, the result might have been quite different. Moreover, the one frame they did have was, for
the most part, filled with brood so young, that little or
none of it hatched while in the hive. If I should try anything in the same line again, I should keep four or five
frames in the hive, and this should be mainly brood well
advanced so that much of it would hatch out to replenish
the wasting numbers.

KEEPING QUEENS CAGED.

Success was reported by others with the plan of keeping queens caged in the hive during part or the whole of the harvest, and although I tried it on a large scale there was no case of success with me.

FASTENING YOUNG QUEENS IN.

The good old-fashioned way of managing afterswarms was to return them as fast as they came out.

Fig. 58.—Movable Shade.

This gave the young queens a chance to fight it out till only one was left, and when only one was left there would be no more swarming. So I planned to let the young queens fight it out without the trouble of returning swarms. I put a queen-excluder between the bottom-board and hive, so that no queen could get out. As no

queen could get out, no swarm could leave   When the
young queens emerged they could settle their little differ-
ences to suit themselves till only one queen was left.   I
would keep track of what was going on inside the hives
sufficiently to take away the excluder after all but one
queen had been put out of the way, so the young queen
could go out on her wedding-trip.   The thing was so certain to work that I spent $37.50 for queen-excluders to
put the plan in practice.

SWARMING GALORE

In due time when queen-cells were sealed the swarms
began to issue   Then they returned   Then they came
out next day   Then they returned again.   After doing
more or less of this, the time came when the young queens
began to emerge   Business became lively   Swarming
once a day did not always satisfy them.   The number of
issues in a day became such that several swarms would
be out at a time, and they were not at all particular to
keep separate.   Neither were they as methodical as
prime swarms about returning to their own hives   Almost any hive seemed to suit them providing there was
a good deal of noise at the entrance, and when swarming
got well under way for the day there were plenty of
hives with noise at the entrance   Whether the excluders
leaked queens, or whatever may have been the reason,
there were some cases of young queens being out, and
when there was a young queen in a swarm there was no
telling how many swarms would unite with it.

ABNORMAL BEHAVIOR.

After a swarm had been balked in its efforts a number of times there seemed to be a reckless disregard in
a good many cases as to the propriety of returning when
they had had plenty of time to discover that no young

queen had come out with them, and sometimes they would settle and remain clustered for half a day, perhaps several swarms in the cluster. Nothing so very bad about that, if I had only been entirely sure that some time they would return; but when I stood gazing on a bunch of bees as big as my body when I'm in best condition, and meditated upon the chance of there being a young queen in the bunch to incite them to sail off into the ethereal blue—well, it was not the sort of meditation most conducive to composure of mind

Inside the hive the program as laid down was pretty generally carried out; at the proper time the excluder was removed, and in due time the young queen was laying. The plan is a good one if one could only induce the bees to refrain from swarming out until only one

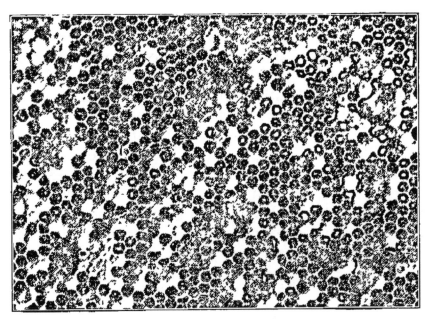

Fig 59 —Brood of Laying Workers

young queen is left in the hive   I could not induce them to do that.

REARING QUEEN IN "PUT-UP."

It is not necessary to tell of all the plans that were tried. One was finally hit upon that proved to be quite satisfactory, so far as tried   When the presence of well-advanced queen-cells showed that a colony was bent on swarming, all but one or two frames of brood were taken from the hive and put in another hive that was "put-up" on top, of course having no communication with the bees below.   In the old hive below the old queen was sometimes left, and sometimes the bees were left without any queen : but in either case care was taken that no queen-cell was left below, and ten days later search was made for queen-cells below, or else the brood was exchanged for brood from a colony where there was no danger of queen-cells, and the old queen was removed   To the "put-up" was given, at the time of putting up, a virgin queen or a ripe queen-cell, and as soon as the young queen was laying the old hive was taken away and the "put-up" hive was put down in its place   Thus the whole force of the colony was kept together, there was a young queen of the current year's rearing, practically reared in the hive, and that colony was past anxiety for the season.   Some, however, say that such a queen will swarm with them.

GETTING BEES TO DESTROY CELLS

I said the brood was put up, but said nothing about the bees or the queen-cells   No attention was paid to the queen-cells, and about half the bees were shaken off the combs—perhaps more than half. Just how many bees to leave in the "put-up" hive was not an easy matter to gauge   If too few there would be chilled brood. If too many the young queen would leave with a swarm. Of course the latter danger could be avoided by destroying all queen-cells in the "put-up," but that would make more work, and if there are few enouugh bees all superf-

Fig. 60.—Top and Bottom Starters in Section.

luous cells will be destroyed by the bees themselves, and there will be no danger of swarming.

NUCLEUS TO PREVENT SWARMING.

A modification of the plan sometimes used was to take a nucleus from somewhere else and put in the place of the colony. But in this case the colony was made queenless two or three days in advance. Either plan left the colony without any diminution of its forces, and with no very great check to its work, and these plans would probably have been continued to the present if it had not been that I struck upon a plan that seemed equally effective but quite a little easier.

FOUNDATION PLAN.

The preliminary work in this plan, which may be called the foundation plan, is precisely the same as the preliminary work done when the last-described plan was used, that is, the plan of putting up a hive to rear a young queen. When speaking of that plan I said nothing about the preliminary work, and I will now give in detail the preliminary work and all the work of the foundation plan.

PRELIMINARY WORK.

As soon as colonies become strong and are working busily, we begin to be on the lookout. This generally will not be till the bees are at work on clover bloom, although it may happen in some seasons that preparation for swarming begins during the last of fruit-bloom Whether it be in apple or clover bloom, we begin to examine some of the strongest colonies to see if any preparations for swarming are made. If we find none in the strongest colonies it is hardly worth while to look through the rest. When, however, we find one or more queen-cells with an egg in each, then it is time to begin a systematic canvas of *all* colonies, and to keep it up in all so long as we continue to find queen-cells in any, except in a case where a colony has already been treated by the foundation plan, or where there is a young queen of the current year

LOOKING FOR QUEEN-CELLS.

We plan to go through each colony about once in ten days to look for queen-cells. I say *about* once in ten days, for it is not always possible to be exact. It may happen that one or two days in succession will be rainy, and then the ten days become eleven or twelve Or, it may be that on account of some interference with our work that we can see in advance, we may think it best to shorten the ten days to nine or less.

Suppose we go through a certain colony and find no queen-cell with as much as an egg in it. The next time around it may be in the same condition, and so it may continue throughout the season. In that case there is nothing to be done with that colony beyond the examination every ten days but to let it alone and be thankful.

Fig. 61.—Cutting Foundation.

Such cases are not as plenty as I should like, but I think they are on the increase.

DESTROYING EGGS.

Suppose, however, that upon one of our visits we find one or more cells containing eggs. We destroy the incipient cells by mashing them, and in the record-book write after the date, "keg," a contraction for the expressive if not very elegant entry, "killed eggs." It is pos-

sible that upon the next visit we may find no more queen-
cells started, and that may be the last of them for the
season. So long as we find only eggs, we do nothing
more than to destroy them.

Generally, however, when eggs are found in cells,
the next visit will find cells with grubs well advanced
When grubs are found in cells, then the colony must be
treated. The treatment is neither elaborate nor difficult

FOUNDATION TREATMENT.

We find and cage the queen, destroy all queen-cells,
remove the hive from its stand, and put in its place a
hive containing three or four frames of foundation The
foundation is on one side of the hive with a dummy next
to it   The rest of the hive is left vacant   Upon this
hive is put a queen-excluder, and over the excluder the
old hive with its brood and bees, and over this the supers
as before (Fig 66). Then the queen is run in at the
entrance of the lower hive, and the colony is left for a
week or ten days.

At the end of the week, or as soon after that time
as we can conveniently reach it, we take away the lower
story with its excluder, and put back the queen in the
old hive, which is left on the stand. When we remove
the lower story with its three or four frames that a week
before contained foundation, there will be less advance
made in those frames than you would be likely to suppose. The vacant part will still be vacant, the amount
of honey will be very small, generally only one or two
frames will have been occupied by the queen, and possibly nothing beyond eggs will be found   If larvæ are
found, they will be still small, and not in large quantity
It appears from this that there is some sulking for a time
on the part of the queen, or else that the bees are rather
slow to prepare the foundation for her. It is possible

that this interim without any laying may be an important part of the treatment. I don't know.

SOME FAILURES.

At any rate, in the first two seasons of using the plan, there was no case of any colony making any further preparation for swarming after being thus treated. The third season (1902) everything did not work so smoothly, but possibly the treatment was not fairly administered in all cases. Some of the colonies did not take kindly to the foundation, and in a few cases it looked as if they might have swarmed out rather than to use the foundation. In one case they built comb and started a brood-nest in the vacant part, leaving the foun-

Fig. 62.—Little Work-table.

dation untouched. But there was some excuse for this, as the foundation was weather-beaten and hard.

If the plan would always work as well as it did the first two years, I could hardly ask for anything better Further trial will prove whether the exceptions of 1902 are to be repeated

WORKING TOWARD NON-SWARMING.

Of course it is no little work to go through the colonies every ten days up to the time of treatment, and I think it likely that it would work all right to treat every colony on the foundation plan early in the honey-flow, whether they had grubs in queen-cells or not But there are some colonies that will go through the whole season with never a grub in a queen-cell—possibly never an egg—and exactly those colonies are the ones most likely to give record-yields To interfere with their work, even for a week in a slight degree, is not desirable. There is also another important reason for allowing every colony willing to do so to go through the whole season without any preparation for swarming and without any interference. I am trying all the time to work at least a little toward a non-swarming strain of bees, and if all colonies were treated on the foundation plan, how would I know which were the non-swarmers from which to choose my breeding stock? Their careful record must be kept

SUPPLANTING UNDESIRABLE QUEENS.

Not every colony, however, that threatens to swarm, is treated by the foundation plan. If a colony that other-wise would receive the foundation treatment has a queen whose workers have the reputation of being very poor storers, if they are vicious in disposition, or if there be any reason why it is not desirable for the queen to be con-tinued in office, the contemplation of swarming on the part of that colony will seal the doom of the queen, and off will come her head.　Very likely a young laying

Fig. 63.—Super-Filler.

queen will take her place after the bees have been queen-less a week or ten days, all cells being killed at the time the queen is killed and at the time the new queen is given.

SUPERSEDING OF QUEENS.

But old age will not be one of the reasons that will always decide the death of a queen.　Some queens do excellent work in their third year, and in rare cases in their fourth.　At any rate, if quite old they will pretty surely be superseded by the bees about the close of the harvest, and if the stock is good the chance for a successor equally good is not bad, and unless it be convenient for me to give them a young queen that I think will be an improvement, the matter of superseding is left to the bees.　An item of some interest is the fact that when

I look through the colonies in the spring to clip any
queen that may have whole wings, I find very little use
for the scissors if the previous season was very poor,
whereas after a big honey-yield I generally find a good
deal of clipping to do   In other words, there seems to
be more superseding at the close of a good than of a
poor year   Has it only happened to come so, or does a
good harvest wear out the queen faster?

THE "JUMBO" HIVE

At one time I had strong hopes that by the use of a
large hive with a large frame I might greatly diminish,
if not entirely suppress, swarming.   Others reported
success with what was called the Jumbo hive.   At Fig.
67 will be seen one of these hives   The frame is $2\frac{1}{8}$
inches deeper than the regular Langstroth frame, and if
you will look at the front of the hive in the picture, you
will see that it is $2\frac{1}{8}$ inches higher than the 8-frame
dovetailed hive by its side   The Jumbo has 10 frames,
and the extra depth makes it equivalent to a 12-frame
Langstroth.

I put bees in two of these hives in the home apiary,
and waited to see what would result the next summer
with much interest   The very first colony to send out a
swarm was in one of these Jumbo hives!   I was sorry,
but it didn't make me sick abed   I had become hardened
to failures and disappointments in following after the
will-o'-the-wisp—non-swarming

PILES OF STORIES.

The problem of prevention of swarming would be
very much easier if I were running for extracted honey
instead of comb   I am very much of the opinion that I
could pile up stories as in Fig 68, and not have one
colony in a hundred swarm, the fact that no such pile

ever swarmed for me confirming that opinion; and I have had a few such piles every year for a number of years..

VENTILATION TO PREVENT SWARMING.

It is not, I think, so much the abundance of room, as the abundance of ventilation that prevents swarming, although the room is important. Notice the opportunity for ventilation in that pile in Fig. 68 The entrance, which you cannot see, is 12 inches wide and 2 inches deep. The second story is shoved forward on the first story so as to make a ventilating space of half an inch at the back, between the two stories. The third story is shoved back to make a space in front; and the ventilating space between the third and fourth stories is at the back. Lastly the cover is shoved forward to make a space of half an inch or more. Thus you see there is a fine chance for a free circulation of air right through the whole pile Alas that such a thing cannot be used for comb honey

SHAKEN SWARM WITHOUT INCREASE.

Another plan that I would enjoy trying if I were running for extracted honey is one variation of forced or shaken swarms It is the simple plan of making a shaken swarm, say from A, and then piling all the brood from A on another strong colony, B European bee-keepers tell us that with this accession of brood B will not swarm S. Simmins, of England, and some others, give A half the bees from B A would be all right for comb honey, but B would not—at least not right away—but it would be all right for extracted honey

ACCIDENTAL SWARMS.

The best I can do, there will sometimes be what might be called accidental swarms. Perhaps a strong colony has in some way lost its queen in the busy season, and when the first reared young queen emerges—if one is allowed to emerge—there will surely be a swarm issue Generally such a thing will be headed off before the young queen has a chance to emerge, but once in a great while she gets ahead of me.

Although there is to me nothing entrancing in the sight of such a swarm whirling through the air, there is one thing I do very much enjoy in it—it is the sight of the seething mass hurrying into the hive when dumped in front of it, as in Fig. 69 You will see that a deep bottom-board has been placed in front of No. 32, on which the swarm was dumped (it had previously settled on a low plum tree), and the bees have flowed all over the sides of the bottom-board, and also over the front of the hive. But I don't want the distress of seeing them pouring out of the hive in a swarm for the sake of the pleasure of seeing them hustle back into the same hive when dumped down in front of it.

TAKING OFF SECTIONS

As fast as supers are filled they are taken off I do not think I could be bothered to take off each section as fast as finished, putting in an empty one to take its place It would take too much time Neither do I like to wait till every section in a super is entirely finished Unless the bees are crowded very much, there will be some uncapped cells in the outside sections which the bees will be very long in sealing If these are waited for, the central sections may lose a little of their snowy whiteness —the thing which, perhaps, helps most to sell them

A super is, then, taken off when all but the outside sections are finished This can be pretty well told by glancing over the top of the super, although sometimes the sections may be all sealed at the upper part and hardly filled below. A look at the under part of the upraised super will decide it. The sharp, circular end of the hive-tool is thrust under the supers to pry apart the attachment of bee-glue.

Unless care is taken, bees will be killed when a super, which has just been taken off, is put back again. Sometimes there may be so few bees in the way that the

Fig. 64.—Load of Forty Supers.

super can be put on quickly without danger. Oftener too many bees are in the way for this, so I put one end on its place, and with a series of rapid up-and-down motions, gradually lower the other end to its place. This gives the bees time to get out of the way, and there are seldom any crushed by it.

CLOSE OF CLOVER HARVEST.

Formerly I took off all supers at the close of the white-clover harvest. Of late there has been a tendency

to leave them on for the later flow.   I am not sure
whether this is wise, except in the few years in which
from some unknown source some exceptionally white
sections were secured at the Hastings apiary.   In other
years at the Hastings apiary, and in all years at the other
apiaries, the honey stored during the cucumber flow is
rather dark in color, and is likely to have an unpleasant
appearance on the surface, as if lightly varnished with
bee-glue.   The darkest of it is generally off in flavor,
but in the past two or three years the flavor was fine, although the honey was dark.   I don't know why   Possibly a greater proportion of sweet clover may have improved the flavor   Although I think my bees get no
inconsiderable quantity of honey from cucumbers, I confess I don't know what pure cucumber honey tastes like,
but I am afraid it does not rank very high in flavor.

LATE HONEY.

As I said, I am not sure that it is ever wise, except
in the Hastings apiary, to allow supers to stay on after
the white-clover harvest is over.   True, a considerable
amount of honey may be got in sections from the late
flow, but it is not all of it of the best, and if it were stored
in brood-combs and saved as extra combs to be crowded
into the brood-chamber the next year before the beginning of the harvest, there might be nearly or quite as
many more sections of white-clover honey stored, to offset what was lost in sections in the fall

GETTING BEES OUT OF SECTIONS

For the purpose of getting bees out of sections I have
tried pretty thoroughly the Porter escape and other
escapes which work on the principle of allowing the
bees to go down out of the supers without the chance
of returning, but they do not work fast enough to suit

me. When I go to an out-apiary, I always want to bring home with me all the honey taken off that day. Even at home I want it taken in the same day it is taken off. I may want to go elsewhere the next morning, and I don't want to be hindered from an early start by having to get it in before starting. Besides, I am just a little afraid that if I should make a practice of leaving honey out over escapes till the next day, some one none too scrupulous might learn the trick and by a night visit save me the trouble of taking off some of the honey. So whatever honey is taken off any day is got into the house before we get to bed that night; for sometimes it happens that when we have a big day's work at an out-apiary we do not get home till 8 o'clock or later.

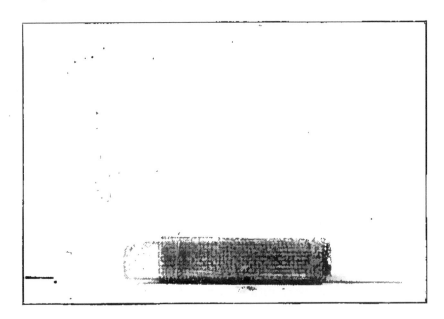

Fig. 65.—One-Cent Cage.

SMOKING BEES DOWN.

When a super is to be taken off, smoke is blown down into it until a sufficient number of bees have gone down out of it. What that sufficient number is depends upon circumstances. If it is early in the day, and we do not care to take the honey home till late, there is no need to drive out so many bees. Other circumstances may also make a difference, and we "cut our coat according to the cloth."

SUPERS STANDING OPEN.

Suppose the honey-flow is in full blast, and we commence to take off supers early in the day, or at least in the forenoon. At such a time there is little need to be very careful about robbers, and it may be that honey may stand exposed for hours without being troubled by them. So when the super has been smoked it is taken off and set on the ground leaning against the hive, the hive-cover is put on the remaining supers, and then our removed super is set on its end on top, so as to project a little over the side of the hive. After a time, perhaps half an hour, the bees are likely to start a trail from the super over the side of the hive to join the bees of the colony below.

A number of supers may be thus standing at a time on their respective hives. Sometimes two supers are taken from the same hive, and, in rare cases, especially late in the season, three

WATCHING FOR ROBBER-BEES.

These supers left standing on the hives, however, are never left entirely out of mind, and a glance is given toward them every few minutes. If at any time bees are seen flying with their heads toward a super, immediate attention is given to the matter, and the supers hustled off the hives. When the bees are nearly all out, or at any time when it is not desirable to leave supers standing on the hives, they are put in piles, preferably not more than ten high.

WHEN ROBBER-BEES TROUBLE.

If fear of robbers does not allow the supers to stand exposed, the super is still put on top of the hive, and a

Fig. 66.—Colony at left treated for swarming.

good many of the bees are at once driven out by smoke. The smoker is held on the side toward the wind, so that the wind will help drive the smoke between the sections, and from time to time the bees are brushed off. The bee-brush generally used is the Coggshall, but if it were not for the trouble of preparing one fresh every day, I think I would prefer a good-sized bunch of asparagus, sweet clover, goldenrod, or something of the kind tied together.

MILLER TENT-ESCAPE.

In piling the supers a sunny place is preferred, to entice out the bees. A deep bottom-board is put on the ground, a super placed on it, and the entrance closed with wirecloth somewhat as a hive-entrance is closed for hauling (Fig. 72). Then over the super is thrown what Root's "A B C of Bee-Culture" has been pleased to call the Miller tent-escape (Fig 73). (Later on I'll tell how it's made) When a second super is brought to the pile, the escape is kicked off, the super placed on the pile and the escape thrown over it When the pile becomes too high to kick off the escape, it is shoved off with the hand, but still allowed to fall to the ground, and afterward picked up

The bees can now make their exit through the top of the escape at their leisure, and from time to time those that have gathered on the wirecloth below are allowed to escape. Matters may be hurried up a little by blowing in smoke below. When there is abundance of time for the bees to get out without being hurried, or if the pile is only five or six high, it is better not to have any opening at the bottom of the pile, but to set the first super on a flat surface that admits no light

KEEPING TALLY OF SECTIONS

The number of the colony from which each super is taken is marked in pencil on one of the middle sections, perhaps when the super is first taken from the hive, certainly before it is taken from the hive entirely A board or a slip of paper is kept where the supers are piled, and as each super is taken to the pile the number of the hive and the number of sections in the super is taken. Occasionally the number of supers in the pile is counted, so as to see whether it tallies with the number taken on the memorandum, for without this there is danger that some super might be forgotten, and the colony not have proper credit When convenient, possibly while we sit resting a little while after the supers are all piled, possibly not till the next morning, the numbers on the memorandum are used to give each colony its proper credit in the record-book.

CREDITING COLONIES.

The credit to each colony is entered *over* the first line that belongs to that colony, so that it may easily be seen at a glance, and so that it may be convenient to have

Fig. 67.—Jumbo Hive (at right).

all the credit on one spot.   If a super containing 24 sections is taken from a colony, the number 24 is entered over its first line.   Then when another 24 sections is taken from that colony, making 48 in all, a line is drawn through the 24 and 48 is written after it.   Then if a super is taken with 15 sections, a line is drawn through the 48, and 63 is written after it, and so on.

WHEELING SUPERS IN

At the home apiary, the piles of supers are generally left till nightfall, so the bees will have abundance of time to be fully out   Then they are taken on a wheelbarrow to the honey-room (Fig. 74).

You will notice that the wheelbarrow is innocent of any box or tray   It is a common railroad barrow, with the tray removed   In this shape it is very convenient for wheeling supers or stove-wood, the principal uses to which it is put. When desired the tray can be replaced to be used for other purposes

HAULING SUPERS FROM OUT-APIARY.

At the out-apiaries the supers must be loaded on the wagon, and sometimes at the close of the season that is a rather ticklish job. When we go to the apiary in the morning, we drive pretty close to the place where the piles of supers are to be—much closer than it will be safe to take the horses at the close of the day's work when the bees are thoroughly stirred up—and after the horses are unhitched the wagon is backed by hand to the most convenient spot for loading on the supers.

LOADING SUPERS ON WAGON

Unfortunately, although the wagon was built especially for the purpose, some irons prevent a perfectly level floor on which to put the supers, so strips of thin board or lath are laid so the supers will be level   The size of the wagon-box is such as to take on one side three supers running crosswise, and on the other side two supers running fore and aft.   Great care is taken to build up the piles true, and when all are on they are fastened together by laths with nails driven partly in, so the nails can easily be drawn upon reaching home. Each pile has a lath vertically, across the top laths are braced in both directions, so that the whole load is practically one solid pile (Fig. 64). As the load comes mainly on

Fig. 68 — Pile of Stories.

the hind axle, 40 supers are as many as we like to haul at one load. We seldom take so large a load.

As I have said, putting the load on the wagon at the close of the season is something of a ticklish job, and is mostly done under cover of smoke, my assistant playing the smoker wherever it will do the most good. The character of the tent-escape comes into fine play here, for it can so quickly and surely be thrown into the right place that the robber-bees have little chance at the piles, so the smoking is mostly done at the wagon A robber-cloth (Fig 75) is even a little better than the tent escape.

When the load is all on, the wagon is drawn away to a distance safe for the horses This may be 8 or 10 rods, or it may be more than twice that distance Fortunately at each out-apiary the ground lies in such a way that after the first few rods the ground is descending, making it easy to draw the load the longer distance Then the horses are hitched on as speedily as possible

HONEY ROOM

Generally, Philo will be ready to take off the load when we get home, unless we get home too near bed-time and Philo has gone home, in which case I am not always a good enough fighter to keep the women from helping to carry the supers into the honey-room This is an addition built onto my dwelling-house. It is 20x15 feet, and the floor-timbers are blocked up with stones so that it will sustain a great weight without breaking

When the supers of sections are taken in, they are piled up near the center of the room with no very great precision, usually being piled crosswise, that is, each super placed across the one under it, for the double purpose of ventilation and to make it easier to lift the supers off the pile than they would be if piled straight and stuck together with bee-glue

PUSH-BOARD

Perhaps the sections will be taken out of the supers the next day, possibly not for a week or more A push-board (Fig. 76) is used to push the sections out of the super. This is made as follows:

Take a board 16⅝ inches long and 11 inches wide. Take boards 12 inches long and ¼-inch thick and nail them across the first board so as to just cover its length, and project ½-inch at each side. This makes a surface 16⅝x12 inches. If this board be now put inside an empty T-super, and the T-super raised, it will be seen that the board will easily drop through the super, except where it is upheld by the three T-tin supports on each side. Places must be cut out of the board so that the supports will present no hindrance. In order to make these places abundantly large, I cut them 1½x½ inch. When cut out, the measure will be, from the corner of the board to the first place or hole, 3¼ inches,

Fig. 69.—Swarm dumped before No. 32.

then 1½ inches for the hole, then 2 13-16 inches to the next hole. Measure the same way from each of the other three corners, and you will have on each side three holes that will allow the supports of the T-tins to pass through without obstruction.

TAKING SECTIONS OUT OF SUPER.

Being now ready to take out the unfinished sections, the first thing is to see whether there are any to take out If a careful inspection shows that all sections in a super are sealed down to the bottom, it goes directly to the pile of finished sections. If any sections are seen that are not finished, the super is placed on the table, and the little sticks removed that were crowded between the ends of the sections on top   A flat hive-cover, or a board a little larger than the super, is placed upon it   Then super and board are both turned upside down, the board being firmly held on the super by one hand while reversing If the super should be reversed without this board being held on it, there might be a possibility of sections tumbling out and breaking   (The board is needed under the reversed super in any case)   The super is now lying upside down on the board, the board even with the edge of the table.   The side of the super having the follower is nearest, and I slide the super toward me enough so that I can push the follower down and let it drop out. I then push the super back on the board and lay the push-board on the bottoms of the sections   Before putting the push-board on the sections, however, I remove any bits of wax that may be on the bottoms of the sections, otherwise the push-board coming down hard upon them will crush the comb enough to make the sealing on the lower part of the sections look watery, if it does no greater damage

As the super now lies, the sections are not resting on the board beneath, there being $\frac{1}{4}$-inch space there

I push the push-board down till the sections rest on the board below.

Fig. 70.—Bee Working on Red Clover.

EXCEPTIONALLY TROUBLESOME CASES.

The sections may fall that quarter of an inch with their own weight, and they may not go down at all without urgent coaxing. If the honey was stored with a rush in the early part of the season, there will be very little gluing, and the sections will come out easily. The later in the season, and the slower the storing, the more gluing, and the more trouble. If there is a lot of glue, and if it is warm, stringy and sticky, it must be humored a little. It can hardly be jerked loose suddenly any more than if it was nailed; but if it is allowed time enough the weight of the sections may be enough to bring them down. Of course a little insistence will hasten matters to some extent, but it seems to be a matter of principle with that kind of glue not to let go too suddenly. Sometimes I take a super of that kind and place it low enough to sit down on the push-board, and then let it take its time. When I feel it give way under me, I give up my seat, unless I continue matters a little longer by taking hold of the super at each end and lifting up while still sitting on the push-board.

WHEN THE GLUE IS BRITTLE.

Sometimes the glue is brittle, especially if quite cold. The case is then quite different. Sitting on it all day would do no good, unless one is heavy enough to bring down the whole thing suddenly If pushing down with the hands on the push-board produces no effect, I pound with the fist on each corner enough to make the start. Then lifting on the super at each end with the fingers, I push the sections out of the super by pushing down on the push-board with the thumbs (Fig. 77).

After the first start is made, perhaps the super is at once lifted off without any trouble, and perhaps further coaxing is needed, and the super must be treated somewhat as one treats a refractory bureau-drawer. I lift on each end alternately, holding down the push-board with one hand and lifting with the other, then with both hands lift off the super (Fig 78)

This sounds a little as if it was hard work getting sections out of supers, because I have spent so much time talking about the troublesome cases, but these are the exceptional ones, and in general the work is easy enough to be done rapidly.

TAKING OUT UNFINISHED SECTIONS.

The empty super being set down and the push-board removed, the unfinished sections are picked off, and the super is put back on the sections as it was before. Then the super and the board under it are reversed, and the board lifted off Finished sections from another super used for that purpose, are put in to take the places of the unfinished sections that were removed, and the super with its 24 finished sections is put on the pile.

BLOCKING UP SUPERS OF SECTIONS.

The piles of finished sections are 22 supers high, the piles being about 6 inches from each other and from the wall. Four blocks ⅞ of an inch thick are placed under the corners of the first super in the pile, and four are put on the corners of each super before the next super is placed over it This for ventilation (Fig. 79) The sun has a fair chance to make this room a pretty warm place, and screened doors and windows allow free passage for the air

FUMIGATING SECTIONS.

Years ago it was very important to fumigate these sections, or else a good many of the larvæ of the bee-moth would disfigure them The trouble gradually faded away until for several years I have done no fumigating whatever, and no harm has come from the omission. I do not know why there should be so much change except a change in the character of the bees that stored the honey. Years ago black blood was present in my bees to a larger extent than now The weeding out of bees too lazy to fight away the wax-moths may have much to do with it.

"GO-BACKS."

The unfinished sections that were taken out are to be disposed of. They are filled into supers and returned to the bees to be finished up, and these supers of sections that are to *go back* to the bees for finishing are called "go-backs," for short. In filling up these supers of "go-backs," no very great care is taken as to assorting them, although it is desirable so far as convenient to have all in the same super at nearly the same stage toward completion.

ARRANGEMENT OF SECTIONS IN "GO-BACKS."

All *except* the two outside rows In these two rows are put the sections that are the least advanced, the four corner sections often containing only foundation

There are two objects in having these outside rows different from the others. The bees will not make as rapid work finishing them as the others, and if all were alike the super would have to be left on too long before all would be finished So there is no expectation of their being finished, and it is not worth while to put in the outside row any that are near completion There is another reason Toward the close of the season, especially, there will be no other supers on a hive that has "go-backs," and these outside rows are needed to give them a chance to do some storing while finishing up the sealing of sections that allow little or no room for storing.

COLONIES FOR "GO-BACK" WORK.

Being more convenient, the "go-backs" are all given to colonies in the home apiary. When the first are given, the honey harvest is usually still in full blast, and a good many colonies in the apiary will have "go-backs," each colony having only one, that being placed on top of its others supers We keep watch to see which colonies make the best work on "go-backs" Some seal faster than others, some seal sections with extra whiteness. In order to help keep track of the rate of progress, each "go-back," at the time it is put on, has marked on one of the middle sections the word "go-back" and the date If the super were not thus marked, the colony would get more credit than it deserved when the super was removed

A little later in the season the number of colonies chosen for this work is limited, only those which do the best being continued at it, and these are not allowed to have any other supers. Generally two supers at a time will be enough for a colony to have; but sometimes three will be given. As fast as one super is ready to come off another takes its place.

ROBBER-CLOTH.

Before fulfilling my promise to describe the tent-escape, I must describe a robber-cloth (Fig. 75), which

Fig. 71.—Shop (looking South).

forms an essential part of the tent-escape. I take a piece of stout cotton cloth (sheeting) large enough to cover a hive and hang down four inches or more at both sides and at each end. This must be weighted down at the side with lath, and for this purpose I take four pieces of lath about as long as the hive. I lay down one piece of lath with another piece on it, and one edge of the cloth between the two pieces of lath. I then nail the two

together and clinch the nails   I use the other two pieces
of lath for the opposite edge of the cloth   This makes
a good robber-cloth just as it is, but it is better to have
the ends also weighted down, especially on a windy day
For this purpose I make a hem in each end, and put in it
shot, nails, pebbles, or something of the kind, stitching
across the hem here and there so the weighting material
will not all run together at one side or the other.

QUICK COVERING WITH ROBBER-CLOTH.

In any case where one wants to cover up a hive
quickly against robbers, as when opening and closing
the same hive frequently for the sake of putting in or
taking out combs, this robber-cloth will be found a great
convenience. No careful adjustment is needed, as in
putting on a regular hive-cover, but one can take hold
of the lath with one hand, and with a single throw the
hive is covered securely, with no killing of bees if any
should happen to be in the way

MILLER TENT-ESCAPE

Having made the robber-cloth, an escape, not in the
shape of a cone, but in the shape of a pyramid, is
fastened centrally upon it (Fig 73)   Take three equi-
lateral pieces of wire-cloth, each of the three sides meas-
uring 11 inches   Put them together in the form of a
tent, sewing the edges together at the three sides by
weaving fine wire through   At the top, however, let
each of the pieces be folded out, so that a hole large
enough to push your finger in will be left   Lay the tent
centrally on the robber-cloth, and mark where the three
corners of the tent come. Now starting at each of these
points, cut the cloth to the center   Cut away the three
flaps of cloth all but about 1¼ inches, and turn this 1¼-

inch margin into the inside of the tent and sew there with heavy thread.

Another way is a little easier to do, and it is a little better, although a little harder to describe.   Take a piece of wire-cloth 22x9½ inches.   Mark a point at the middle of one of the longer sides, and on the other side mark a point 5½ inches from each end, as shown in the figure.   Make a fold at each of the dotted lines.   The wire-cloth may be cut away at the two outside dotted

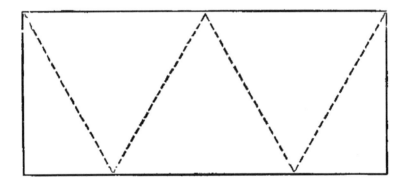

lines, or, what is better, the end pieces may be folded over and sewed down.   Now bring the two parts of the upper margin together and sew with wire, and then proceed to fasten the tent in place as before.   In this latter case, of course, a hole must be cut at the top of the tent.

When one of these tent-escapes is placed on a pile of supers, or on a hive containing bees, the bees will pass out freely at the top, but the bees that try to get in attempt to make the entrance farther down.   Once in a great while there will gather a bunch of the outgoing bees at the top so as to clog the exit, and then the robbers will settle on this bunch of bees and work their way in, but a little smoke will scatter the bunch of bees.

"ONCE A THIEF NOT "ALWAYS A THIEF

For many years I believed what perhaps is generally believed, that the saying, "Once a thief, always a thief" was true of any bee ever guilty of robbing. There is, no doubt, some ground for such a belief, for a bee that has spent to-day robbing from a certain hive will very likely start in on the same business to-morrow, if any more plunder is to be had in the same place, but it is not true that a bee that has been engaged in one robbing scrape will never after return to honest labor.

Indeed, so far as the bee is concerned, getting honey out of another hive probably seems just as honest work as to gather nectar from the flowers And the more active a bee is when engaged in the field, the more active might we expect to find it in trying to rob when there is nothing more to be had in the field

Many a hive is robbed out in spring, and many a bee is engaged in the robbing, yet the first day in which an abundance of stores can be had in the field, every bee of sufficient age gleefully joins in the quest abroad, and the fact that honey may be exposed with little danger shows that the bees that were formerly so intent upon robbing are now afield with the others

LEAVING SOMETHING FOR ROBBERS.

A practice that is just as far from right as the theory about which we have been talking is the practice of taking away whatever the robbers are working upon, without leaving anything in its place. If by carelessness I have left a section of honey on a hive, and find the robbers at work upon it, I can hardly do a worse thing than to take it away.

If I leave it, the bees will stick to it, and clean it out, and for some time a number of robbers will stick to it after the honey is all gone, but they stick to that one spot, and if the empty comb is left there, they keep hunting it all over and over, and by and by conclude the honey is all used out of it and go about their business. If the section is taken away and nothing left in its place, they seem to think they have made a mistake as to the place and hunt all around for the missing section, until they force their way into the nearest conquerable colony.

If a weak colony is attacked, I may sometimes take it away, but if I do, I immediately put in its place an empty hive in which I put some scraps of comb containing a little honey. They will rob this out and that will be the end of it. It is possible that dry comb without any honey might answer.

Fig. 72.—No. 12 Closed for Hauling.

ROBBING, FAULT OF BEE-KEEPER.

Except in case of queenless colonies, I am somewhat of the opinion that most cases of robbing have been

through my own carelessness. When there is nothing
to do in the fields, the bees may be seen busily trying to
enter cracks about hives so small that there is no possibility of their entering, and they are sharp to observe any
change If, at such times, a fresh opening be left any-
where about a hive, it is sure to be discovered. An entrance at the top of brood-chamber, at the back end, may
be left open all the season without being disturbed by
robbers. But if it has been kept closed until a time when
robbers are troublesome, and then opened, whether it be
that the robbers are stirred up by seeing the change, or
whether the bees of the colony are not in the habit of
protecting themselves in that quarter, the robbers are
pretty sure to give the new entrance especial attention;
and if the colony be not very strong there may be serious
trouble

STARTING ROBBING BY FEEDING.

As feeding is done only in a time of scarcity, it is
one of the most common causes of robbing among careless bee-keepers. When general feeding is done with
Miller feeders, there is little danger, no matter what time
of day the work is done, but if some weak colony is short
of stores, I try to be somewhat careful to do nothing
to attract especial attention to it. I have sometimes fed
at night, and so far as convenient prefer to feed late in
the day, but convenience does not always allow it

One time I found a colony at the close of the honey
harvest, by some means about at the point of starvation
With more carelessness than was excusable, I gave them,
I think in the forenoon, two or three combs filled with
sugar syrup Some time after, I happened to look toward that end of the apiary and saw what looked like a
swarm. The bees had become excited over their new-
found stores; the robber-bees had joined in and the bees

of the colony seemed to think forage was so plentiful
that it wasn't worth while to be mean about it, there was

Fig. 73.—Miller Tent-Escape.

enough for all; so the robbers were doing a land-office
business without let or hindrance.

STOPPING ROBBING WITH WET HAY.

I closed the entrances of the other hives in the immediate neighborhood, so that only two or three bees
could pass at a time, and then threw a lot of loose, wet
hay at the entrance of the besieged hive.

Not only did I put hay at the entrance, but piled it
up all around to the top of the hive. For some time I
kept every thing very wet all around the hive by pouring on pails of water, and then left them till next day.

No other hives were attacked. I somewhat expected to find the queen killed, but she was all right
next day, and no further trouble occurred, as the colony

was a strong one, and when in its right mind, capable of taking care of itself.

DO ROBBED-BEES JOIN THE ROBBERS?

One of the venerable traditions that is perhaps generally accepted without question is that when a colony is being robbed it is a quite common thing for the bees that are robbed to join the robbers and help carry off the stores. I am very skeptical as to there being any truth in the tradition. I do not say such a thing never happened, but I never saw such a case, and I have seen from first to last quite a number of cases of robbing. I have known a number of cases in which all the stores were emptied out of the combs by robbers, and the bees of the colony seemed to be all left, and generally by taking the right kind of pains I have succeeded in re-establishing such a colony. In such cases there was certainly no joining the robbers

I have found other cases in which the bees were entirely gone, and I could only guess what had become of them. My guess was that after being robbed of all their stores, and having used up all the honey in their honey-sacs, perhaps some time after the robbers had ceased to pay any attention to them, they had swarmed out as any hunger-swarm will do, and had united, or tried to unite, with some other colony. Would they not be likely to join some colony other than the one that had treated them so unkindly?

PILES SOMETIMES A TARGET FOR ROBBERS

Piles of four or five stories with abundant ventilation at each story are in no danger from robbers under ordinary circumstances; but if you ever have such piles, and are so unfortunate as to get the robbers once started at them, you "better watch out." Even if there should be a dearth for some time, robbers are not likely to attack a pile; for they have probably got into the habit of thinking that such a pile is not to be meddled with, but just you do something to call particular attention to the pile, such as letting a comb of honey stand by it exposed, and there are so many exposed places to defend that the robbers are likely to have things their own way.

Fig. 74.—Wheeling Load of Supers.

A BAD CASE OF ROBBING.

One time George W. York was here when bees were not busily at work in the fields, and I opened up a pile of four stories, for what purpose I do not now remember; very likely I was trying to show off in some way. At any rate I showed him a fine case of robbing, for the robbers pounced down upon every exposed point, and before I had noticed what was going on they were having a gay time. Of course I couldn't build a haystack about the four stories, but I had to do something, for although the colony was a powerful one it was utterly inadequate to the protection of four exposed stories, and without any interference on my part its doom was sealed   I closed all entrances except the lower one, and then applied the hay and water to the lower story successfully.

PILES IN LATE SUMMER

During the usual working season there is need of some foolishness on the part of the bee-keeper to start robbing at a pile having a strong colony, but after the weather becomes quite cool toward fall, the case is different.   Of course, all but the lower entrance should be closed before cold nights come, but sometimes there is a case of neglect   In a cold night the colony shrinks down into the lower or the lower two stories—all the more because there is a current of air right through the hive —and the two or three upper stories are left without any bees

In the following morning they do not go up again into the upper stories till some time after the weather has warmed up   The robbers, however, do not wait so long, but finding an upper entrance unprotected go to work in lively style.

As late as October 6, in the year 1902, a pile was left with an upper entrance or ventilating space still open, and on the forenoon of that day I observed lively work at that place, while all was quiet at the lower or regular entrance   I shoved the cover back so as to close the space, and then took a snap-shot of the bees trying to get in, as shown in Fig 81.   Only two stories show in the picture, although the pile was four stories high Fortunately no other place was open except the regular lower entrance, and it was so far from top to bottom that the robbers made no attempt below—indeed I suppose they would have been promptly repulsed if they had— so after trying for a time to get in the place I had closed, they gave up and left the hive.

PLAYING BEES AND ROBBERS.

I think I can tell by carefully looking at bees when flying with unusual commotion at the entrance of a hive, whether it is a case of robbing or bees at play, but I am not sure I could tell someone else the difference in appearance. Looking at bees at play in Fig. 82, and comparing with Fig. 81, there appears little difference. In actual life there will be seen the same excited eagerness in each case.

Fig. 75.—Robber-Cloth.

The time of day helps to decide. During the middle of the day, say from noon till the middle of the after-

noon, playing is common ; earlier or later than that time,
if there is big excitement at the entrance of a weak colony, the likelihood is that robbing is going on

SIGNS OF ROBBING

One pretty sure sign of robbing, when there is a
good deal of stir at the entrance, is to see bees working
frantically to force an entrance under the cover or at
some other part of the hive   Just why they should do
this at times when they seem to have plenty of chance
to get in at the regular entrance I do not know—it seems
to be a way they have

A sure sign of robbing is to find the bees entering
the hive with empty sacs and coming out with their sacs
full.   The contents of the sac can be told by killing the
bee, pulling it in two, and squeezing out the contents of
the sac   Indeed, the squeezing is hardly needed

BEES STICK TO THE SAME ENTRANCE

A glance at the hive shown in Fig 81 would show
that it is a case of robbing, for the flying is at an opening
never used for an entrance   It is a somewhat curious
fact that bees are very persistent in continuing to use
the same place for an entrance

After the bees have become used to going in and
out at the regular place, if I make an opening at the
back end of the hive, no matter if it be as large as the
front entrance, that back opening will never be used as
an entrance   One would think that young bees taking
their first play-spell would be as likely to use the back
as the front opening, but when I made a practice of having ventilating openings at the backs of the hives I do not
remember to have seen bees playing at the back.   Per-

haps the noise of the regular traffic in front attracts them there.

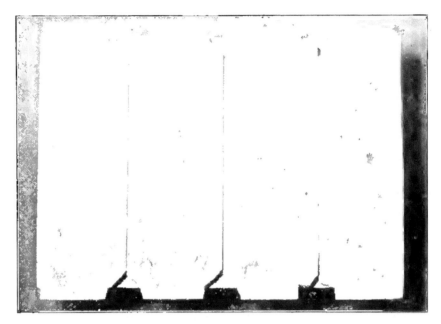

Fig. 76.—Push-Board.

LOSING THE ROBBERS.

I make it a rule to stop operations usually when robbers are very bad, but sometimes it seems necessary to fight it out. I have sometimes taken advantage of the plan of making cross bees or robbers lose themselves, or rather lose the object they are after by rapidly changing the base of operation. One day at the Wilson apiary I had taken off some wide frames of sections and wanted to take them from the place where they were piled up, so as to put them on the wagon. The robbers were so fierce and persistent that it seemed impossible to open a crack without their immediately forcing their way in. My wife was provided with a smoker in full blast, and a big bunch of goldenrod or other weeds A robber-cloth covered the pile. With one hand I lifted the cloth and with the other took out a frame of sections, then quickly dropped the robber-cloth in its place, my wife keeping a cloud of smoke in the way of any robbers which should attempt to enter the pile while the cloth was raised. Instantly the frame was out of the super, the robbers made for the frame of sections. I made for the wagon and my wife made for me. Running in a zig-zag, circuitous course, my wife followed me, puffing and switching at every step, and by the time we got to the wagon the robbers were lost, the frame was slipped quickly into the super on the wagon, and the robber-cloth dropped over it. The Scotch folks at the house had a good laugh over the crazy couple chasing one another through the orchard, but we beat the bees. Under ordinary circumstances it would be better to take an easier plan or wait till dark.

PROTECTION FROM STINGS.

I have been a bee-keeper for forty-one years, during the last twenty-four of which I have made the production of honey my sole business, aside from writing about bees, and yet I have not reached that point where I care nothing for protection from stings. When I first commenced keeping bees, a sting on my hand was a serious affair, swelling to the shoulder, and troubling fully as much the second day as the first. Now, if I receive a half-dozen stings or more, I cannot tell an hour or two later where I was stung, except as a matter of memory. Yet I think that a sting gives me fully as much pain for the first minute now, as it did forty years ago. Sometimes the pain is so severe that it literally makes me groan, especially if no one is within hearing. I sometimes wonder at those who scout at any sort of protection, and query whether there may not be just a little of a spirit of bravado about it. I think I *could* go through a year without any sort of protection, but I do not think I ever shall. A bee inside my clothing makes me very nervous, and I cannot go on in comfort at my work with a feeling of uncertainty as to where and when its little javelin shall pierce my flesh. If I feel it crawling on me, and then cease to feel it because it is on the clothing and not on the skin, I am in momentary dread as to where it shall turn up next; and it is a real relief when it stings me, for I know then the precise spot where it is, and have no further expectations from it.

BEE-VEIL.

So I seldom go among the bees without a veil. I may not have it over my face, but it is on the hat, ready to be pulled down at any time. The veil is made of inexpensive material, called by milliners cape-lace or cape-net. It is 21 inches wide. A piece is cut off as long as the circumference of the brim of a straw hat, and both ends sewed together. Shirr a rubber cord in one end of this open bag, thoroughly soak or wash out the starch, and sew the other end on the edge of the hat-brim. It is important for the eye-sight that the stuff of the veil be black, but the black coloring crocks one's clothing. So of late years a border of white cloth is sewed on the veil to receive the rubber cord.

The rubber cord holds the veil close about one's neck, yet not close enough but what a bee sometimes gets under it. Although a bee is not at all likely to sting when it gets inside a veil, it is just as well to have it remain outside. So my assistant devised the plan of drawing the veil down very tightly in front, and pinning it to her waist with a safety-pin. Seeing it work so well with her, I have also adopted the plan, pinning to my suspenders on one side, or to my vest if I have one on.

Sometimes a face-piece of silk net is sewed in the veil. Instead of having the veil sewed to my hat, so that the bee-hat must be taken along when we go to an out-apiary, I sometimes have in my pocket a veil made with a rubber cord shirred into each end, and when I reach the apiary the veil is slipped on over the hat I am wearing.

The openings at the wrist and neck of my shirt are small, the cloth lapping over so as to give a bee little chance for entrance. If bees are likely to be on the ground, my pants are put inside my stockings. I get a great many stings on my hands, but the inconvenience and discomfort of any sort of gloves would be to me worse than the stings.

My assistant prefers to wear gloves, not only to avoid the stings, but to avoid the bee-glue I may say in passing that I am not always very particular about getting the bee-glue off my hands, but when I do clean them I usually give the bee-glue a good rubbing with butter or grease, and then wash off with soap and water. I confess I don't very much mind having bee-glue on my hands unless there is so much of it that it sticks to the bed-clothes at night But I do abhor the sticky feeling of honey on my hands, and when they get daubed, if I have no water I pick up some soil to rub them with. That at least takes away the sticky feeling Perhaps you think the soil is worse than the honey I don't.

BEE-GLOVES

For some time Miss Wilson wore a kind of cheap white glove that I think was made of pig-skin She dislikes the smell of oiled canvas gloves, although to me the smell is not very bad, and the smell of the pig-skin is horrid Latterly she wears light buckskin. They are free from smell, and wash well.

GETTING OUT STINGS.

I like to get a sting out of my skin as soon as possible, if not too busy.   A little trick in this direction is,
I think, not known to all bee-keepers.   I am not sure

Fig. 77.—Pushing Sections out of Super.

whether I learned it by instinct, or from the writings of
G. M. Doolittle.   If a bee stings my hand, I instantly
strike the hand with much force upon my leg, with a
sort of quick, wiping motion.   This mashes the bee,
generally, and rubs out the sting at the same time.

SCOLDING BEES.

If one thinks of the thousands or millions of bees in a large apiary, it will be seen that comparatively few bees make any attack Sometimes a single bee will threaten and scold me by the hour, perhaps finally sting-ing me by getting into my hair or whiskers, and for aught I know the same bee may keep up the same thing for days—I mean the scolding, not the stinging It is sometimes worth while to get rid of the annoyance by stepping to one side and knocking it down with a stick by a few rapid strokes back and forth in front of my face. I often mash it by slapping my hands together

CROSS COLONIES

Sometimes the bees have seemed, very cross, and a little observation has shown these bees to proceed from a particular part of the apiary, and really from only one hive. A careless observer might have said all the bees in the apiary were cross I have had a few colonies so cross that merely walking by the hive was the signal for a gen-eral onslaught Truth obliges me to say that I have some-times been so badly stung by one of these, when working at them, that I have taken refuge in inglorious flight, glad to get a respite and scrape out the stings Just why there should be one or two of these in a year in such marked contrast with others I cannot say. The only remedy I had was to kill the queen

DRESS FOR THE HOTTEST WEATHER

During the principal part of the honey-flow, a promi-nent element of hardship is the endurance of the heat Sometimes the heat really has made me sick so that in spite of a press of work, I have been obliged to give up and lie down for an hour or more. At such times you may be sure I am not very warmly clad. One straw hat and veil, one cotton shirt, one pair cotton overalls, one pair cotton socks and one pair shoes, comprise my entire wearing apparel (Fig. 83). Before noon, shirt and pants are both thoroughly wet with perspiration.

Fig. 78.—Lifting off the Super.

SPONGE-BATH AT NOON.

In this heated condition, I sponge myself off with cold water before dinner, put on dry pants and shirt, and hang up the wet ones in the sun to be put on next day. I am sure that by this refreshing change, I am able to do

more work   It might be thought that applying cold
water all over the body when every part is dripping with
perspiration might make me take cold.   I have never
found it so, even if followed up every day.   The body is
so thoroughly heated that it easily resists the shock, and
a brisk rubbing leaves one in a fine glow.

My overalls are white, such as painters or masons
use   I do not enjoy being so conspicuous when I happen to be on the streets clad in white, but I would rather
be conspicuous than to be stung; and I feel sure that I
do not get so many stings as I would with darker clothing.

WOMAN'S BEE-DRESS.

My assistant is not dressed so coolly as I.   Her desire to keep her dress clean makes her warmer than she
otherwise would be, for she wears an apron that covers
all the dress except the sleeves (Fig. 84).   This apron is
made of denim, and has two large pockets.   It is made
after pattern No 3,696 of the Butterick Publishing Co.
To cover the sleeves of her dress, she uses a pair of white
sleeves fastened together by a strap sewed to each sleeve
across the back, a similar strap in front being sewed to
one sleeve and buttoned to the other   The wrists of
these sleeves are sewed to the wrists of her gloves, and
ripped off whenever it is necessary to wash either gloves
or sleeves.   For convenience, several pairs are kept.

QUEEN-REARING—BREEDING FROM BEST.

My sole business with bees being to produce honey,
I am not particular to keep a popular breed of bees, only
so far as their popularity comes from their profitableness
as honey-gatherers.   I am anxious to have those that are
industrious, good winterers, gentle,   and   not   given   to
much swarming.   For some years I got an imported

Italian queen every year or two, but for several years I have preferred to rear from queens of my own whose workers have distinguished themselves as being the most desirable.

IMPORTANCE OF SELECTION.

The queen being the very soul of the colony, I hardly consider any pains too great that will give better queens. The first thing is to select the queen from which to rear, for generally all rearing will be from the same queen, whether for the home apiary or an outside apiary. The records are carefully scanned, and that queen chosen which, all things considered, appears to be the best. The first point to be weighed is the amount of honey that has been stored. Other things being equal, the queen whose workers have shown themselves the best storers will have

Fig. 79.—Supers of Sections Blocked Up.

the preference. The matter of wintering will pretty much take care of itself, for a colony that has wintered

poorly is not likely to do very heavy work in the harvest.
The more a colony has done in the way of making preparations for swarming, the lower will be its standing
Generally, however, a colony that gives the largest number of sections is one that never dreamed of swarming.

BREEDING FROM BEST.

I am well aware that I will be told by some that I am
choosing freak queens from which to rear, and that it
would be much better to select a queen whose royal
daughters showed uniform results only a little above the
average. I don't know enough to know whether that is
true or not, but I know that some excellent results have
been obtained by breeders of other animals by breeding
from sires or dams so exceptional in character that they
might be called freaks I know, too, that it is easier to
decide which colony does best work than it is to decide
which queen produces royal progeny the most nearly uniform in character. By the first way, too, a queen can be
used a year sooner than by the second way, and a year
in the life of a queen is a good deal. I may mention that
a queen which has a fine record for two successive seasons is preferred to one with the same kind of a record
for only one season At any rate, the results obtained in
the way of improvement of stock as a result of my practice have been such as to warrant me in its continuance,
at least for a time.

The danger from inbreeding must not be lost sight
of entirely. With two or three hundred colonies kept in
three different apiaries it is perhaps not great Should
signs of degeneracy at any time appear, it will not be
difficult to introduce fresh blood.

CONDITIONS FOR QUEEN-REARING

Having chosen the queen from which to rear, I have
kept in mind that unless conditions are favorable the

royal progeny of the best queen in the world may be very poor. Queen-cells must be started when the weather is

Fig. 80.—Cleated Smoker.

sufficiently warm, when bees are gathering enough to make them feel that there is no need to stint the royal larvæ in their rations, and until near the point of emergence it is much better that the cells shall be in the care of a strong colony. So I do not begin operations for queen-rearing until about the time that bees inclined to swarming would begin to make preparations therefor.

REARING QUEENS IN HIVE WITH LAYING QUEEN.

It would be too long a story to enumerate all the plans I have used in queen-rearing. I have reared excellent queens, and many of them, by the Alley plan, and by the Doolittle cell-cup plan, together with its modifications by Pridgen and others. I think I was the first one to report rearing a queen in a colony having a laying queen; and I have reared them in stories under as well as over the story having the laying queen   Neither is it absolutely necessary to have a queen-excluder between the stories   In lieu of an excluder I have used a cloth with room for passage at the corners   Neither excluder nor cloth is absolutely necessary, distance is enough   That first reported case was on this wise:

Upon a hive containing a colony had been piled four stories of empty combs for safe keeping. To make sure that the bees would not neglect the care of the most distant combs, I put a frame of brood in the upper story. A few weeks later I found a laying queen in the upper story with the old queen still below   A hole in the upper story had allowed the flight of the young queen without invading the domains of her mother. For those who produce extracted honey this plan might be used to advantage

UNQUEENING COLONY TO START CELLS.

I have reared good queens by the old and simple plan of taking away the queen of a strong colony   Of course this must be a choice queen   Previous to the removal of the queen the colony is strengthened   Frames of well-advanced brood are from time to time given from other colonies until it has two—perhaps three—stories of brood. None of this brood, however, is given less than five or six days before the removal of the queen. The queen is taken with two frames of brood and adhering bees and put on a new stand in an empty hive, an empty comb and one with some honey being added.

TIME TO START NUCLEI.

In nine or ten days from the removal of the queen it is time to break up the queenless colony into nuclei. It might generally be left till a day or two later before a young queen would come out to destroy her baby sisters

Fig. 81.—Robber Bees.

in their cradles, but it is best to take no chances. If it were true, as formerly believed, that queenless bees are in such haste to rear a queen that they will select a larva too old for the purpose, then it would hardly do to wait even nine days. A queen is matured in fifteen days

from the time the egg is laid, and is fed throughout her
larval lifetime on the same food that is given to a
worker-larva during the first three days of its larval existence So a worker-larva more than three days old, or
more than six days from the laying of the egg, would be
too old for a good queen. If, now, the bees should
select a larva more than three days old, the queen would
emerge in less than nine days I think no one has ever
known this to occur

BEES DO NOT PREFER TOO OLD LARVAE

As a matter of fact bees do not use such poor judgment as to select larvæ too old when larvæ sufficiently
young are present, as I have proven by direct experiment and many observations It will not do, however,
to conclude from this that all queen-cells started by a
queenless colony left to themselves will be equally good
Bees have a fashion of starting cells for a number of
days in succession, and will continue to start them when
larvæ sufficiently young for good queens are no longer
present So some means must be taken to make sure
that no nucleus has for its sole dependence one of these
latest cells If several cells can be afforded for each
nucleus, there is little danger they will all be bad
Neither is there great danger if a cell is chosen which is
large and fine-looking Perhaps the safer way is to
give the queenless colony a frame with eggs and young
brood three or four days after the removal of the queen,
and then they will not be obliged to use the older larvæ
of the other combs

PLACING QUEEN-CELLS.

Two or three frames of brood with adhering bees
are taken for each nucleus If one of the frames has a

cell or several cells in a good location, well and good.
If not, the lack must be supplied. But the cells must be
where they will be sure to be well cared for. They must
not be on the outer edge of a comb, with the chance to be
chilled, neither must they be on the outer side of the
comb, but on the side of the comb that faces the other
comb. Any cells that are not just where they are
wanted must be cut out. For this purpose I like a tea-
knife with a very thin and narrow blade of steel.

STAPLING CELLS ON COMB.

A staple, such as is used to fasten a bottom-board to
a hive, is used to fasten a cell in place. The cell is placed
where it is wanted, then the staple is placed over it, one

Fig. 82.—Bees Playing.

leg of the staple close to the cell, and the other leg is
pushed deep into the comb (Fig. 85).

MAKING BEES STAY IN NUCLEI

Each nucleus is put upon a stand of its own, and the entrance is plugged up with leaves so that no bee can get out. One of the nuclei, however, is left without having its entrance closed, and this is put in the place of the hive which contains the queen, and the hive with the queen is put back on the old stand from which the queen was first taken. The entrances may be left closed until the shrinking of the leaves allows the bees to make their way out, but I generally open them in about twenty-four hours, first pounding on the hive to make the bees mark their location upon emerging. Although queen-less bees are much better than others at staying wherever they are put, there will be still fewer bees return to the old place if the nucleus is fastened in twenty-four hours or longer.

LOOKING FOR EGGS.

Twelve or fourteen days after forming the nuclei I look to see if the queens are laying. I might find eggs in less time, but not always, and at any rate not in considerable number, and it saves time on the whole not to be in too much of a hurry. If no eggs are found a comb of young brood is given as an encouragement to start the young queen to laying, and a day or two later, if queen-cells are started on this young brood, a mature queen-cell is given.

KEEPING BEST QUEEN IN NUCLEUS.

Instead of having my best queen in a strong colony, as in the plan just given, she is usually kept in a two-frame nucleus throughout the summer, the nucleus being strengthened into a full colony in the fall for wintering. One object of this is to make the queen live longer.

Lately I have used a plan that I think I like better

than any other I ever tried, although if I were rearing queens on a large scale I might prefer the plans now so well known among those who rear queens to sell. The plan of which I speak gives me just as good queens, and with less trouble.

Fig. 83.—Bee-Dress.

STARTING BROOD FOR CELLS.

Having my breeding queen in a two-frame nucleus, I take away one of the combs, and in its place put a frame in which are two small starters two or three inches long and an inch wide. One of these starters is put about six inches from each end (Fig 86)   A week later this frame will have a comb built in it that will fill most of the frame, the comb being fairly well filled with eggs and young brood (Fig. 88)   It is taken away, and another frame with two small starters put in its place as before   Thus this nucleus will furnish once a week a frame of comb with brood of the best sort for queen-rearing   It will be a day or so after the frame is given before the queen lays in it, so that the brood will not be too old even if the bees were so foolish as to prefer it

The comb being new and tender makes it probably an easier job for the bees to build queen-cells upon it; at any rate they always show a preference for such comb, and perhaps start on it a larger number of cells than they would on older comb

PREPARING BEES FOR CELL-BUILDING.

Having now arranged for the right kind of brood and eggs to be ready on the same day of each week, the next thing is to provide the right kind of bees to start the cells   Old bees are not as good as young for the purpose, so there must be a goodly number of young bees each time a fresh comb is given, and it is better to have matters arranged so that the bees shall be conscious of their queenlessness at the time the comb is given, so that work on the cells may begin at once

Two colonies are used, their hives standing back to back, one facing east, the other west   This is in the home apiary, for queen-rearing after this plan is all done at home and when queens are needed at the out-apiaries they are taken from home   One of the colonies has a queen, the other is queenless, and the queen is changed from one side to the other each week   Two stories are on each stand, the lower story having combs in which the bees can store if they are getting anything to store.

If there is nothing to store, and perhaps not enough sometimes coming in for daily needs, a feeder is kept on the queenless colony. The upper story on the one stand contains, of course, the queen with her complement of brood-combs; the other has six combs more or less occupied with honey and pollen, besides the one or two frames containing the brood for cells.

Suppose we go into the apiary to operate Wednesday, June 11.

NUCLEUS WITH BEST QUEEN.

We first go to the hive containing our best queen Perhaps I ought to say more fully what is in this hive. At the one side is one frame next the wall filled with brood sealed and unsealed, and next to it the frame that a week before was given empty, now nearly filled with new, white comb containing the very young brood and eggs (Fig. 88) Next to this comes a dummy, possibly a partly filled frame coming first Next the wall on the other side of the hive are two combs containing some honey, there being empty space between them and the dummy aforesaid. If the bees need any honey, they can get it here; if they need a place to store, they can store here. You might think the queen will cross over, or that the bees will build in the vacant space, but I have not had that trouble If these outside combs should become filled with honey, of course they can be exchanged for others not so filled.

BROOD FOR QUEEN-CELLS

We take out the frame with the virgin comb, and replace it with an empty frame with its two little starters, brushing back into the hive the bees from the comb taken out, and closing the hive. Looking at the comb taken out, you will see that instead of the oldest brood being in the center, it will be in the two places where the two little starters were put. It was for this purpose the two starters at the sides were given rather than a central one. For by this means the waving contour will give opportunity for a larger number of queen-cells on the edge of the comb than would otherwise be the case.

TRIMMING THE BREEDING-COMB.

For a little distance at the edge, the comb contains eggs only. This part is trimmed away, leaving the youngest of the brood at the edge of the comb (Fig. 89). One reason for this is that, other things being equal, the bees show a decided preference for building on the edge of a comb. Another reason is that I decidedly prefer to have cells on the edge, thus making them easier to cut out when wanted. The part cut away would only be in the way of both of us

BEES USING YOUNG LARVAE ONLY.

When a queen is taken away from a full colony, the bees start cells from young brood, and as I have already said, they continue to start fresh cells for several days, and until after there is no longer brood of the proper age, so that the last cells started will contain larvæ too old to make good queens. But on these combs prepared as I have described, they do not do so. Rarely, if ever, will a cell be found elsewhere than on the edge of the comb, and I have never known the bees to start a cell after the larvæ were too old   I do not know why there is this difference   I only know the fact. But it is a very convenient fact

AGE OF LARVAE FOR QUEENS.

Scientists tell us that a worker-larva is fed for three days the same as a queen-larva, and then it is weaned

Theoretically, then, up to the time a larva in a worker-
cell is three days old, it ought to be all right to rear a
queen from. Practically, I do not believe a larva three
days old is as good as a younger one. The only reason
I have for so believing is the expressed preference of

Fig. 84.— Woman's Bee-Dress.

the bees themselves. Give them larvæ of all ages from
which to select, and they always choose that which is
two days old, or younger. Indeed, it will be seen that
in the comb from which I have trimmed the edge (Fig.
89) the larvæ on the edge of the comb have been out of

the egg but a short time, for I merely trimmed away the eggs, and possibly not all of them.

PREPARING BEES FOR CELL-BUILDING

Having our frame ready, we go to our queenless colony. Suppose the east colony is the queenless one. We make the hives exchange places, putting the queenless one on the west stand, and the one with the queen on the east stand. Opening the west or queenless one, we take out the frame that now contains queen-cells, this frame having been given the Wednesday previous. On the top of this frame is penciled "14," for on Saturday the 14th the cells must be distributed lest being left longer one of the young queens should emerge and kill the rest. This frame is put for safe keeping in some queenless nucleus strong enough so that the cells will be well protected against a possibly cool night They will be left three days in this safe keeping, that is, till Saturday, June 14. The prepared frame is put in place of the one taken out, and on the top-bar is penciled "21," the day on which the prospective cells must be distributed

The east hive is now opened, and all the bees in the upper story brushed into the west hive, taking care to leave the queen in the east hive, and the hives are closed up The queen may appear lonesome in the east hive, but there are bees left in the lower story, and the field-force that have been flying from the east side will all return there The west hive will be seen to have a strong force of bees of the right sort to start queen-cells

The same performance is repeated the next Wednesday, the hives change places, and fresh brood from the choice queen takes the place of the queen-cells removed, and this is repeated each Wednesday so long as more cells are desired

The next thing is to distribute the cells to the nuclei.

This is Saturday's work. The day for the distribution of the cells having been marked in advance on the top-bars, there is not much chance for mistake.

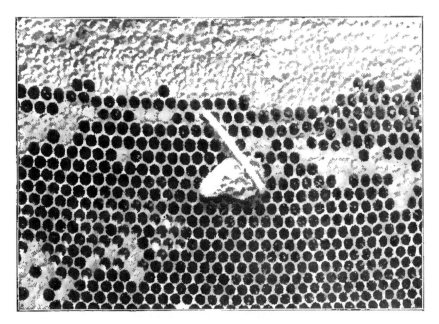

Fig. 85.—Queen-Cell Stapled on Comb.

MORE THAN ONE NUCLEUS IN HIVE.

The frames for nuclei are the regular full-sized frames, and a full hive may be used for each nucleus, but I find it economy to have the hive divided up into two or three compartments for as many nuclei. Three nuclei in one hive are mutually helpful in keeping up the heat, and thus it is possible to have the nuclei weaker than if each nucleus was by itself, while results are as good with the three weaker nuclei in the one hive as with three stronger nuclei in three separate hives.

NUCLEUS-HIVE.

For many years I have had hives divided into two or more compartments, and have had much trouble from

the bees finding a passage from one compartment to another, but my latest nucleus hives have not troubled in
that way   They are made from ordinary 8-frame hives
together with the 2-inch-deep bottom-board. First two
pieces are nailed on the inside of the bottom-board, each
piece 18¼x1¾x⅞.   One piece nailed 4½ inches from
one side, the other 4½ inches from the other side   These
pieces do not lie flat in the bottom, but stand on edge,
with 1⅜ inches between them   Then the hive is fastened on the bottom-board with the four usual staples.
Two division-boards, each 18¼x9¾x5-16, are now put
in place and crowded down tight upon the two pieces in
the bottom-board.   These two division-boards are 4⅝
inches from each side, leaving 2¼ inches between them.
The four spaces at the top, at the ends of the division-
boards, are closed by blocks ¾x½x5-16 whittled enough
to allow them to be wedged into place   Light 1¼ inch
wire-nails are driven through from the outside to hold
the division-boards in place. A block 10x2x⅞ is pushed
into the entrance centrally, and held there by a nail lightly driven in front of it   That leaves an entrance at each
end of the block for the two side compartments, but no
entrance for the middle compartment   For this purpose
an inch hole is bored in the back end of the hive midway
between the two corners, its center being about three
inches from the upper surface of the hive   Three boards
of half-inch stuff cover the three compartments, and over
this is an ordinary hive-cover

At Fig 90 will be seen a bottom-board for a nucleus
hive You will notice that the two pieces that run lengthwise through the center of the bottom-board are a quarter of an inch shallower than the rim of the bottom-
board. If they were 2 inches deep instead of 1¾ the
bottom-bars of the frames would rest directly on them.
Of course the division-boards are deep enough to come
clear down upon these two pieces.

Two nucleus-hives will be seen at Fig. 91. The one at the right faces us, showing the entrance at each side. The back of the left hive is toward us, showing the round hole near the top, which serves as an entrance to the middle compartment.

LARGE SPACE FOR MIDDLE FRAME.

In one of these side compartments there is abundant room for two frames and a dummy, and three frames

Fig. 86.—Starters in Breeding Frame.

without the dummy can with care be crowded in. The central compartment will of course take only one frame. It seems as though 2¼ inches is quite too much space for one frame, but I use that space advisedly. Many years ago I made a nucleus hive with six compartments, and at that time not having had much experience I made each compartment 2¼ inches wide. .Years afterward I made another nucleus hive, and smiling at my former ignor-

ance and congratulating myself upon the superior knowledge I had gained with the passing years, I made the
compartments more nearly in accord with the usual space
occupied by each frame in a hive, making each compartment—I'm not sure whether it was 1⅝ or 1¾   At any
rate, the bees swarmed out of these limited quarters to
such an extent that I could not use them, whereas they
had not swarmed out of the 2¼ compartments.   Neither
have they swarmed out of these later ones.   Having so
much room in these central compartments, the bees sometimes build pieces of comb on the sides which I must
clean away, but that is better than to have them swarm
out.

CONTENTS OF NUCLEUS-HIVE.

A nucleus hive is tenanted by a two-frame nucleus
on each side and a one-frame nucleus in the middle. Care
is taken to choose one of the best frames of brood for the
middle nucleus, and perhaps a few extra bees are brushed
in.   A third comb may be put in each of the side compartments, or a dummy, the same as the dummies used in
the regular hives .

MAKING THE BEES STAY.

When populated, the entrances of the nuclei are
plugged up with green leaves.   These are generally
taken away twenty-four hours later, after the hives are
pounded to stir up the bees, but if they are neglected the
leaves will dry and shrink so the bees can make their
way out   It is better to form nuclei with queenless bees,
for they are not so much inclined as others to go back to
their old place.

QUEEN-CAGE

When we go to give queen-cells to the nuclei, we
are provided with introducing queen-cages (Fig 92).

These are an improvement over the Miller introducing cage quoted in the catalogs of supply-dealers. Two blocks 3 inches by ½ by ¼ and a piece of wire-cloth 6½x1⅞, form the material for the cage. Lay the two blocks parallel on their edges, and nail on these one end

Fig. 87.—Putting Foundation in Sections.

of the wire-cloth, the end of the wire-cloth corresponding with the ends of the blocks. Fold the wire-cloth around the ends of the blocks and nail it on the other side, and you have a cage 3x1⅞x½, outside measure. The plug to close the cage is not so simple, for the cage is to be provisioned, and the plug holds the candy. Two blocks

1¼x½x¼, a piece of tin and a piece of section stuff each 1¼ inches square form the material for the plug. Lay the two blocks parallel on their sides, with ¼ inch space between them   On these nail the piece of tin, turn over, and nail on the section stuff   Near one end drive a tack partly in to prevent the plug going too far into the cage. That makes all complete.

DISTRIBUTING QUEEN-CELLS.

When the queen-cells are to be distributed on Saturday, the first thing is to provision a number of queen-cages with the usual queen-candy, tacking a piece of pasteboard on the end of the plug.   Then we go to the nucleus where the cells are stored, cut out the cells, rejecting any that do not appear satisfactory, and put the cells in the cages   Some cells, however, are left uncaged. When we come to a nucleus that has had no queen for a day or more, there is no need of caging the cell.   It is put against the comb in a good place, and fastened there with a hive-staple (Fig 85).   Coming to a nucleus with a queen which we wish to remove, we put the queen in a cage, and give the nucleus a caged cell, laying the cage against the comb and nailing it there with a 1½ or 1¾ wire nail (Fig 93)   This nail is slender so as to push easily through the meshes of the wire-cloth   Then the young queens that we have removed are used wherever needed

BRUSHING BEES OFF QUEEN-CELLS.

Before cutting cells from the comb the bees must be removed, and it would mean the ruin of the cells to shake the bees off   Brushing with a Coggshall brush, although it might do with extreme care, would be likely to result in torn cells.   Even something no stiffer than goldenrod or sweet clover needs much care.   I like best a bunch of long and soft June grass—a very flimsy affair to use as a brush, but it is safe.

ADVANTAGE OF CAGING CELLS.

Of course the object of caging the cells is to prevent the bees from tearing them down. At the time of taking a queen out of a nucleus, if a cell were merely stapled on, the bees would be pretty sure to destroy it, for not yet realizing that their young laying queen has been taken from them, they feel no need of anything like a queen-cell. So the cage saves the time and trouble of waiting and making a second visit another day.

There is, however, another advantage in using the cage, making it somewhat desirable to use it in all cases. We often want to know what has been the fate of a cell,

Fig. 88.—Comb for Queen-Cells.

and can generally tell pretty well by its appearance. If it has the appearance of most of those in Fig. 94, we

know that a young queen has emerged and must be in
the nucleus   If it is torn open in the side, like the one
at the extreme right, we are sure that the young queen in
it was destroyed by the bees.

If the cells have merely been stapled on, the bees are
so prompt about removing them as soon as they are no
longer of any use that scarce a vestige of them is left,
so we have nothing to judge by.   But when a cell is enclosed in a cage, the bees are very slow about removing
it, so the cage gives us a better chance for judging

APPEARANCE OF VACATED CELLS

In Fig. 94 the first three cells at the left have the cap
still adhering by a neck, showing that it has been only a
short time since the queen emerged, providing the cell
has not been caged; if it has been caged the queen may
have been out some time.   The fourth cell looks entire,
as if it yet contained a young queen   But it is decep-
tive.   The bees have a trick of fastening the cap back
again as if it were a great joke, sometimes thus impris-
oning one of their own number   A very close look will
generally show a little crack, and a very little
force   will   be   needed   to   pick   the   cap   loose
The   next   six   cells   show   plainly   that   a   young
queen has emerged from each, and finding a cell of that
kind is just as good evidence as a sight of the queen,
only I would a little rather see the queen for the bare
chance that she may not have perfect wings   As already
mentioned, the cell at the extreme right shows by the
hole in its side that no queen ever came out of it alive

QUEENS FOR OUT-APIARIES

On any day when we are going to an out-apiary and
expect to use young queens, we take them from any nucleus that will furnish them, never putting any escort

bees in the cage with the queen, and generally one or more extra queens are taken along, for we are never sure they may not be needed.

Fig. 89.—Comb for Queen-Cells, Trimmed.

Care is taken that the record-book shall always show the condition of each nucleus; so we always have some idea as to which nucleus will furnish a laying queen, which one needs a cell, and so on.

I may remark in passing that at one time I tried having virgin queens caged to give in place of the cells. One would reason that matters ought to be hurried up a little by having virgins instead of cells, but actual practice did not seem to prove it so, and it seemed on the whole better to give the cells.

INTRODUCING QUEENS.

Latterly I usually introduce a queen in a provisioned cage, nailing the cage directly over the brood, as in Fig.

93. Often, however, when it is convenient, I take from a nucleus the frame on which the queen is found, and put frame and all in the queenless hive If this is done at a time when honey is yielding, there is little or no danger, providing the colony has been queenless long enough to be fully conscious of its queenlessness. Indeed, I have introduced many a queen during the harvest into a colony conscious of its queenlessness, by merely taking out a frame of brood and dropping the queen among the bees on the middle of the comb If I wish to run no risk whatever, as in the case of a valuable imported queen, I put in a hive without any bees several frames with no unsealed brood, but with plenty of sealed brood, some of it just emerging, and then closing the hive bee-tight put it where there is no danger of the brood being chilled. One way to do this is to put it over a strong colony, wire-cloth preventing the passage of the bees from one hive to the other. At the end of five days the hive can be set on its own stand, and these five-day-old bees, under the stress of necessity, will soon be seen carrying in pollen.

ARTIFICIAL INCREASE.

Fighting so bitterly against all increase by swarming, I would run out of bees entirely if I did not resort to artificial increase. Without pretending to give all the ways by which increase has been made, I may tell just a little about it

One can make increase by drawing brood or bees, or both, from colonies that are working for honey, and thus keep all the old colonies storing, and at the same time make the desired increase In that way the largest number of colonies possible are kept at work on the harvest, and one might have a feeling that all the increase was clear gain But the feeling is a delusive one.

It is not the number of colonies at work storing, but the number of *bees,* that count   And 60,000 bees in one hive will store more honey than will the same number of bees equally divided in two hives   So in planning for increase, I generally count that the colonies that are drawn upon for increase shall make that their business without being expected to be called upon to store surplus, while those that work for surplus are to be left in the fullest strength possible throughout the season.   You cannot make something out of nothing, and if increase is to be made you may as well devote a certain number of colonies to that business

INCREASING BY TAKING TO OUT-APIARY.

The case may be different in a locality where there is a long and late flow, but I am talking about this locality with white clover as the dependence for a harvest In the year 1880 I took 1,200 pounds of honey from twelve colonies and increased them to eighty-one; but the honey taken was extracted buckwheat, and I never knew such a buckwheat harvest before or since   Perhaps it will be well to tell more explicitly how that increase was made   The success achieved will be somewhat diminished when I say that the bees were supplied with ready-built combs, so they had no combs to build   But they had no help from other colonies in the way of bees or brood except a few eggs from which to rear queens

The twelve colonies were taken from the home apiary to the Wilson apiary, and were prepared in advance for dividing.   From part of them the queens were taken and queen-cells thus secured   Ten-frame hives were used at that time, and by some help from others of the twelve, a hive would contain ten frames of brood and bees without any queen, a sealed queen-cell on each frame of brood.   After standing a day or so this hive

would be taken to the out-apiary, and the ten frames put
in ten different hives   Of course every bee staid just
where it was put.   To each of these was added another
frame of brood and adhering bees that had been brought
along, and whether these bees were queenless or not there
was nothing for them but to stay where they were put.
In the course of time these first-formed nuclei were
strong enough to help others, and the latest nuclei were
built up at once into fair colonies.

INCREASING 9 WEAK COLONIES TO 56.

In the year 1899, at the Hastings apiary, I increased
nine colonies to fifty-six, making them rear their own
queens, and building up mostly on foundation.   No advantage was taken in the way of hauling colonies from
home to divide, and the same plan would work just as
well if I had had only one apiary.   The increase was
very satisfactory, considering how   weak   the   colonies
were at the start.   May 29 there were only forty-one
combs containing any brood in the nine colonies, counting each comb with brood, even if the patch of brood
were no larger than a silver dollar   I doubt if the nine
averaged any more than three and a half good frames
of brood each   On the other hand, the year was unusually favorable for increase, for there was a continuous though not strong flow right through until, I think,
in September.

No attempt could be made at increase until the colonies were stronger, and the first step looking in that
direction was not made until June 12   On that date No
237 with its seven frames of brood and bees was taken
from its stand, and a hive of empty combs set on the
stand   The queen was found and put in the hive of
empty combs, which by this time had a good many bees
returning from the field.   The queen of No. 237 was

considered the best in the apiary. No. 237 was now set on the stand of No. 235, and No. 235 was set in a new place. Please understand that the stand holds its number, and that when the hive that was on stand 237 is moved as stated it is now No. 235. We now have on 235 a hive full of brood and bees without any queen, and while it will lose the old flying force it had, it will get the flying force that belongs to its present stand. The

Fig. 90.—Nucleus Bottom-Board.

colony that was moved from 235 will, of course, lose its flying force, and will take its time to recuperate.

The bees on these two stands—235 and 237—were the principal actors throughout the season, the other colonies in the apiary merely serving as feeders from which to draw brood from time to time. On 237 was left the hive of empty combs, the queen, and the constantly increasing flying force. We now go to the other colonies and draw from them what brood they can spare without depleting them unwisely, leaving foundation in place of the brood. Looking at the record I find this was only four frames of brood. No bees were taken with this brood. An upper story was put on 237 and these four frames of brood put in it with four empty combs. Of course the queen and bees would soon be up in this upper story

Matters were left in this shape for nine days, the plan being to visit the apiary every nine days throughout the summer. A stormy day, however, might extend the time to ten days, or Sunday coming on the ninth day might shorten the time to eight days

At the expiration of the nine days, June 21, we returned   We took the brood with queen-cells and all bees from 235, and formed two nuclei. Just why we did not start three I don't know, for usually we started a nucleus with two frames of brood, and we must have had more than four frames of brood. No measures were taken to make these bees stay where they were put; it was not necessary with such queenless bees.

Then we took the upper story of 237, with all its brood and bees, and put it on 235, taking out the queen and putting her back in the lower story on 237. Then we looked to see what brood we could get in the seven colonies that acted as feeders, without reducing any of them to less than four or five brood This time we found six brood, which we took without any bees, and put on 237.

This was the regular program each time · forming nuclei with the brood, bees, and cells on 235; putting all brood and bees from 237 on 235, always leaving the queen at 237; and then getting for 237 a fresh stock of brood wherever it could be spared

As none of the assisting colonies were overdrawn, they would be getting stronger, so that up to a certain point more brood could be drawn each time. July 18, for the first time, more brood was drawn than it was thought wise to give to 237, there being twenty frames in all. Sixteen of these, or two hives full, were taken for 237, the other four were used to strengthen some of the nuclei. Not the weakest nuclei were strengthened, but

Fig. 91.—Nucleus Hives.

the earliest and strongest, for by being helped these would become strong enough to be helpers in turn. In fact, toward the last of the season, when there was little time for nuclei to grow up, the earlier nuclei rendered substantial aid to the later ones, at least one of them yielding as many as nine frames of brood. The first nu-

clei were formed June 21, as already mentioned; the last
were formed August 23.

I have gone thus fully into detail, because I believe
this plan can be used successfully by any one who has
only a small number of colonies and is desirous of increase. The first nuclei are formed early enough in the
season so that they have more than time enough to become strong colonies, and the latest must be formed
only in sufficient numbers so that they can be strengthened up as soon as the queen gets to laying

NUCLEUS PLAN OF INCREASE

With nucleus hives for queen-rearing, as already
described, it is easy to carry out the nucleus system in
the strictest sense I go to a nucleus with a laying queen,
preferring a nucleus with two or three frames, take all
the frames with queen and adhering bees, put them in
an empty hive, and set the hive on an empty stand A
week later a frame of brood may be added. It will be
better if it can be given with adhering bees, and still better if the bees can be queenless. Still, there is no great
danger to the queen in any case, although the weaker the
nucleus when strange bees are given, the greater the
danger to the queen A week later on, two frames of
brood and bees may be added, and the queen will be safer
if these two frames are taken from two different colonies
The colony will then be strong enough to be left to its
own devices.

NUCLEUS BUILDING UP WITHOUT HELP.

Indeed, it is not necessary to do anything more than
to let a nucleus stand without any help in a fair season,
if it can stand *long enough* My assistant is inclined to
be quite optimistic in some things, and one August she
expressed her belief that a nucleus of two frames with a

laying queen would be able without any assistance, if
started on that date, Aug. 6, to build up into a colony
strong enough to winter. I said that would be asking
too much, and we would put the matter to the test. So
two frames of brood with adhering bees were put in a
hive on a new stand, and two days later a laying queen
was given. The two frames of brood were rather better
than the average, for I wanted her to see that even with
an extra chance it was too late in the season for any such
growth. I don't know whether she watched that colony
on the sly or not, but I did. Looking at it every few
days, I could see no gain—if anything it grew weaker.
Then I thought I could see a little gain, and in twelve
days from the time it was started the two frames of

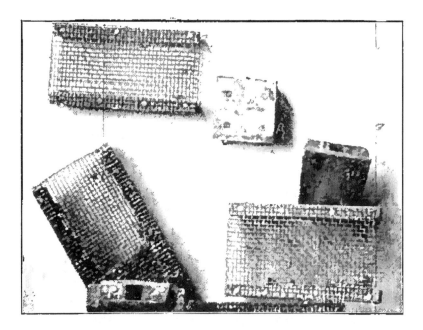

Fig. 92.—Improved Miller Queen-Cages.

brood had increased to two and a half. Five days later
there were three brood, and from that on it walked right

along to a fair colony, although it had to be fed up for winter. But I would not want to count on starting for a full colony so late as that in all seasons, especially if the frames of brood were not the very best.

INCREASE WITHOUT NUCLEI.

These different ways are all on the nucleus plan. Just one more way I want to mention, and it is not on the nucleus plan, but if queens are on hand I think I like it as well as any. We take four colonies, and the first thing is to have all four strong before anything is done Then we take an empty hive-body without any bottom-board, and into it we put two frames of brood without any bees from the first hive (a few bees will do no harm), the same from the second, and the same from the third, filling out the hive with two empty combs or combs with some honey Upon one of the central frames we nail a provisioned introducing cage containing a laying queen. Upon the fourth hive we put a queen-excluder, and on this we set our hive full of brood, and cover it up. Three or four hours later, or twenty-four hours later if more convenient, this hive is set upon a bottom-board on a new stand, and the work is all done. A way that is easier, and nearly as good, is to set the hive with the six brood immediately in place of the fourth hive, setting the fourth hive in a new place. The returning field-bees will populate the new hive Ten days or two weeks later the performance may be repeated if the season is prosperous, and this may be repeated a number of times. Of course empty combs or foundation will take the place of the two frames of brood drawn from each hive. An advantage of this plan is that it makes a strong colony at once, and there is no danger of being caught with a number of weaklings on a sudden cessation of the harvest Each new colony formed will in its turn soon be able to take its part in the game to start still others.

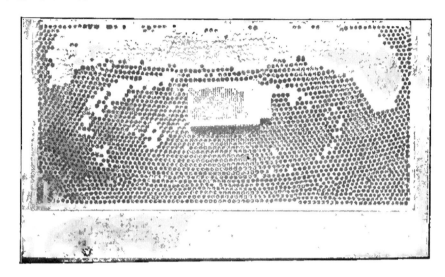

Fig. 93.—Cayed Queen-Cell.

SHAKING BEES OFF COMBS.

In this last plan, since the frames of brood are taken without bees, there is a good deal to be done in the way of cleaning bees off the combs. While it does not matter if a few bees should be left on the combs, it does matter greatly that care be taken to make sure that the queen is not among the bees taken. So it is well to *brush* the combs tolerably clean, and then one can easily see whether the queen is present. Before brushing, however, most of the bees should be *shaken* off, for if this is rightly done it will be a saving of time.

FINAL TAKING OFF OF SECTIONS.

When the time comes that the bees are expected to do no more work in the sections, whether that be immediately at the close of the clover harvest or later, the supers with their sections are all brought home and piled up in the honey-room. On some accounts it is better if the sections can be taken out of the supers at once and taken care of, and on other accounts it is better they should stand for some time It is a very difficult thing to scrape the bee-glue from sections while the weather is still hot, and as disagreeable as it is difficult. There may be some unsealed cells of honey in the outer cells of some sections, and this will have little chance to evaporate if it is thin, after the sections are in the shipping-cases. So the sections are likely to stand for some time in the supers after all are taken off, being blocked up as in Fig. 79.

FUMIGATING SECTIONS

Formerly it was necessary to fumigate the sections with sulphur after they were brought into the house, the fumigation being repeated two or three weeks later. I suppose I should now prefer bisulphide of carbon to sulphur for fumigation, but for several years I have not found it necessary to fumigate. Formerly the larvæ of the bee-moth would make bad work if fumigation were omitted, and sometimes in spite of it, but now there is no trouble I don't know what makes the difference, unless it be that formerly there was so large a percent of black blood in my bees.

When the time does come for taking the sections all out of the supers, the work is gone at in earnest and continued until all the marketable sections are in their shipping-cases ready for market. It will be understood that all supers taken off before the last, have been handled as heretofore mentioned, the marketable sections having all been piled up in the honey-room and the others returned as "go-backs," and the last lot taken off will consist of every sort, from foundation untouched by the bees up to sections entirely filled and sealed.

SORTING THE SECTIONS.

Philo sorts the sections into four classes as he takes
them out, although some supers are assigned to one class
or another without being taken out, because all in the
super are of one kind. One lot consists of dry sections,
or those in which the foundation either has not been
touched by the bees, or else has been drawn out so little

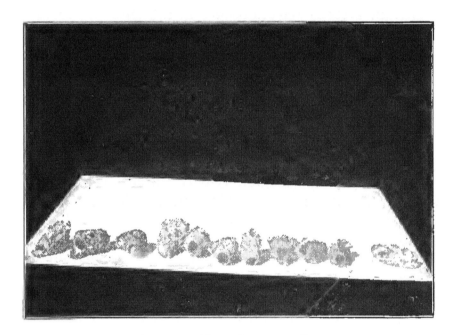

Fig. 94.—Vacated Queen-Cells.

that no drop of honey has been put in it. These are put
in a pile by themselves.

FEEDER SECTIONS.

The second lot consists of those which have just a
few drops of honey in them, up to those which are not
more than half filled. Some entire supers will be assigned to the first or second lot without being taken out
of the super at all. When a super feels pretty light, it is

inspected with some care by looking through it from the under side. If it is found that there is no honey in any section in the super, it goes to the dry pile without any taking out. If there is honey in the super, but no section in it more than half filled, it goes to the second pile without being emptied, even if there is only one section in the super containing any honey, and that section having only a few drops.

BEES EMPTYING SECTIONS.

The supers of sections in this second pile are called "feeders," because the honey in them is to be fed back to the bees (Fig. 96) Usually this feeding is not done until all the "feeders" are ready for the bees. They are taken into the shop cellar, and if there are only a few of them they are put in piles bee-tight with an opening at the top and another at the bottom only large enough for one or two bees to pass at a time If the number of supers is sufficiently large, say half as large as the number of colonies in the home apiary, then the supers are set singly all around against the wall of the cellar so as to make them as easily accessible to the bees as possible. When there are only a few sections, if the bees have free access to them they will tear the combs to pieces.

When all the "feeders" are in the cellar, then the door is opened wide, and the bees help themselves The reasons for having these "feeders" in the cellar rather than outdoors are, first, that I want to keep the bees away from them until the whole of them are ready for the attack; second, that in the cellar they are safe from the rain. The best of these emptied "feeders" furnish "baits" for the following season

UNMARKETABLE SECTIONS.

The third pile Philo makes consists of those which are more than half filled with honey, but not good enough to be marketable (Fig. 97). This pile is never very large, and is easily gotten rid of at home, together with some help from relatives. Some of it will make as fine appearance as any honey when placed on the table, although the under side on the plate may have too many unsealed and unfilled cells to admit it into the marketable class. There may also be some broken sections, for sections have a fashion of falling with half a chance.

BEES CLEANING DAUBY SECTIONS.

Sometimes it happens that a section otherwise good is spoiled, and badly spoiled, in appearance by having

Fig. 95.—Miller Frame.

honey from some section above leak all over one or both of its faces. Miss Wilson hit upon a plan for having

such sections cleaned up in short order, and with very little trouble. She puts them in a super, puts the super over a colony of bees, and an hour later, if the bees are active, they are taken from the hive as good as new.

The rest of the sections that do not go into one of these three piles are merchantable sections. That makes four kinds into which Philo sorts them, and you will see that it is possible out of one super to take sections that will go into all four of the piles. Of course there is always standing a super ready for any odd sections of each kind, that is, a super for dry sections, another for "feeders," etc.

FIRST PART OF CLEANING SECTIONS

Having now told how Philo sorts the sections, let me further tell what he does with them. When he comes to a super that does not go entire to the first or the second pile, the sections are taken out in the manner described on previous pages, leaving the contents of the super upside down on a board. The T tins are lifted off, and any sections that are not marketable are picked off and their places supplied with those that are marketable. Then the super that was taken from them is replaced by a box without top or bottom, that is, it is much like the super, only it is perhaps an inch longer, an inch wider, and an inch shallower than a T super, the exact size not being important. A piece of board is wedged into one side, and another into one end, so as to hold the sections firmly in place (Fig. 98). A case-knife with the whole length of its edge held at right angles to the sections sweeps back and forth, and when this has made the surface fairly clean, No 2 sandpaper is used. Then a board similar to the one under the sections is laid on top, and with one hand under the under board and the other over the upper board he turns the whole upside down. The knife and sandpaper now do their work on the tops of the sections. Then the wedges are taken out, the box removed, and the boardful of sections is slid along the table to the one who is scraping. This table, which is very convenient, is 8 feet long, and 3 ft. 9 in. wide.

FINAL SCRAPING OF SECTIONS

Miss Wilson generally does all the scraping; that is, all the scraping besides what Philo has done, and sometimes his part, as in Fig. 98. She sometimes scrapes on a board on her lap, but usually on one of the small tables heretofore mentioned (Fig 99). If the section should rest upon the table, the knife used in scraping could not freely reach the lowest parts, so a loose block lies on the board, on which the sections rest. Another advantage of the block is that the accumulation of propolis is not so much in the way The size of this block is not material, it may be an inch thick, four inches long or longer, and two inches wide or wider The block could be nailed down, but it is more convenient to have it loose, so as to scrape the propolis off the table from time to time. The scrapings have generally been thrown away, but with a steam wax-press it may pay well to get the wax out of it. Possibly propolis may yet be a marketable commodity.

The knife used is a steel case-knife kept very sharp. The sides and edges of the sections are to be scraped, and, if necessary, sandpaper follows the knife. The finishing touches are put on Philo's work, knife-marks, pencil-marks, and any discolored spots being carefully removed.

A scraper should be a careful person, or in ten minutes' time he will do more damage than his day's work is worth. Even a careful person seems to need to spoil at least one section, before taking the care necessary to avoid injuring others. But when the knife makes an ugly gash in the face of a beautiful white section of honey, that settles it that care will be taken afterward

PACKING SECTIONS IN SHIPPING-CASES.

The scraper has in easy reach two shipping-cases. In one, as fast as they are scraped, are put all sections that are not in any way faulty, such as appear in Fig 100   In the other are put any which are a little off color, either as to comb or honey, or which have some cells un-sealed   These must be sold as second-class at a reduc-tion of about 2 cents a pound.   In Fig 101 are shown six such sections, the upper three having the best side out and the lower three having the poorest side out.

KIND OF SHIPPING-CASES

For some years I used double-tier shipping-cases holding twenty-four sections each, the upper tier resting on a little board supported by two other little boards, so that no weight came upon the lower tier   A pile of such cases showed a greater proportion of honey in its surface than a pile of single-tier cases, and for this reason I liked it, but it was odd goods, and so I changed to single-tier cases   I have used mostly the twelve-section case, as shown in Fig. 102   But please do not think that all my honey looks as well as that in Fig 102   The specimens in Fig. 100 are fairer samples, although they are pos-sibly a little below the mark

I have used some single-tier cases holding twenty-four sections (Fig 103).   These are not so nice and firm to handle as the smaller cases, but it costs less to pack a ton of honey in the larger than in the smaller cases.   Grocers who sell by the case are inclined to pre-fer the larger case, for they say a customer who buys a case at a time will as readily buy a twenty-four-section case as a twelve-section case

VENEERING.

The most difficult thing about the packing is to prevent veneering. It seems to come so natural, when a

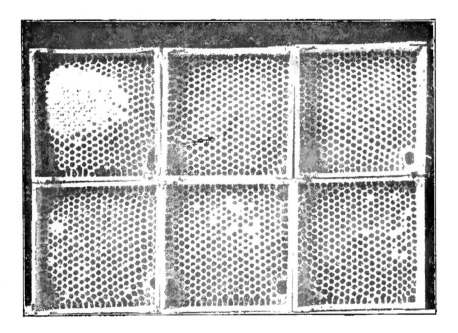

Fig. 96.—Feeder-Sections.

particularly white and straight section goes into the case, to put it next the glass, best side out at that. But it is especially desirable that the outside shall be a fair index of the entire contents of the case. In the long run there is money to be made by it, to say nothing of the feeling of satisfaction.

HONEY-SHOW.

When the cases are filled and weighed, they are stacked up in piles, and these piles are mostly—perhaps always—so arranged as to make the best show possible. There is no object in this beyond the pleasure it gives the family to see it for a few days, perhaps only for a

day   But the sight is a beautiful one so long as it lasts,
as I think you will agree with me if you look at Fig 104

PLACE TO KEEP HONEY

I have sold a crop of honey before it was off the
hives, and sometimes I have kept part of a crop over till
spring.

In any case the honey for home use in spring must
be kept over. It is not the easiest thing in the world to
keep it through the winter in good shape If kept cold
it is apt to granulate or candy, as it is usually called If
allowed to freeze, the combs crack and look bad, and in
time the honey oozes out of the cracks Honey is
deliquescent, absorbing from the atmosphere a large
amount of water if conditions are favorable. Try putting some common salt in a place where you think of
keeping honey, if the salt remains dry, so would honey.
But a place that is suitable at one time may not be at
another. Years ago I filled the back end of the honey-
room with honey It was a good place for it, the outside
walls were thin and the heat of the sun made it a hot
place When cold weather came, however, it was a bad
place, and the lower sections at the back part—beautiful,
snowy-white, when first put in—became watery and
dark-looking A fire for cooking was kept in the adjoining room, and although there seemed but very little
steam in the air, by the time it got to the back end of the
room, and settled to the lower part, there was enough to
spoil hundreds of sections You see, warm air is like
a sponge to take up moisture, and cold squeezes the
moisture out of it The point to see to, then, is to have
no air coming from a warmer place to the place where
the honey is I would sooner risk honey in a kitchen
with a hot fire and plenty of steam, than in a room without fire and with a door partly opened into a sitting-

room where no water or steam is ever kept. Indeed, a kitchen is quite a good place to keep honey, the higher up the better.

KEEPING HONEY IN GARRET.

It is well known that a cellar, except in particularly dry localities, is about the worst place in which to keep

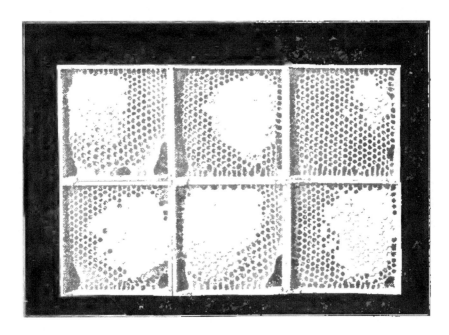

Fig. 97.— Unmarketable Sections.

honey; but it is not so well known that the place the farthest removed from the cellar—the garret—is one of the very best places. My mother kept some sections throughout the latter part of summer in a garret, and after enduring the freezing of the following winter they were as fine as when first put there. The roasting heat of the summer in that garret had so ripened the honey as to make it proof against injury from freezing.

GRANULATED HONEY.

If comb honey becomes granulated or watery, I know of no way to restore it If for home use, or if one happens to have a market where extracted honey sells for a good price, the sections may be put in stone crocks *slowly* melted, being sure it is not overheated, and then when cool, the cake of wax may be lifted off the honey

The best place to keep comb honey is also the best place to keep extracted; but if extracted honey becomes granulated or watery, it may be restored to its former, or even a better condition If thin and not granulated, by setting it on the reservoir of a cook-stove and letting it remain days enough, it will become thick I suppose you may have known this, and also that extracted honey, when granulated, may be liquefied by slowly heating, but did you know that when thin honey is warmed for a long time the flavor is improved? I have had the flavor improved and could attribute it to nothing but remaining a couple of weeks on the reservoir. I do not mean by this that if fine-flavored honey in good condition is placed on the stove reservoir it will be improved Most people, however, who have had much to do with honey, must have noticed that when extracted honey becomes thin from attracting moisture from the atmosphere, it seems to acquire a different flavor—perhaps I might say it has a sharp taste—and the slow heating seems to restore it partly if not wholly to its former condition.

RIPENING HONEY

The same thing is true of honey which is taken thin from the hive, not yet having been brought to proper density by the bees

There is a difference of opinion as to whether honey, or perhaps nectar, evaporated outside of the hive, is equal to that which remains in the hive till thick Of course, no large amount could be evaporated on a stove reservoir. Some bee-keepers have large tanks in which to evaporate honey by the sun or other heat.

It must not be understood that when honey has really soured it can be made good by the process mentioned.

Fig. 98.—Sections Wedged for Scraping.

The only thing is to use it for vinegar; and fine vinegar it will make.

DRAINING EXTRACTED HONEY.

There is another plan which I have used to secure some extra-fine extracted honey for our private use.

Whether it could be used profitably on a large scale, I cannot say   There are, however, always people who are ready to pay a high price for an extra article   After a crock of clover honey has granulated, I turn it on its side or upside down, and let it remain days enough to drain off all the liquid part   If drained long enough, the residue—and this will be nearly all the crockful—will be as dry as sugar, and when this is liquefied by slow heating it makes a delicious article   It will, however, granulate very easily a second time   On a larger scale, the liquid might be drained off by boring a hole at the lower part of a barrel of granulated honey   I spoke of treating clover honey in this way; I do not know what other kinds may be treated the same way, but I have had some granulated honey of smooth, even texture, from which no liquid part could be drained   When set to drain, the whole mass would roll slowly out.

MARKETING HONEY.

I have had no uniform way of marketing honey. I should prefer in all cases to sell the crop outright for cash, if I could get a satisfactory price; but some years I can do better to sell on commission   Judgment must be used as to limiting commission-men to a certain price. Some commission-men will sell off promptly at any price offered, and when sending to such men it is best to name a certain figure, below which the honey must not be sold I have sold in my home market, as well as in towns near by, and have shipped to nine of the principal cities, and it would be an impossibility for me to say what would be my best market next year. Prices vary according to the yield in different parts of the country. If shipping to a distant point in cold weather, I keep up a hot fire to warm the honey twenty-four hours before shipping   If very cold I wait for a warm spell.

LOADING SECTIONS WHEN SHIPPING.

On a wagon, the length of a section should run across the wagon—on a car lengthwise of the car. Convenience of packing in a wagon, however, is of first consideration, for with careful driving it matters little which

Fig. 99.—Scraping Sections.

way the sections are placed. On the other hand, no matter what the inconvenience, I would have the sections in a railroad car so that when a heavy bump comes the sections must take it endwise. I always prefer, if possible, to load the honey directly into the car myself. Then I know that it will carry well, unless the engine does an unreasonable amount of bumping

PACKING SECTIONS IN A CAR.

Very likely a number of cases of honey packed in a crate do not need any special care in loading; but if I can make sure that the honey will go through to its destination without any reloading, I prefer to put the cases in the car one by one. If the number of cases is so small that there is no need to pile one case on another, then the cases are put in one end of the car and kept in place by a strip of common inch lumber nailed on the floor If there are enough cases so they must be tiered up, then the lower tier has a strip nailed on the floor as before, but each of the upper tiers is fastened differently. On each side of the car is nailed a cleat to support a fence-board which runs across the width of the car, resting flat like a shelf on these cleats. Another cleat is nailed on the side of the car over the board, so it can move neither up nor down The board is up tight against the cases, perhaps a little above their middle. Then a third cleat is nailed on each side of the car against the board to prevent the board from moving in the least.

If there is a space at the side of the car, straw is packed hard into it beside the cases. If the space is very small, pieces of old wooden separators may be wedged in. Newspapers are laid on the bottom of the car under the cases, and newspapers tacked on top of them.

HOME MARKET.

Much has been said about cultivating a home market, but there are two sides to the matter If bee-keepers from neighboring towns come in and supply my home market at 2 cents per pound less than my honey nets me when shipped to a distant market, about all I can do is to leave the home market in their hands. I suspect, however, that it would have been to my advantage to have paid more attention to developing my home market for extracted honey..

HOME VERSUS DISTANT MARKET.

In deciding between a home and a distant market, there are more things to be taken into consideration than are always thought of. There is breakage in transportation, and the greater the distance the greater the risk. If I can load my honey into a car myself, and it goes to its destination without change of cars, I do not feel very anxious about it. On this account a car-load is safer than a small quantity, for a full car-load may be sent almost any distance without re-shipping. If re-shipped, it

Fig. 100.—Sections Ready for Casing.

is not at all certain how it will be packed in a car. I once sent a lot of honey to Cincinnati, and when it ar-

rived at its destination, the sections were actually lying
on their sides ! I suppose the railroad hands who packed
it in the car at the last change, thought the glass was
safest from breaking if the case was put glass side down.
The strangest part about it was that I lost nothing by
the breakage The dogged persistence of a German
consignee obliged the railroad company to pay all damage; for the consignee was that staunch German and
genial friend of bee-keepers—the late C F Muth. It is
the only case in which I have known a railroad company
to pay for breakage of honey

There is less danger of breakage by freight than by
express Besides danger of breakage, there is risk of
losing in various ways. You may not be able to collect
pay for your honey. If sent on commission, the price
obtained may be less than the published market report
You have no means generally to know how correct the
claims for breakage may be In fact, unless you know
your consignee to be a thoroughly honest man, you are
almost entirely at his mercy. A quarter or half a pound
may be taken off each case by the claim that it is custom
to reject fractions,

PRICES IN HOME AND DISTANT MARKET.

Taking all these things into consideration, together
with the cost of freight and shipping-cases, it must be
a good price that will justify a man to ship off honey to
the neglect of his home market If shipped to be sold
on commission, providing he ships to a near market, the
price should be at least $2\frac{1}{2}$ cents per pound more than he
can get in his home market, to justify his shipping If
he ships to a distant market the difference should be still
more, as the additional freight may make a difference
of 1 cent per pound or more, and the risk of breakage
becomes greater.

Not always, however, must I be willing to sell in my home market for less than I can get abroad. If there is

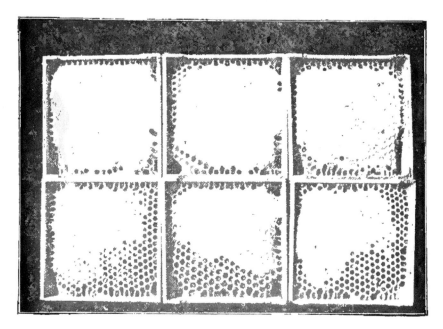

Fig. 101.—Second-Class Sections.

a year of dead failure in my locality, or so nearly a failure that the home market must be at least partly supplied from elsewhere, then I should get more for my honey than the grocers will have to pay in the large city markets, for they must add freight to the price they pay there.

FALL FEEDING.

Some seasons are so poor that the bees do not get enough throughout the whole season to carry them through the winter. One year I took no surplus, and fed 2,800 pounds of granulated sugar for winter stores. Some years the clover crop will be a failure, but plenty of stores will be gathered later in the season to carry the bees over winter. It is not always easy to tell in advance just what will be, but it is best to err on the safe side ; and it is no harm to have more stores on hand than are actually needed.   It is also better to have the feeding done early.   If the feed is given so early that it can be given thin enough, the bees make chemical changes in it that make it better for winter

FEEDING SYRUP.

Formerly I did not take this into account, and syrup was prepared that approached the consistency of honey. Water was put in a vessel on the stove, and when at or near the boiling-point granulated sugar was slowly stirred in at the rate of five pounds of sugar to a quart of water.   When the sugar was about dissolved, an even teaspoonful of tartaric acid for every twenty pounds of sugar previously dissolved in water, was stirred into the syrup, for without the acid the syrup is likely to turn into sugar in the combs when fed so thick   If I were to feed late in September, or in October, I think I should prefer the same syrup now.

FEEDING EARLY FOR WINTER.

But by feeding in August or early in September the work can be made much easier, and at the same time the food will be better for the bees   For they will so manipulate the thin feed given them that no acid will be needed, making their winter stores much more like the stores they obtain from the flowers.   There is nothing complicated about the feeding, and there is not the same trouble with robbers as when syrup is made   First, the feeders are all put on, and left standing uncovered. Then the amount of sugar needed in each feeder is put in dry, whether that be two pounds or fifteen pounds   Then I go around to each feeder, and, making a depression in the center of the sugar, put in half a pint or more of water. I do this rather than to put in the full quota of water at first, because in the latter case it is possible that the water would force its way into the reach of the bees without having much sweetness in it, for I forgot to say that I use the Miller feeder. I am not sure that this precaution is necessary, but it can do no harm. I now go around and put in each feeder about as much water as will balance the sugar, counting either by pints or pounds. Of course, if twelve pounds or more of sugar should be in the feeder, it will be impossible to balance the sugar with water. In that case I put in all the water I can. Next day or so the liquid will be used out, and I can fill up again. Indeed, in many cases where equal parts of sugar and water are given, the water will be mostly out by the next day, leaving only damp sugar in the feeder, and more water must be added. Practically, this is giving the feed very thin, and I suspect it is all the better. I have never had any trouble from robber-bees while leaving the feeders open in the way mentioned, of course covering up as soon as water is all in; although I have had trouble by leaving a cover on a feeder that was not bee-tight, and with such a cover it is better first to put on a cover of cotton cloth that hangs down all around.

SELECTING COLONIES TO FEED.

I have spoken as if a feeder was put over each colony lacking stores. That is by no means always the case—indeed, not often the case. There are reasons why it is better to have a comparatively small number of colonies do the storing, taking sealed combs from these to give to the weaker ones. It is a good deal less trouble, when the feeding is begun in good season, to have one colony store enough for five or ten others besides itself than it is to have feeders on all of the five or ten colonies.

Some colonies will store better than others, and the best can be chosen

FEEDING IN FALL FOR SPRING.

For some reason, bees seem to store from a feeder much better late in the season than they do before the harvest time. The greater strength of the colonies and the warmer weather would make one expect a difference, but it has always seemed to me that there was more difference than could be accounted for without some other reason. So it is desirable at this time to have not only enough combs filled to bridge over the winter, but to supply any possible deficiency up to the harvest time.

An upper story of empty combs is put on, possibly two. As fast as combs are completely filled and sealed they can be removed and replaced by empty ones. If it is desired to have combs filled out upon foundation, beautiful work will be done upon them in these upper stories. It will easily be seen that it is less trouble to add sugar from time to time as needed, also to add water as needed, than it is to apportion the smaller amounts to a number of colonies No great matter if too much or too little of one or the other is present; the thing will regulate itself. For with cold water there is no danger of the feed being too thick, and all the harm of too large a proportion of sugar is that the bees will have to wait for more water when it is too dry to give down. On the other hand, they will continue taking it down when it is much thinner than half-and-half, and perhaps it is all the better manipulated when very thin.

Perhaps it would do as well to feed as described under wholesale feeding in spring, but in that case I should want the feed quite thin, and there would be more danger from robbers, and more danger of having thin feed left in the feeders to sour.

DIFFICULTY OF DECIDING ABOUT STORES.

It is not an easy thing to determine just what amount of stores is needed to carry a colony through to the next harvest. Some colonies use more than others under apparently the same conditions. Experience will enable one to judge fairly well by inspection as to the amount of stores present, but one can be more exact

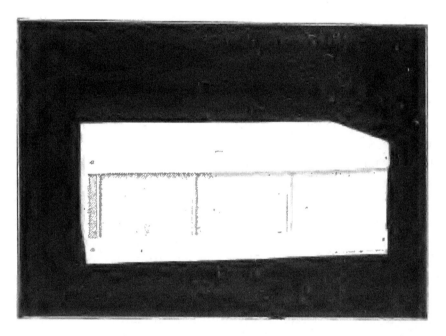

Fig. 102.—12-Section Shipping-Case.

about it by actual weighing. Besides, with proper conveniences for it, the weighing takes less time. But two colonies may weigh exactly the same, and one may have abundance and the other may starve, because, although weighing the same, one had much more honey than the other. One had much pollen, the other little. Or, the combs of one were new, and the combs of the other very old and heavy. The only safe way is to have all so heavy that under any and all circumstances there will be no danger. So we aim to have each hive with its contents, its cover, and its bottom-board, weigh as much as fifty pounds. Some will weigh so much more than this that hefting will show that there is no need of weighing. Even a strong colony that stored well throughout the season in a prosperous year may have had the brood-chamber so stocked with brood that not enough honey was in the brood-chamber, so it is well to heft and weigh even in the best seasons, and to do this late enough so that storing from flowers need no longer be taken into account, and so early that there will be abundance of time for the bees to arrange matters to their liking in the brood-chamber.

Whether it would not be best always to provide in advance to have the bees store enough honey in extra combs so there would never be any need to feed sugar except in years of downright failure, is a question that might be considered.

WEIGHING COLONIES.

A common spring balance with a capacity of eighty pounds is used for weighing (Fig. 105) An endless rope passes around the hive under the cleat at each end, then the hook of the spring balance passes under the two parts of the rope over the hive, and the slack is taken up by tying a string around the two parts under the hook. A hickory stick used as a lever passes through the ring of the upper part of the spring balance, the short end of the lever being supported by a light frame-work that stands on the adjoining hive When all is properly adjusted. the long end of the lever is raised, and the weight is read, and then taken down, so that a comb or combs may be added to bring up to the desired weight. If no precaution is taken, the spring balance, when first raised, will slide on the lever down against one's hands or shoulder. To prevent this a stout string has one end tied to the short end of the lever, and the other end tied to the ring of the balance, so as to keep it within bounds.

NUCLEI IN FALL.

When the time for rearing queens is over, the nuclei will be in various conditions. Some will be weak, some strong, some queenless. Here will be a nucleus hive containing three strong nuclei with a good laying queen in each nucleus. Nothing is to be done in such a case but to leave the three nuclei as they are, to be carried into the cellar without any further preparation, unless it be to give some honey if it be needed. In the case of the middle nucleus, that will mean exchanging their comb for one as

Fig. 103.—24-Section Case.

much as two-thirds or three-quarters full of honey. In the nuclei at the sides of the hive, the heaviest frames of

honey will be toward the center of the hive This will en-
courage the bees to cluster in that direction, thus con-
centrating the warmth of the three nuclei.

UNITING NUCLEI.

But the hives with three strong nuclei and three
queens will be exceptional Some will have only two
queens, some one. If a nucleus hive has in it only one
queen, it may be that a full hive is set in place of the nucleus hive, the contents of the three apartments of the
nucleus hive put into this full hive, and, if necessary,
enough nuclei added from elsewhere to make a fair colony If none of the nuclei in any one nucleus hive be
sufficiently strong where there is only one queen in the
hive, then the nucleus with the queen is likely to be put
in some nucleus hive that has contained only two queens
In some cases one of the division-boards is taken away,
making one of the compartments large enough to receive
five frames, besides the other with the three frames. Thus
the nucleus in the larger compartment may be built up to
a tolerably fair colony

Thus you will see that there is little or no destroying
of queens, the effort being to have each queen supported
by a good force of bees, considering the size of her compartment No attention is paid to the matter of trying to
make bees stay where they are put If they don't like to
stay they don't need to, they'll count somewhere But as
they are mostly queenless bees that are moved, they are
not bad about returning

DOUBLE HIVES FOR WINTER.

Not only have I wintered nuclei two and three in a
hive, but a few years ago I had considerable experience
in wintering full colonies in double hives If I had not
changed from ten-frame to eight-frame hives I should

have continued the practice, but an eight-frame hive makes too cramped quarters for two full colonies, even

Fig. 104.—Honey-Show.

in winter. Still, I approximate it with five frames on one side and three on the other, and of course the hive could be divided to take four frames on each side.

There is nothing new or original about two colonies in one hive, among others Dzierzon's twin hives having been highly esteemed by him and others for many years. These, however, are used the same all the year around, and my use of them is only during the time of year when bees can be crowded into a less space than a full hive.

From the time the bees are fed in the summer or fall, till perhaps the middle of May, most of my colonies would have room enough in one-half of a ten-frame hive. I am not sure that any of them ever need more room through the fall and winter, and in the spring they need no more till more than four frames are needed for brood. With some, this may come quite early, but I think I should be

well satisfied if I could get all my colonies to contain
four combs well filled with brood by the middle of May.
Some of them may have at that time brood in nine or
ten frames, but more of them could have all their brood
crowded into three or four combs

ADVANTAGE OF DOUBLE HIVES.

Now, if during the time I have mentioned, we can
have two colonies in one hive, we shall, I think, find it
advantageous in more than one direction. It is a common thing for bee-keepers to unite two weak colonies
in the fall. Suppose a bee-keeper has two colonies in the
fall, each occupying two combs   He unites them so they
will winter better   If they would not quarrel and would
stay wherever they were put, he could place the two
frames of the one hive beside the two frames in the
other hive, and the thing would be done   Now suppose
that a thin division-board were placed between the two
sets of combs, would he not see the same result? Not
quite, I think, but nearly so. They would hardly be so
warm as without the division-board, but nearly so, and
both queens would be saved   In the spring it is desirable to keep the bees warm   If two colonies are in
one hive, with a thin division-board between them, they
will be much warmer than if in separate hives.   The
same thing is true in winter   I have had weak nuclei
with two combs come through in good condition during
a winter in which I lost heavily, these nuclei having no
extra care or protection other than being in a double
hive   You would understand the reason of all this easily
if in winter you would look into one of these double
hives in the cellar. On each side the bees are clustered
up against the division-board, and it looks exactly as if
the bees had all been in one single cluster, and then the
division-board pushed down through the center of the
cluster.

Now suppose we have 100 colonies that are all fed
up for winter and they are then put into double hives.
Please understand that there is little or no extra expense
for these double hives.   They are just the regular hives,
only we take special pains to see that the division-board
is perfectly bee-tight.   If the hives are to be hauled
home, as I haul mine each fall, there are only 50 instead of 100 to haul; just half the bulk, and a much less

Fig. 105.—Weighing Colonies.

weight than the 100 would be.   Just half the hives are
to be handled in taking in and out of winter quarters;
just half the room is occupied in winter quarters; and I
think, although I do not know, that the bees will winter
better than if only one colony in a hive.   If they are to
be taken, in the spring, to a distant apiary, there is the
advantage of hauling only 50 hives instead of 100.   If,
in the spring, any colony be found queenless it is in fine
position to be united with its fellow colony.

CHANGING FROM SINGLE TO DOUBLE HIVES

Possibly you may be ready to agree with me so far as to say, "Certainly, the thing looks desirable, but is it feasible? Will not the trouble counterbalance all advantage?" I know it is usually a matter of some trouble to change a colony from one location to another in the same apiary. I think, however, that I have reduced the trouble to a minimum I will give you my plan and you can judge for yourself.

As I have already told you, my hives stand in pairs, and I kept them so, years before I thought of double hives. Some time before the change is made to double hives, the entrances of the hives are closed at one side, so that the bees become accustomed to using the same side of the entrance that they will use when thrown into the double hive, that is, the right hand colony will use the right hand side of its entrance, and the left hand colony will use the left hand side of its entrance. Each colony will have four of its combs so solid with honey that it will be well provisioned.

Remembering that the two colonies of a pair are on the same stand, we now remove both hives from the stand and set the double hive on the middle of the stand Then the four combs from the right hand hive will be put with their bees in the right hand side of the double colony, and the rest of the bees brushed from the other combs. The left hand side is treated the same way. Some bees will still be left in the depopulated hives; so these hives can be set at each side, the entrance of the empty hive at the proper entrance of the double hive, and left there long enough for the bees to crawl in and join their companions.

The matter is now accomplished and it has been no long or difficult job. The bees use the new entrance *almost* as readily as the old. To them their hive seems moved less than its width to one side, and there is no possible danger of their entering the wrong place. I have tried it, and watched the result, therefore I speak of not what the bees *ought* to do, but what they *do* do.

CHANGING FROM DOUBLE TO SINGLE HIVES.

Can we as easily get them back into two hives in the spring when they become crowded in this double hive? Just exactly as easily. We simply reverse the operation. Take the double hive from its place and re-place it with the two hives, then remove the contents of the double hive and put them in the proper single hives, and the bees will go every time to the right place. I

Fig. 106.—Colonies Home from Out-Apiaries.

speak again from personal observation as to what the bees actually do.

BRINGING BEES HOME IN THE FALL.

In the fall, the bees must be brought home from the out-apiary so as to be wintered in the cellar

There are always a few things upon which bees can work till quite late; so it is desirable to be as late as possible bringing them home   They must, however, be brought home early enough so they will be sure of a good flight after being brought home and before being put in the cellar.   Some say they may be safely put into the cellar without the flight, but one winter part of mine were put in without a flight, and that part wintered distinctly worse than the others.   At the latest, I want them home before Nov. 1.   When brought home they are placed conveniently near the cellar door (Fig. 106).

WHEN TO PUT BEES INTO CELLAR.

It is a thing impossible to know beforehand just what is the best time to take bees into the cellar.   At best it can be only a guess   Living in a region where winters are severe, there are some years in which there will be no chance for bees to have a flight after the middle of November till the next spring, and I think there was one year without a flight-day after the first of November   One feels badly to put his bees into cellar the first week in November, and then two or three weeks later have a beautiful day for a flight. But he feels a good deal worse after a good flight-day the first week in November to wait for a later flight, then have it turn very cold, and after waiting through two or three weeks of such weather to give up hope of any later flight and put in his bees after two or three weeks' endurance of severe freezing   So it is better to err on the side of getting bees in too early.

Theoretically, the right time to cellar bees is the

next day after they have had their last flight for the season, and one must do the best one can to judge after any

Fig. 107.—Dripping-Pan Wax-Extractor.

flight-day whether it is the last or not. More than one reason can be given for taking in next day after a flight. The hives are dry; there are no accumulations of frost or ice inside; and the bees are unusually quiet. All the better if the next morning is cool, as it is likely to be. Sometimes, however, one cannot have everything as one wants it, and I have been caught taking in bees in a snow-storm. Better take them in during the storm than after it is all over and constantly growing colder. But it seems to do no harm for them to be taken in covered with snow.

PREPARING THE CELLAR.

For twenty-four hours before taking in—perhaps for several days—doors and windows of the cellar are kept wide open, so as to air it out thoroughly, and perhaps the walls are whitewashed and the floor limed, although this is generally done after taking out in the spring. Strips of boards are placed on the ground so that the bottom hive has its bottom-board an inch or two above the ground at the front end, and an inch more at the back end.

CARRYING IN HIVES.

Hives are carried in just as they are, because before the time for hauling bees home all false bottoms were removed, and the bottom-boards fastened to the hives where necessary. With the large ventilating space at the entrance, and with abundance of stores, there is no need to loosen the gluing of a cover from before the time a colony is hauled home till after the time for hauling back in spring

PILING HIVES IN CELLAR.

The hives are piled five high, each pile independent of the others, so jarring one hive can jar only four others. First a row of piles is put at the farther side of the cellar, the hives close side by side, entrances facing the wall, with a space of about two feet between them and the wall. Then another row is placed back to back close up against this row. Then comes a space of about two feet, and another row facing the space, so that entrances face each side of the space Then comes another row, back to back, and so on That makes the hives in double rows, back to back, with a two foot space in which to get at the entrances

As far as convenient, the heavier hives are put at the bottom, and lighter at top. It is easier work to do so, and the lighter ones have perhaps the advantage by being higher up, where it is a little warmer.

CARRYING IN BEES WHEN ROUSED UP.

Often the bees get so warmed up by the middle of the forenoon, that they fly out when their hive is lifted to be carried into the cellar.. In this case the hive is put back on its summer stand, and another colony, less wide-awake, is taken. But if the rousing up becomes general, operations must cease until the after-part of the day or the next morning. If for any reason, as the lateness of the season, or the fear of an approaching storm, it is thought best to carry in a hive whether the bees are willing or not, the entrance must be stopped. For this purpose—as there is no danger of suffocation from stopping for a short time—I know of nothing better than a large rag or cloth which will easily cover the entire entrance. The rag must be dripping wet In this condition it can be very quickly laid at the entrance, and being cold and wet the bees seem to be driven back by it, and when the rag is removed in the cellar, few if any bees come out If dry, the bees would sting the rag, and upon its removal in the cellar a crowd of angry bees would follow it.

WARMING THE CELLAR.

Some think it a bad thing to have fire in cellar I would rather have the right temperature without the fire. So I would in my sitting-room. But when the temperature in the sitting-room without a fire gets down in the neighborhood of zero, I would rather have the fire Same way in the cellar. In this latitude, 42 degrees north, I have known the mercury to reach 37 degrees below zero, and some winters there is very little of the time when my cellar is warm enough for the bees. A thermometer hangs centrally in the cellar, and I try to keep it at about 45 degrees. Sometimes it goes to 36 degrees, but not often, and not for long. Oftener it reaches 50 degrees, but that is neither often nor long.

STOVE IN CELLAR

Whenever the thermometer appears to have any fixed determination to stay below 45 degrees, a fire is started I would not think of using an oil-stove, or anything of the kind that would allow the gases to escape in the cellar. A chimney goes from the ground up through the house, and a hard-coal stove is used. Until last winter I used a common small cylinder stove, having an inside diameter of about 8 inches between the fire-brick Last winter I used a low-down open or Franklin stove, and I think I like it as well or better With either stove there is the open fire, and one might fear that the bees would fly into it, but they do not appear to do so   Neither does any harm come to the hives that stand within two feet of the stove, for the stove is right in the same room as the bees   A few minutes attention each morning and evening will keep the fire going continuously, in case it is needed continuously   There have been winters when fire was kept going nearly all the winter through, and other winters when little was needed The winter of 1901-02 was one of the mild ones   A fire started Dec. 21 was kept for three days   Another, Jan 27, lasted one day. A third started Feb 3 lasted seventeen days   I think the outer temperature was at no time more than 15 degrees below zero

HEAT FOR DIARRHEA.

I do not know for certain, but I *think* I have had good results at a time when diarrhea began to trouble the bees in the cellar, by making a hot fire and running up the temperature above 60 degrees   The bees would become very noisy, but after the cellar cooled down to the normal 45 degrees they were quieter than before, and I suspect the bees felt better.

VENTILATION OF CELLAR.

I believe heartily in the doctrine of pure air and plenty of it for man, beast, and bee. So I consider ven-

Fig. 108.—Screwing Down Wax-Press.

tilation a very important affair. With a two-inch space under the bottom-bars and a 12x2 entrance, there is no trouble about the ventilation of the *hive;* but no matter how well ventilated a hive may be, if the cellar in which it is placed contains nothing but foul air, how can the air in the hive be sweet?

FIRE FOR VENTILATION.

I am not sure but I should want a fire in a cellar for the sake of ventilation even if not needed for heat.

For the purpose of ventilation alone, the warmer the weather the more the fire in the cellar is needed. Of course there must be some limit to this, for when the temperature of the cellar goes above 60 degrees, the bees show signs of uneasiness.

WARM SPELLS IN WINTERING.

The most difficult time to keep the bees quiet in the cellar, is when a warm spell comes in the fall soon after taking them in, or early in the spring. At such times I open up the cellar at dark. If very warm, all doors and windows are opened wide and by morning generally all are quiet. I leave all open as long as possible in the morning, sometimes till noon; when the bees begin to fly out all must be darkened. Very likely it would be better if there were a way to admit air in abundance without admitting light.

COOLING AND AIRING CELLAR.

Years ago, when the temperature became too high in the cellar in spring, and I wanted to keep the bees in the cellar still longer, I tried cooling down with cakes of ice. But it was not satisfactory. The trouble was not so much with the *temperature* as the *quality* of the air. Then I learned that opening the cellar was more effectual.

OPENING CELLAR AT NIGHT.

The first time I tried that trick I got a pretty bad scare. It was in the spring, and there came a warm spell, lasting perhaps two or three days. It kept getting warmer in the cellar, and the bees kept getting noisier. At the same time I kept getting more uneasy, not knowing just what the end might be. After the trouble got pretty bad, I thought I would venture to open the cellar wide in the evening, hoping that it might become cooler through the night. I think it was 50 or 60 degrees outside, and not far from that in the cellar. The bees were quite noisy when the cellar was opened, and I listened closely for the quieting down. It didn't come On the contrary, the noise increased to a roar that could be heard some distance from the cellar, and the bees were running all over the hives, some of them hanging out in great clusters as if getting ready to swarm. I felt afraid they would all leave their hives and make a wreck I assure you I was badly frightened; but I didn't know of anything to do, so I didn't do anything As nearly as I now remember, I did not go to bed till I could recognize a little subsiding, and in the morning the bees were back in their hives as quiet as mice More than once since then I have gone through the same performance without being troubled by it; only the cellar is not allowed to get so bad before it is opened.

LETTING LIGHT IN CELLAR.

Here is a memorandum written March 14, 1902: "During the past eight days the weather has been unusually warm for the season, varying from 29 to 65 degrees The doors have been wide open day and night except on the two warmest days, and the (east) window part of the time. Three days ago it was 65 degrees in the afternoon. Within twenty-four hours the ground was covered with snow, and yesterday morning the mercury stood at 29 degrees. At 7 a. m to-day, it was 35 degrees without and 44 degrees in the cellar, doors and window having been open all night. At 9 a. m. it was

46 degrees outside and 45 degrees in the cellar   The sun
shone directly into some of the entrances near the window
without disturbing the bees.   At 10:30 a m it was 52
degrees outside and 47 degrees in the cellar; the bees
still quiet   At 11 a. m it was 53 degrees without and
48 degrees in cellar   In five minutes by the watch I
counted fifteen bees which flew to the window.   I then
closed the window, leaving the doors wide open.   At 12
o'clock it was still 53 degrees without and 49 degrees
in the cellar   In five minutes I counted five bees flying
to the door.   The light does not shine directly into the
room where the bees are, they being in an inside room.
I can see to read easily at the hives nearest the door   At
3 20 it was 55 degrees outside and 50 degrees in cellar
In five minutes I counted three bees flying to the door
It was then getting cloudy, the sun having been shining
most of the day.   I opened the window for five minutes
and twelve bees flew to it.   At 6 p m the window was
opened again, leaving all wide open till it should again
become bright enough on the next or some following day
to make the bees fly out, or cold enough to bring the
mercury down too far in the cellar."

I have not given this as an example of the perfection
of wintering.   It is far from that   But it shows that
after 119 days of confinement the bees will stand a good
deal of light and warmth without showing much insubor-
dination, providing they have an abundance of good air.
It must be higher than 45 degrees to induce them out
when in good condition.

SUB-EARTH VENTILATOR.

Some years ago I put in a sub-earth ventilator of 4-
inch tile, 100 feet long and 4 feet deep   It was of common porous drain-tile, and becoming a little skeptical of
the quality of the air admitted I allowed it to become

filled up. I am not sure that I did wisely. I am strongly of the opinion that an air-tight pipe large enough and deep enough would be a great aid to successful cellaring.

MICE IN BEE-CELLARS.

Mice are troublesome denizens of cellars in winter. Even if a cellar should be entirely free from them, they are likely to be brought into the cellar with the bees when the hives are brought in. Some winters I have closed the entrances with heavy wire-cloth having three meshes to the inch. This shuts out mice without hindering the free passage of bees. Even if a mouse is shut up in a hive, it will not be so bad as to let it have the free run of

Fig. 109.—Emptying Out Slumgum.

the cellar. Other winters traps have been used and various poisons, perhaps the most satisfactory poison being strychnine thinly spread upon very thin slices of cheese, the cheese being then cut into tiny squares.

CLEANING OUT DEAD BEES.

Aside from attending to warming and ventilating my cellar, and waging war against the mice, I think of no other attention given to the bees through the winter, except cleaning out the dead bees. For cleaning them out of those hives which have them—for some reason of which I am not yet sure, there are some hives which contain scarcely a dead bee—I have a very simple tool It is a piece of round, ¼-inch or smaller iron rod, with one end hammered flat for about two inches and bent at right angles, making something like a hook. With this hook I can reach into the hive under the frames and scrape out the dead bees.

I have a common kerosene hand-lamp with a sheet-iron chimney having a little mica window on one side—such as is used for heating water on lamps. This serves as a dark-lantern, making little light except in one direction. Holding the lamp in my left hand, I look in to see whether any live bees are in sight Often I see the cluster near the front of the hive, oftener at the center or back part of the hive, the bees looking as if dead, so still are they; but in a few seconds some one will be seen to stir. Sometimes the cluster will come clear down so as to touch the bottom-board, and sometimes not a bee will be seen below or between the bottom-bars When the cluster comes clear down, there may or there may not be bees on the bottom-board In any case, all the dead bees are cleaned out that can be got without disturbing the living. There is, as has been said, a difference as to the number of dead bees in different colonies, and there seems also a difference in different winters. In some cases perhaps the **dead** bees all reach the cellar bottom, in others staying in the hive. Last winter, 1901-02, the number on the bottom-boards was so small that it did not seem worth while to clean them out at all—perhaps the first time of such an occurrence.

SWEEPING UP DEAD BEES.

It is very unpleasant to have the dead bees under foot on the cellar bottom Some fasten them in the hive. Some sprinkle sawdust on the floor In either case they are left in the cellar to foul the air. It seems much better to sweep out the cellar. During the first part of the winter very few bees will be on the floor, and sweeping once a month will be enough, or more than enough. Toward spring the deaths will be very much more frequent, and the sweeping must be more frequent. Last winter the cellar was not swept till Jan. 29—seventy-five days after the bees were taken in Then it was swept again after respective intervals of twenty-one, nineteen, and five days, the quantity swept out each time being about the same That gives some idea of the greater mortality as spring approaches. Referring to the record, I find that one winter, when the bees were confined 124 days, the dead bees for each colony amounted to four-fifths of a quart or three-fifths of a pound, which made about 2,130 bees for each colony. I think the mortality is usually greater than that.

TOO-WARM CELLAR.

Heretofore one of the chief elements in the problem of wintering has been to keep the bees warm enough. Beginning with the winter of 1902-3 a new and different problem confronts me—that of keeping the bees cool enough. The coal famine following the great anthracite strike caught me with four hard-coal stoves and no coal to put in them—indeed, no prospect of getting any, and winter close at hand.

FURNACE IN CELLAR.

About that time my friend, E. R. Root, happened to be here, and strongly advised as the best way out of the dilemma to have a furnace put in—one big enough to heat the whole house, and of such character as to burn wood, green or dry, coal, hard or soft, and indeed anything having any inclination toward combustibility. I followed his advice, or rather I outran it, for I got a larger furnace than he thought advisable, the fire-pot being 27 inches in diameter. I am not sorry the furnace is so large so far as heating the house is concerned, for it makes a delightful summer temperature in any part of the house, no matter how cold the weather, without any of that unpleasant and unwholesome burnt-air effect. But it makes a matter of impossibilty for me to think of keeping the temperature of the bee-room down to 45 degrees and I am looking forward with some anxiety as to how the bees will come out in the spring.

UNFAVORABLE CONDITIONS.

Conditions, however, have been exceptionally unfavorable, so that if there should be a considerable loss in wintering it does not follow that such will usually be the case

The workmen that set up the furnace were late in finishing up the last part of the work in the cellar, so that the bees were not put in till the 8th of December. On that day the temperature was 8 degrees below zero. It would have been much better to have left them out for another flight if I had been sure of a day warm enough without waiting too long. But I was not sure of that, and I thought it better for them to be taken in in rather bad condition than to run the risk of leaving them out longer. The sequel showed I was wise in so doing, for no day warm enough for a flight came within a short time.   Indeed, no such day has come up to the first of February, and there is no great prospect of it till spring.

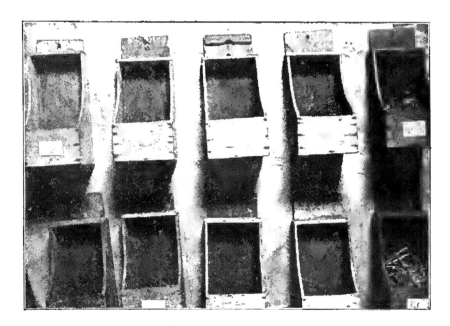

Fig. 110.—Nail Boxes.

A thin partition of lath and plaster is all that separates the bee-room from the room in which the furnace is located, and the thermometer in the bee-room generally shows a temperature of 50 degrees.   Some of the hot-air pipes pass through the bee-room overhead, and a thermometer laid on one of the two hives directly under one of these pipes nearest the furnace shows a temperature of 70 degrees.   The pipe is covered with asbestos paper, but there is only a space of about three inches between the pipe and the top of the hives.   There is plenty of room to set these colonies in a cooler place, but they will be allowed to stay right where they are to see what the result will be.   The first half of their winter's confinement does not seem to show that they are faring worse than other colonies.

The winter has been unusually warm, no day since the bees were taken in being as cold as the day on which they were taken in Keeping the doors more or less open all the time, and the window part of the time, the cellar cannot be kept entirely dark.

All these things are against successful wintering, but, as already said, even if the bees should come out in the spring in poor condition it is no proof that another winter would show the same result They are not likely to be taken in another winter after having suffered so much from cold, and the winter is not likely to be again so warm

VALUE OF PURE AIR.

But amid the discouraging circumstances there is one strongly redeeming feature—the bees have not suffered from impure air The simple fact that the air in the cellar is much warmer than it would be without the furnace gives assurance of better ventilation

I suspect that the value of pure air for wintering bees is underestimated, and that the reason that bees outdoors can stand confinement at a much lower temperature than they can in the cellar is not so much because of occasional flights as because of purer air So I am not without hope that notwithstanding unfavorable conditions the great compensation of pure air may help the bees to pull through.

KEEPING CELLAR OPEN.

At present writing a thaw of a few days' duration has kept the doors of the cellar open to their widest, night and day, the window being open but shaded, and the thermometer stands at 53 degrees in daytime, going down to 50 degrees at night. Being so warm and so light, a few bees are flying out all the time, and of course they fly out only to meet their death. But it would probably make matters still worse to make the cellar dark, for the increased heat, together with air less pure, would probably kill more bees, even if they should not fly out of the hives.

DRIPPING-PAN WAX-EXTRACTOR.

Before the introduction of the solar wax-extractor, the rendering of wax was generally reserved as winter's work, and indeed after the introduction of the solar it was often convenient to work up in winter some of the material saved up A very simple arrangement on a small scale did excellent work on much the same principle as the solar extractor, only the heat of the stove was used in place of solar heat.

An old dripping-pan (of course a new one would do) had one corner split open, and that made the extractor. The dripping-pan is put into the oven of a cook-stove with the split corner projecting out (Fig. 107). The opposite corner, the one farthest in the oven, is slightly raised by having a pebble or something of the kind under it, so that the melted wax will run outward. A dish set under catches the dripping wax, making the outfit complete Of course the material to be melted is put in the pan the same as in the solar extractor.

SOLAR WAX-EXTRACTOR

I do not know that the solar extractor has any advantage over the dripping-pan arrangement, except that the sun furnishes free heat. In either case, when old combs are melted, a good deal of wax remains in the refuse or slumgum, because the cocoons act much like sponges. Especially is this the case if more than a single thickness of comb is placed for melting.

STEAM WAX-PRESS

So when the German steam wax-press came, leaving the slumgum practically free from wax, the solar extractor had to take a back-seat, leaving wax-rendering again a proper thing for winter work.

The wax-press is placed upon the cook-stove (Fig. 108), and the work is done according to the instructions sent out with the machine. I find that time is an important element in the work, and that there is nothing to be gained by trying to hurry up matters by screwing down very hard. If the screw be turned down as tight as can be done without sliding the can around on the stove, that is all that is necessary. Then when the wax ceases to run it can be turned down again. Continuing in this way till no more wax runs, when the slumgum is turned out (Fig 109) it is so free from wax that it is not worth working over again. The wax saved by using the steam wax-press will pay immense interest on the money invested in its purchase.

OTHER WINTER WORK.

The work of getting sections ready for the hoped-for harvest of the coming summer has already been mentioned, and the winter affords opportunity for making up hives, supers, or any fixtures that may be needed. As these things are bought mostly in the flat, the chief part of the work is nailing, and it is a great convenience to have the different kinds of nails in their proper places ready for immediate use. A set of nail-boxes, part of which are seen in Fig. 110, serves the purpose excellently. The boxes are patterned somewhat after a tin nail-box I saw at a tin-shop. When a box is taken from its nail on the wall, laid flat and slightly shaken, the nails are easily picked up from the shallow part of the box.

Truth compels me to say that so many different persons find it convenient to use these boxes and inconvenient to return them, that of late the boxes are not always found in their proper places, and when the picture was taken they were assembled for that special occasion.

READING BEE-JOURNALS.

Most of the winter-time, however, is occupied with reading and writing. There are some thirty or forty bee-journals to be read, and a large part of them are printed in the German and French languages. I am a poor

Fig. 111.—" Busy at the Typewriter."

scholar in either German or French, so it is not strange if I sometimes get behind in my reading, to bring up in winter. I wish I could find the time to read over again at my leisure in winter all the bee-journals that I read more or less hurriedly in summer. But I never find the time. I used to think that if I ever lived to be fifty years old I would take things very leisurely. But I am now past fifty, and I never was so crowded in my life before.

WRITING FOR THE BEE-JOURNALS.

Besides the reading, there is the writing. Some extra writing usually to be done each winter, besides the regular work in that line   I have written "Stray Straws" for Gleanings in Bee-Culture ever since December, 1890, and four years later I began writing answers to questions in the American Bee-Journal. The thought of keeping up that work year in and year out, with never a vacation summer or winter, would be somewhat wearisome if it were not that I delight in the work. If any one of my readers should hesitate about sending to me any question connected with bee-keeping because of the thought that it will be unpleasant to me, let him disabuse his mind of any such thought   The receipt of such questions is a real pleasure.

One thing, however, that gives pain instead of pleasure, is to find a stamp enclosed upon opening a letter, for then I know that the writer expects an answer by mail, and, in justice to others, answering bee-questions by mail is a thing I cannot do. If I should answer one by mail I must answer others, and the only fair way is to treat all alike   The request for me to answer a question in the regular "Questions and Answers" department in the American Bee-Journal will always be cheerfully complied with without any stamp accompanying the request

Possibly some one of my readers might desire a picture of the office in which I do my work   That would take a number of pictures   According to circumstances, my office may be on the back porch seen in Fig 1, or it may be in anyone of nine different rooms inside   A look at the furnishings in Fig 111 will show that it is no serious undertaking to move my 'office" whenever desired   I never like to be far from the rest of the family, and when at work I enjoy the sound of their voices, even though I may pay no attention to what they are saying.

They are generally quite considerate in refraining from interrupting my work by remarks directed personally to me, but sometimes they forget.

I count myself singularly blessed in having a home where all the members of the family are so united in their tastes and enjoyments. One of our chief earthly pleasures is the love of flowers. At our quiet country home we have room unlimited for producing summer roses by the bushel, and the bay window of the sitting-room brightens the days of winter with its bright colors and luxuriant green. If you were here, I am sure you would enjoy a sight of that window, and then I would take pride in displaying to you my set of china honey-dishes shown in the first picture in the book. They were painted by my sister, each dish showing a separate honey-plant, one-half the dish being covered by a honey-comb

I desire to record my deep gratitude to a loving Heavenly Father for giving me so busy and happy a life, and for you, dear reader, I can hardly express a better wish than that your life may be as happy, if not as busy, as mine.

Some years ago, at the instigation of Editor E. R. Root, I wrote a honey-leaflet which has been circulated by hundreds of thousands. It has been thought well that it should be reproduced in more permanent form by having a place in the present work, and here follows·

HONEY AS A WHOLESOME FOOD.

About 60 pounds of sugar on the average is annually consumed by every man, woman and child in the United States Of course, many use less than the average, but to make up for it some consume several times as much It is only within the last few centuries that sugar has become known, and only within the last generation that refined sugars have become so low in price that they may be commonly used in the poorest· families. Formerly honey was the principal sweet, and it was one of the items sent as a propitiatory offering by Jacob to his unrecognized son, the chief ruler of Egypt, 3,000 years before the first sugar-refinery was built.

It would be greatly for the health of the present generation if honey

could be at least partially restored to its former place as a common article
of diet   The almost universal craving for sweets of some kind shows a
real need of the system in that direction, but the excessive use of sugar
brings in its train a long list of ills   Besides the various disorders of the
alimentary canal, that dread scourge—Bright's disease of the kidneys—
is credited with being one of the results of sugar eating   When cane-
sugar is taken into the stomach, it cannot be assimilated until first changed
by digestion into grape sugar. Only too often the overtaxed stomach fails
to properly perform this digestion, then comes sour stomach and various
dyspeptic phases   Prof A J Cook says

"If cane-sugar is absorbed without change, it will be removed by the
kidneys, and may result in their break-down, and physicians may be correct in asserting that the large consumption of cane-sugar by the 20th
century man is harmful to the great eliminators—the kidneys—and so a
menace to health and long life "

Now, in the wonderful laboratory of the bee hive there is found a
sweet that needs no further digestion, having been prepared fully by those
wonderful chemists—the bees—for prompt assimilation without taxing
stomach or kidneys   As Prof Cook says   "There can be no doubt but
that in eating honey our digestive machinery is saved work that it would
have to perform if we ate cane-sugar, and in case it is overtaxed and
feeble, this may be just the respite that will save from a break down "

A I Root says· "Many people who cannot eat sugar without having
unpleasant symptoms follow, will find by careful test that they can eat
good, well ripened honey without any difficulty at all "

HONEY THE MOST DELICIOUS SAUCE.

Not only is honey the most wholesome of all sweets, but it is the most
delicious   No preparation of man can equal the delicately flavored product
of the hive   Millions of flowers are brought under tribute, presenting their
tiny cups of dainty nectar to be gathered by the busy riflers, and when
they have brought it to the proper consistency, and stored it in the won-
drously wrought waxen cells and sealed it with coverings of snowy whiteness, no more tempting dish can grace the table at the most lavish banquet,
and yet its cost is so moderate that it may well find its place on the tables
of the common people every day in the week

IT IS ECONOMY TO USE HONEY

Indeed, in many cases it may be a matter of real economy to lessen
the butter-bill by letting honey in part take its place   A pound of honey
will go about as far as a pound of butter, and if both articles be of the
best quality the honey will cost the less of the two   Often a prime
article of extracted honey (equal to comb honey in every respect except
appearance) can be obtained for about half the price of butter   Butter
is at its best only when "fresh," while honey, properly kept, remains in-
definitely good—no need to hurry it out of the way for fear it may become
rancid.

GIVE CHILDREN HONEY.

Prof. Cook says "We all know how children long for candy This longing voices a need, and is another evidence of the necessity of sugar in our diet . . . Children should be given all the honey at each meal-time that they will eat. It is safer, will largely do away with the inordinate longing for candy and other sweets; and in lessening the desire will doubtless diminish the amount of cane-sugar eaten Then if cane-sugar does work mischief with health, the harm may be prevented"

Ask the average child whether he will have honey alone on his bread or butter alone, and almost invariably he will promptly answer, "Honey." Yet seldom are the needs or the tastes of the child properly consulted The old man craves fat meat; the child loathes it He wants sweet, not fat. He delights to eat honey, it is a wholesome food for him, and is not expensive Why should he not have it?

HONEY BEST TO SWEETEN HOT DRINKS.

Sugar is much used in hot drinks, as in coffee and tea The substitution of a mild-flavored honey in such uses may be a very profitable thing for the health Indeed, it would be better for the health if the only hot drink were what is called in Germany "honey-tea"—a cup of hot water with one or two tablespoonfuls of extracted honey The attainment of great age has in some cases been attributed largely to the life-long use of honey-tea

COMB AND EXTRACTED HONEY

At the present day honey is placed on the market in two forms— in the comb, and extracted "Strained" honey, obtained by mashing or melting combs containing bees, pollen, and honey, has rightly gone out of use Extracted honey is simply honey thrown out of the comb in a machine called a honey extractor The combs are revolved rapidly in a cylinder, and centrifugal force throws out the honey The comb remains uninjured, and is returned to the hive to be refilled again and again For this reason extracted honey is usually sold at a less price than comb honey, because each pound of comb is made at the expense of several pounds of honey

DIFFERENT KINDS AND FLAVORS

Many people think "honey is honey"—all just alike; but this is a great mistake Honey may be of good, heavy body—what bee-keepers call "well-ripened"—weighing generally twelve pounds to the gallon, or it may be quite thin It may also be granulated, or candied, more solid than lard. It may be almost as colorless as water, and it may be as black as the darkest molasses The flavor of honey varies according to the flower from which it is obtained It would be impossible to describe in words the flavors of the different honeys. You may easily distinguish the odor of a rose from that of a carnation, but you might find it difficult to describe them in words so that a novice smelling them for the first time could tell which was which But the different flavors in honey are just as distinct as the odors in flowers Among the light colored honeys are white clover, linden (or basswood) sage, sweet clover, alfalfa, willow-herb, etc, and among the darker are found heartsease, magnolia (or pop-lar), horse-mint, buckwheat, etc

ADULTERATION OF HONEY

In these days of prevailing adulteration, when so often "things are not what they seem," it is a comfort to know that *strictly pure* honey, both extracted and comb, can still be had and at a reasonable price The silly stories seen from time to time in the papers about artificial combs being filled with glucose, and deftly sealed over with a hot iron, have not the slightest foundation in fact For years there has been a standing offer by one whose financial responsibility is unquestioned, of $1,000 for a single pound of comb honey made without the intervention of bees The offer remains untaken, and will probably always remain so, for the highest art of man can never compass such delicate workmanship as the skill of the bee accomplishes

With extracted honey the case is different When you see in the grocery a tumbler of liquid honey with a small piece of comb honey in the center, you may be pretty sure the liquid honey is not honey at all, but glucose. If not familiar enough with honey to detect it by the taste, your only safe course is to buy of some one who *knows* as to its source, and upon whose honesty you can rely

CARE OF HONEY—WHERE TO KEEP IT.

The average housekeeper will put honey in the cellar for safe-keeping —about the worst place possible Honey readily attracts moisture, and in the cellar extracted honey will become thin, and in time may sour, and with comb honey the case is still worse, for the appearance as well as the quality is changed The beautiful white surface becomes watery and dark-ened, drops of water ooze through the cappings, and weep over the sur-face Instead of keeping honey in a place moist and cool, keep it dry and warm, even hot It will not hurt to be in a temperature of even 100 degrees Where salt will keep dry is a good place for honey Few places are better than the kitchen cupboard Up in a hot garret next the roof is a good place, and if it has had enough hot days there through the sum-mer, it will stand the freezing of winter, for under ordinary circumstances freezing cracks the combs, and hastens granulation or candying

GRANULATED HONEY—TO RELIQUEFY

When honey is kept for any length of time it has a tendency to change from its clear liquid condition, and becomes granulated or candied This is not to be taken as any evidence against its genuineness, but rather the contrary Some prefer it in the candied state, but the majority prefer it liquid It is an easy matter to restore it to its former liquid condition. Simply keep it in hot water long enough, *but not too hot* If heated above 160 degrees there is danger of spoiling the color and ruining the flavor

Remember that honey contains the most delicate of all flavors—that of the flowers from which it is taken. A good way is to set the vessel containing the honey inside another vessel containing hot water, not allowing the bottom of the one to rest directly on the bottom of the other, but putting a bit of wood or something of the kind between Let it stand on the stove, but do not let the water boil It may take half a day or longer to melt the honey If the honey is set directly on the reservoir of a cook-stove, it will be all right in a few days In time it will granulate again, when it must again be melted

HONEY-COOKING RECIPES.

HONEY-GEMS.—2 quarts flour, 3 tablespoonfuls melted lard, ¾ pint honey, ½ pint of molasses, 4 heaping tablespoonfuls brown sugar, 1½ level tablespoonfuls soda, 1 level teaspoonful salt, 1-3 pint water, ½ teaspoonful extract vanilla

HONEY-JUMBLES.—2 quarts flour, 3 tablespoonfuls melted lard, 1 pint honey, ¼ pint molasses, 1½ level tablespoonful soda, 1 level teaspoonful salt, ¼ pint water, ½ teaspoonful vanilla
The jumbles and the gems immediately preceding are from recipes used by bakeries and confectioners on a large scale, one firm in Wisconsin alone using ten tons of honey annually in their manufacture.

AIKIN'S HONEY-COOKIES —1 teacupful extracted honey, 1 pint sour cream, scant teaspoonful soda, flavoring if desired, flour to make a soft dough

SOFT HONEY-CAKE.—1 cup butter, 2 cups honey, 2 eggs, 1 cup sour milk, 2 teaspoonfuls soda, 1 teaspoonful ginger, 1 teaspoonful cinnamon, 4 cups flour.—*Chalon Fowls.*

GINGER HONEY-CAKE —1 cup honey, ½ cup butter, or drippings, 1 tablespoonful boiled cider in half a cup of hot water (or ½ cup sour milk will do instead) Warm these ingredients together, and then add 1 tablespoonful ginger and 1 teaspoonful soda sifted in with flour enough to make a soft batter Bake in a flat pan.—*Chalon Fowls*

OBERLIN HONEY FRUIT-CAKE —½ cup butter, ¾ cup honey, 1-3 cup apple jelly or boiled cider, 2 eggs well beaten, 1 teaspoonful soda, 1 teaspoonful each of cinnamon, cloves, and nutmeg, 1 teacupful each of raisins and dried currants Warm the butter, honey and apple jelly slightly, add the beaten eggs, then the soda dissolved in a little warm water, add spices and flour enough to make a stiff batter, then stir in the fruit and bake in a slow oven Keep in a covered jar several weeks before using.

HONEY POPCORN BALLS —Take 1 pint extracted honey, put it into an iron frying-pan, and boil until very thick, then stir in freshly popped corn, and when cool mold into balls These will especially delight the children

HONEY SHORTCAKE —3 cups flour, 2 teaspoonfuls baking-powder, 1 teaspoonful salt, ½ cup shortening, 1½ cups sweet milk Roll quickly, and bake in a hot oven When done, split the cake and spread the lower half thinly with butter, and the upper half with ½ pound of the best-flavored honey (Candied honey is preferred If too hard to spread well it should be slightly warmed or creamed with a knife) Let it stand a few minutes, and the honey will melt gradually, and the flavor will permeate all through the cake To be eaten with milk

OBERLIN HONEY LAYER-CAKE —2-3 cup butter, 1 cup honey, 3 eggs beaten, ½ cup milk Cream the butter and honey together, then add the eggs and milk Then add 2 cups of flour containing 1½ teaspoonfuls baking powder previously stirred in Then stir in flour to make a stiff batter Bake in jelly-tins When the cakes are cold, take finely flavored candied honey, and after creaming it, spread between the layers

HONEY NUT-CAKES —8 cups sugar, 2 cups honey, 4 cups milk or water, 1 lb almonds, 1 lb English walnuts, 3 cents' worth each of candied lemon and orange peel, 5 cents' worth citron (the last three cut fine) 2 large tablespoonfuls soda, 2 teaspoonfuls cinnamon, 2 teaspoonfuls ground cloves. Put the milk, sugar, and honey on the stove to boil 15 minutes, skim off the scum, and take from the stove Put in the nuts, spices, and candied fruit Stir in as much flour as can be done with a spoon Set away to cool, then mix in the soda (don't make the dough too stiff) Cover up and let stand over night, then work in enough flour to make a stiff dough Bake when you get ready It is well to let it stand a few days, as it will not stick so badly Roll out a little thicker than a common cooky, cut in any shape you like

This recipe originated in Germany, is old and tried, and the cake will keep a year or more —*Mrs F Smith*

MUTH'S HONEY-CAKES —1 gallon honey (dark honey is best), 15 eggs, 3 pounds sugar (a little more honey in its place may be better), 1½ oz baking soda, ⏤ oz ammonia, 2 lbs almonds chopped up, 2 lbs citron, 4 oz cinnamon, 2 oz cloves, 2 oz mace, 18 lbs flour Let the honey come almost to a boil, then let it cool off and add the other ingredients Cut out and bake The cakes are to be roasted afterward with sugar and white of eggs

OBERLIN HONEY-COOKIES —3 teaspoonfuls soda dissolved in 2 cups warm honey, 1 cup shortening containing salt, 2 teaspoonfuls ginger, 1 cup hot water, flour sufficient to roll

HONEY TEA CAKE —1 cup honey, ½ cup sour cream, 2 eggs, ½ cup butter, 2 cups flour, scant ½ teaspoonful soda, 1 teaspoonful cream-of tartar Bake 30 minutes in a moderate oven —*Miss M Candler*

HONEY-GINGER-SNAPS —1 pint honey, ¾ lb butter, 2 teaspoonfuls ginger Boil together a few minutes, and when nearly cold put in flour until it is stiff Roll out thin, and bake quickly

HONEY-CARAMELS —1 cup extracted honey of best flavor, 1 cup granulated sugar, 3 tablespoonfuls sweet cream or milk Boil to "soft crack," or until it hardens when dropped into cold water, but not too brittle—just so it will form into a soft ball when taken in the fingers Pour into a greased dish, stirring in a teaspoonful extract of vanilla just before taking off Let it be ½ or ¾ inch deep in the dish, and as it cools, cut in squares and wrap each square in paraffine paper, such as grocers wrap butter in To make chocolate caramels, add to the foregoing 1 tablespoonful melted chocolate, just before taking off the stove, stirring it in well For chocolate-caramels it is not so important that the honey be of best quality --*C C Miller*

HONEY GRAPE JELLY —Stew the grapes until soft, mash and strain them through cheese-cloth and to each quart of juice add one quart of honey, and boil it until it is thick enough to suit Keep trying by dipping out a spoonful and cooling it If you get it too thick it will candy. Any other fruit-juice treat just the same

MOORE'S HONEY GINGER-SNAPS —One pint of honey, one teaspoonful of ginger, and one teaspoonful of soda, dissolved in a little water, and two eggs Mix all, then work in all the flour possible, roll very thin, and bake in a moderately hot oven. Any flavoring extracts can be added, as you may wish.

MOORE'S HONEY JUMBLES OR COOKIES are made in the same way as the above, without any sugar or syrup, but add some shortening. In using honey for any kind of cakes, the dough must be as stiff with flour as possible, to keep them from running out of the stove

TO SPICE APPLES, PEARS OR PEACHES.—One quart of best vinegar, 1 quart of honey, ½ ounce each of cloves and stick cinnamon Boil all together 15 minutes, then put in the fruit, and cook tender. Put in a stone jar with enough of the syrup to cover the fruit It will keep as long as wanted.

FOR SUGAR CURING 100 POUNDS OF MEAT —Eight pounds of salt, 1 quart of honey, 2 ounces of saltpeter, and 3 gallons of water Mix, and boil until dissolved, then pour it hot on the meat

MRS BARBER'S HONEY-CANDY.—One quart honey, 1 small teacup of granulated sugar, butter size of an egg, 2 tablespoons strong vinegar Boil until it will harden when dropped into cold water, then stir in 1 small teaspoonful of baking soda Pour into buttered plates to cool Without the vinegar and soda it can be pulled or worked a long time, and is just the thing for an old-fashioned candy pull, as it is not sticky, and yet is soft enough to pull nicely.

SCRIPTURE HONEY-CAKE —One cupful of butter—Judges v 25, 3½ cupfuls of flour—I Kings iv 22, 2 cupfuls of sugar—Jeremiah vi 20, 2 cupfuls of raisins—I Samuel xxx. 12, 2 cupfuls of figs—I Samuel xxx. 12, 1 cupful of water—Genesis xxiv 17, 1 cupful of almonds—Genesis xliii 11, little salt—Leviticus ii. 13, 6 eggs—Isaiah x 14; large spoonful of honey—Exodus xvi 31, sweet spices to taste—I Kings x 2.
Follow Solomon's advice for making good boys, and you will have a good cake—Prov xxiii 14 Sift two teaspoonfuls of baking powder in the flour, pour boiling water on the almonds to remove the skins, seed the raisins, and chop the figs. It makes one large or two small cakes

MRS BARBER'S HONEY-COOKIES —One large teacupful of honey. One egg broken into the cup the honey was measured in, then 2 large spoonfuls sour milk, and fill the cup with butter or good beef dripping Put in one teaspoonful of soda and flour to make a soft dough. Bake in a moderate oven a light brown

GOTHAM HONEY GINGER-CAKE.—Rub ¾ of a pound of butter into a pound of sifted flour, add a teacupful of brown sugar, 2 tablespoonfuls each of ground ginger and caraway seed. Beat 5 eggs, and stir in the mixture, alternately, with a pint of extracted honey Beat all together until very light Turn into a shallow square pan, and set in a moderate oven to bake for one hour. When done, let cool and cut into squares.

MRS AIKIN'S HONEY APPLE BUTTER —One gallon good cooking apples, 1 quart honey, 1 quart honey vinegar; 1 heaping teaspoonful ground cinnamon   Cook several hours, stirring often to prevent burning   If the vinegar is very strong, use part water

HOWELL'S HARD HONEY-CAKE —Take 6 pounds of flour, 3 pounds honey, 1½ pounds of sugar, 1½ pounds butter, 6 eggs, ½ ounce saleratus, ginger to your taste   Have the flour in a pan or tray   Pack a cavity in the center   Beat the honey and yolks of eggs together well.   Beat the butter and sugar to cream, and put into the cavity in the flour, then add the honey and yolks of the eggs   Mix well with the hand, adding a little at a time, during the mixing, the ½ ounce of saleratus dissolved in boiling water until it is all in   Add the ginger, and finally add the whites of the 6 eggs, well beaten   Mix well with the hand to a smooth dough Divide the dough into 7 equal parts, and roll out like gingerbread.   Bake in ordinary square pans made for pies, from 10x14 inch tin   After putting into the pans, mark off the top in ½-inch strips with something sharp Bake an hour in a moderate oven   Be careful not to burn, but bake well Dissolve sugar to glaze over top of cake   To keep the cake, stand on end in an oak tub, tin can, or stone crock—crock is best   Stand the cards up so the flat sides will not touch each other   Cover tight   Keep in a cool, dry place   Don't use until three months old, at least   The cake improves with age, and will keep good as long as you will let it   Any cake sweet ened with honey does not dry out like sugar or molasses cake, and age improves or develops the honey-flavor   This recipe has been used with unvarying success and satisfaction for 100 years in the family that reports A year's supply of this cake can be made up at one time, if desired

MARIA FRASER'S HONEY-JUMBLES —Two cups honey, 1 cup butter, 4 eggs (mix well), 1 cup buttermilk (mix) 1 good quart of flour 1 level teaspoonful soda or saleratus   If it is too thin, stir in a little more flour If too thin it will fall   It does not want to be as thin as sugar cake   Use very thick honey   Be sure to use the same cup for measure   Be sure to mix the honey, eggs and butter well togther

HONEY FRUIT-CAKE —Take 1½ cups of honey, 2-3 cup of butter, ½ cup of sweet milk, 3 eggs well beaten, 3 cups of flour, 2 teaspoonfuls of baking-powder, 2 cups raisins, 1 teaspoonful each of cloves and cinnamon

HONEY GINGER-SNAPS —One pint honey, ¾ pound of butter, 2 tea spoonfuls of ginger, boil together a few minutes, and when nearly cold put in flour until it is stiff, roll out thinly and bake quickly

MRS. MINNICK'S SOFT HONEY-CAKE —Put scant teaspoonful soda in teacup, pour 5 tablespoonfuls hot water on the soda, then fill the cup with extracted honey   Take ½ cup of butter and 1 egg and beat together, add 2 cups of flour and 1 teaspoonful of ginger, stir all together, and bake in a *very slow* oven

HONEY-CAKE —One quart of extracted honey, ½ pint sugar, ½ pint melt ed butter, 1 teaspoonful soda, dissolved in ½ teacup of warm water, ½ of a nutmeg and 1 teaspoonful of ginger   Mix these ingredients, and then work in flour and roll   Cut in thin cakes and bake on buttered tins in a quick oven

---

REMEDIES USING HONEY

HONEY AND TAR COUGH-CURE —Put 1 tablespoonful liquid tar into a shallow tin dish, and place it in boiling water until the tar is hot   To this add a pint of extracted honey, and stir well for half an hour, adding to it a level teaspoonful pulverized borax   Keep well corked in a bottle.   Dose,

1 teaspoonful every one, two, or three hours, according to severity of cough

HONEY AS A TAPE-WORM REMEDY—Peeled pumpkin seeds, 3 ounces; honey, 2 ounces, water, 8 ounces Make an emulsion Take half, fasting, in the morning, remaining half an hour later. In three hours' time two ounces castor-oil should be administered Used with great success—*Medical Brief*

HONEY FOR ERYSIPELAS is used locally by spreading it on a suitable cloth and applying to the parts The application is renewed every 3 or 4 hours. In all cases in which the remedy has been employed, entire relief from the pain followed immediately, and convalescence was brought about in 3 or 4 days

HONEY FOR DYSPEPSIA—A young man who was troubled with dyspepsia, and the more medicine he took the worse he became, was advised to try honey and graham gems for breakfast He did so, and commenced to gain, and now enjoys as good health as the average man, and he does not take medicine, either. Honey is the only food taken into the stomach that leaves no residue, it requires no action of the stomach whatever to digest it, as it is merely absorbed and taken up into the system by the action of the blood Honey is the natural foe to dyspepsia and indigestion, as well as a food for the human system

HONEY FOR OLD PEOPLE'S COUGHS—Old people's coughs are as distinct as that of children, and require remedies especially adapted to them It is known by the constant tickling in the pit of the throat—just where the Adam's apple projects—and is caused by phlegm that accumulates there, which, in their weakened condition, they are unable to expectorate

Take a fair sized onion—a good strong one—and let it simmer in a quart of honey for several hours, after which strain and take a teaspoonful frequently It eases the cough wonderfully, though it may not cure.

HONEY FOR STOMACH COUGH—All mothers know what a stomach cough is—caused by an irritation of that organ, frequently attended with indigestion The child often "throws up" after coughing.

Dig down to the roots of a wild cherry tree, and peel off a handful of the bark, put it into a pint of water, and boil down to a teacupful Put this tea into a quart of honey, and give a teaspoonful every hour or two It is pleasant, and if the child should also have worms, which often happens, they are pretty apt to be disposed of, as they have no love for the wild-cherry flavor

HONEY AND TAR COUGH CANDY—Boil a double handful of green hoarhound in two quarts of water down to one quart, strain, and add to this tea two cups of extracted honey and a tablespoonful each of lard and tar. Boil down to a candy, but not enough to make it brittle Begin to eat this, increase from a piece the size of a pea, to as much as can be relished It is an excellent cough candy, and always gives relief in a short time

SWISS REMEDY FOR A COLD SETTLING ON THE CHEST.—Boil a quart of pure spring water, add as much camomile as can be grasped in three fingers, and three teaspoonfuls of honey, and cover tight The vessel is then to be quickly removed from the fire and set on a table at which the patient can comfortably seat himself Throwing a woolen cloth over the patient's head so to include the vessel, he is to remove the cover and inhale the vapors as deeply as possible through the mouth and nose, occasionally stirring the mixture until it is cold, and then retire to a warmed bed In obstinate cases the treatment should be repeated for three evenings.

HONEY CROUP REMEDY —This is the best known to the medical profession, and is an infallible remedy in all cases of mucus and spasmodic croup   Raw linseed oil, 2 oz , tincture of blood root, 2 drs , tincture of lobelia, 2 drs ; tincture of aconite, ½ dr , honey, 4 oz   Mix   Dose, ½ to 1 teaspoonful every 15 to 20 minutes, according to the urgency of the case   It is also excellent in all throat and lung troubles originating from a cold   This is an excellent remedy in lung trouble   Make a strong decoction of hoarhound herb and sweeten with honey   Take a tablespoonful 4 or 5 times a day

HONEY ON FROST-BITES —If your ears, fingers or toes become frozen nothing will take the frost out of them sooner than if wrapped up in honey The swelling is rapidly reduced, and no danger occurs

HONEY AND CREAM FOR FRECKLES —Have you tried a mixture of honey and cream—half and half—for freckles? Well, it's a good thing. If on the hands, wear gloves on going to bed

DR KNEIPP'S HONEY-SALVE —This is recommended as an excellent dressing for sores and boils   Take equal parts honey and flour, add a little water, and stir thoroughly   Don't make too thin   Then apply as usual

SUMMER HONEY-DRINK —1 spoonful of fruit-juice and 1 spoonful honey in ½ glass water, stir in as much soda as will lie on a silver dime, and then stir in half as much tartaric acid, and drink at once

DR PEIRO'S HONEY-SALVE—for boils and other diseases of a similar character—is made by thoroughly incorporating flour with honey until a proper consistency to spread on cloth   Applied over the boil it hastens suppuration, and the early termination of the painful lesion.

HONEY AS A LAXATIVE —In olden time the good effects of honey as a remedial agent were well known, but of late little use is made thereof A great mistake, surely   Notably is honey valuable in constipation   Not as an immediate cure, like some medicines which momentarily give relief only to leave the case worse than ever afterward, but by its persistent use daily, bringing about a healthy condition of the bowels, enabling them properly to perform their functions   Many suffer daily from an irritable condition, calling themselves nervous, and all that sort of thing, not realizing that constipation is at the root of the matter, and that a faithful daily use of honey family persisted in would restore cheerfulness of mind and a healthy body —Le Progres Apicole

COUGHS, COLDS, WHOOPING COUGH, ETC —Fill a bell metal kettle with hoarhound leaves and soft water, letting it boil until the liquor becomes strong—then strain through a muslin cloth, adding as much honey as desired—then cook it in the same kettle until the water evaporates, when the candy may be poured into shallow vessels and remain until needed, or pulled like molasses candy until white

HONEY FOR SORE EYES —A neighbor of mine had inflammation in his eyes   He tried many things and many physicians, was nothing better, but rather grew worse, until he was almost entirely blind   His family was sick, and I presented him with a pail of honey   What they did not eat he put in his eyes, a drop or two in each eye two or three times a day In three months' time he was able to read coarse print, and after four months' use his eyes were almost as good as ever   I have also found honey good for common cold-sore eyes —S C PERRY

INDEX.

ILLUSTRATIONS.

Lightning Source UK Ltd.
Milton Keynes UK
UKHW030633220321
380773UK00009B/769